THE ROCKINGHAM SHOOT
AND OTHER DRAMATIC WRITINGS

JOHN McGAHERN

The Rockingham Shoot
and other dramatic writings

edited and with an introduction by
STANLEY VAN DER ZIEL

FABER & FABER

First published in 2018
by Faber & Faber Limited
Bloomsbury House
74–77 Great Russell Street
London WC1B 3DA

Typeset by Country Setting, Kingsdown, Kent, CT14 8ES
and Agnesi Text, Hadleigh, Suffolk
Printed in the UK by CPI Group (UK) Ltd, Croydon, CR0 4YY

A CIP record for this book
is available from the British Library

ISBN 978-0-571-33663-0

2 4 6 8 10 9 7 5 3 1

Contents

Introduction
MCGAHERN THE DRAMATIST

Many of these plays deal with the unresolved legacy of Ireland's colonial past, and with the difficult transition to nationhood that followed the achievement of independence in 1922. John McGahern, the son of a Sergeant in the new state's police force (the *Garda Síochána*, or 'Guards'), spent much of his formative years in the shadow of the great houses of North Roscommon in the 1940s, and witnessed first-hand the final stages of decline of the old Anglo-Irish gentry. He would later write about this world and its fate in a number of his essays – perhaps most lucidly towards the end of his life in the opening paragraphs of his review of Valerie Pakenham's *The Big House in Ireland*:

In the North Roscommon I grew up in, the high demesne wall of Rockingham extended for several miles. All the stone gatehouses were picturesque and no two were alike, and from their gates the long avenues ran to the Nash mansion that overlooked Lough Key . . . With a retinue of servants, farmhands, stable lads, gardeners and gamekeepers, the estate was a closed world within a world. The social occasion of the year was the pheasant shoot and the great annual ball when the gentry gathered from several counties and the British ambassador came from Dublin. Rockingham House burned down in 1957 and the estate was split into farms.

A few miles away stood Woodbrook House. It had one tiny gatehouse and no walls and it was given fame by David Thomson's book *Woodbrook*. The Kirkwoods lived there, under the leaking roofs, and occasionally they were rescued from their habitual genteel penury by their racehorses. The only annual ball was when they gave their barns to the local wrenboys on St Stephen's Night for their dance. Around the same time as Rockingham burned down, Woodbrook passed into the hands of the gentle Maxwells, old retainers of the Kirkwoods.[1]

1. John McGahern, *Love of the World: Essays*, ed. Stanley van der Ziel (London: Faber and Faber, 2009), p. 416.

The fate of the Protestant ascendancy in the twentieth century was not just a question of passing historical or sociological interest for McGahern; he also felt he owed the beginnings of his development as a reader and writer to the influence of the gentle Protestants who lived in one of these houses. In the autobiographical essay 'The Solitary Reader' (1991), and later in *Memoir* (2005), he recalled how he had become a reader when he was 'given the run' of a nineteenth-century library in an old stone manor house where a Protestant father and son called Willie and Andy Moroney lived 'in royal untidiness'. There the future novelist read indiscriminately, taking and returning volumes one shopping bag at a time. There he was also introduced to the notion of leisure in an environment where ideas were freely discussed and independent thought was valued. All of this was in stark contrast with the general atmosphere of philistinism, intolerance and 'Moral Idleness' which seemed to prevail in the rest of the country.[2] The contrast between these worlds, and the sometimes fraught attitudes that attended their co-existence, is a theme in much of his work.

In his childhood, the 'Big House' was both literally and metaphorically a point of light in the darkness. In a 1987 interview about the origins of the television film *The Rockingham Shoot*, McGahern remembered how, as a child, 'We used to look at the lighted windows [of Rockingham House] from away behind the main walls.'[3] What was inside those walls was as exotic and exciting to the young McGahern as it is to the children in the film, who marvel over the luxuries on offer in the buffet tent. In his maturity, the remnants of the Protestant ascendancy and their crumbling estates remained to him not just reminders

2. Ibid., pp. 87–8; see also John McGahern, *Memoir* (London: Faber and Faber, 2005), pp. 172–3.
3. Ciaran Carty, 'Out of the Dark', *Sunday Tribune*, 6 September 1987, p. 18.

of the history of British imperial conquest and oppression, as they had been for the revolutionary generation just a few decades earlier; they were also significant, as they had been for the mature Yeats of 'Meditations in Time of Civil War' and *Purgatory*, as much needed repositories of culture, civilisation, civility and refinement. During the filming of *The Rockingham Shoot*, McGahern became intrigued by one example of this mixture of military command and aesthetic refinement that set the old ruling class apart from the rest of the country. When *The Rockingham Shoot* was shot on location at Crom Castle, the seat of Lord Erne near Enniskillen in Northern Ireland, the Earl and Countess took an interest in the filming on their estate. McGahern's wife Madeline remembers how at some point during the crew's preparation of the costly scene in which the lovers are strolling in front of the lit castle in the background, the Earl was heard to ask someone, in a voice of command, 'Everything under control?'[4] McGahern loved that; but he would also always remember the sound of the swish of the Countess Erne's delicate silk raincoat as she walked with her husband at a slight distance from the beehive of activity, a glass of Beaujolais in her hand.[5]

In broader terms, many of McGahern's works are concerned not only with the slow process of coming to terms with Ireland's colonial past, but also with the difficulty of

4. McGahern was interested in this difference in voice and bearing that distinguished the two Irelands. It is a subject in the story 'The Conversion of William Kirkwood', in which the illegitimate child of a servant who has been taken in by the last member of an aristocratic family develops a 'voice and laugh closer to the clipped commanding accents of the Kirkwoods than to her mother's soft obscured speech, vowel melting into vowel'. John McGahern, *High Ground and Other Stories* (London: Faber and Faber, 1985), p. 122.

5. This anecdote draws on Madeline McGahern's recollections, communicated in an email to the editor, July 2017. Mrs McGahern does not remember the Countess carrying a glass of Beaujolais; that detail is drawn from Carty, 'Out of the Dark', p. 18.

establishing or maintaining a sense of civilisation, or even civility, in the wake of independence. The loss of established social structures, either through the destruction of the Big House or through the dispersal of tight-knit village communities in the wake of the Great Famine in the nineteenth century and the mass emigration of the mid-twentieth (as described by McGahern in the story 'Oldfashioned' and essays like 'Whatever You Say, Say Nothing'), led to a civic vacuum, in which an emergent nationalism might restore political sovereignty but could not establish a shared ethical code or a sense of manners.

This is a recurring subject across all of the dramatic works collected in this volume – even in a play like *The Power of Darkness*, which deals with the ruthless realities of survival among the peasant classes in which social niceties are but the thinnest veneer.

In much of McGahern's other work, the lack of manners in the Irish countryside in the mid-twentieth century can be a source of comedy. In his 1975 screenplay for *Swallows*, for example, the women at the Countrywomen's Association function are disparaged for their lack of social graces and their boring and predictable topics of conversation by the Sergeant who, with delicious irony, is himself devoid of the same qualities as he turns up for the function drunk and lectures the baffled villagers on the life and work of Paganini, while only the priest has some of the tact required to diffuse the situation. Similarly, in his 1972 radio adaptation of his first novel, *The Barracks* (1963), Elizabeth Reagan (the spelling of the name in the radio play is different from that in the novel) is repeatedly exasperated with the chattering Mrs Casey, wondering whether 'That woman will never learn that everybody lives alone' (p. 83). Like so many characters in both McGahern's fictional and dramatic oeuvre, Elizabeth feels oppressed by the proximity of too many people who all make demands on her solitariness, and who lack the capacity to read

4

another's need for quiet and solitude. (Elsewhere in this volume, both Reilly in *The Rockingham Shoot* (p. 238) and Maggie in *The Power of Darkness* (p. 282) humorously compare the unwanted busy-ness of their surroundings to the traffic of Dublin's main thoroughfare, O'Connell Street.) And when Guard Mullins and Sergeant Reagan in the same play confront a man found urinating against the chapel wall during a nocturnal raid on the village pubs, they are more concerned with teaching the man about manners and civility than in threatening law (p. 133). In fact, even despite compounding his initial offence by insulting a police officer on duty, he gets away without being charged, much to the chagrin of the Superintendent. Perhaps the invocation of legal measures would have been less than fully respected, in any case, in a country like Ireland in the 1940s where the populace had long race memories of colonial subjugation, where law and order were still connected in the national psyche with an alien power to be resisted, and where crimes and transgressions were for that reason seen as *de facto* patriotic acts.[6] It takes more than a generation to reverse such long-ingrained ways of thinking, if they can ever be reversed at all. Even Reagan's own dalliances with his superior, Quirke, bear the hallmarks of this same inherited attitude towards authority; a high-ranking state official is somebody to be outwitted like an enemy rather than a colleague or an ally.

McGahern even introduced the need for manners and civility into his 1973 television screenplay adaptation of the opening story of James Joyce's *Dubliners. The Sisters* is probably primarily of interest to readers of McGahern not so much for the way in which its plot follows that of Joyce's story, but for the original elements that McGahern adds to the Joycean frame. In some respects, his adaptation of 'The

6. This characteristic of the national psyche of a colonised people is a subject in the plays and prose of J. M. Synge, and in many of Frank O'Connor's stories.

Sisters' is as much a chapter in the 'moral history' of *McGahern*'s Ireland in the third quarter of the twentieth century as it is of Joyce's at the turn of the century.[7] It is clear from the screenplay that McGahern not only found themes and ideas in Joyce's stories that could be adapted in his own literary endeavours (there are echoes of *Dubliners*, *A Portrait* and *Ulysses* everywhere in his fiction), but that he also projected certain idiosyncratic McGahernesque elements on to the Joycean text. His pre-occupation with the lack of manners in mid- and late-twentieth-century Ireland is one such element.

Following the appearance of *High Ground* and *The Rockingham Shoot* in the mid-1980s, one journalist observed how 'The comparative intellectual refinement and urbanity of the clerical characters in [McGahern's fiction] is always contrasted with the philistinism and coarseness of some of their flock.'[8] This is certainly true of Father Flynn in *The Sisters*, written more than a decade earlier, who emphasises to the boy protagonist (who is nameless in Joyce's story, but who becomes 'Stephen' in McGahern's screenplay) that when the time comes for him to follow his religious vocation he must go to the Irish College in Rome rather than pursue his studies in one of the domestic centres of religious training, because 'the places here I'm sorry to have to say are not fit places, football seminaries' (p. 164). The snobbishness of the priest's remark is further amplified by an additional line of dialogue written in McGahern's handwriting in the margin of one copy of the typescript: 'You must never, never, Stephen, play on the street or mix with the common boys for commonness begets commonness.'[9] The sense of class-

7. *Selected Letters of James Joyce*, ed. Richard Ellmann (London: Faber and Faber, 1983), p. 83.

8. Cathy Herbert, 'Window on the World', *Magill*, vol. 10, no. 13 (October 1987), pp. 56–62, at p. 60.

9. John McGahern, typescript of *The Sisters*. James Hardiman Library, National University of Ireland, Galway: P71/748, p. 9. (Hereafter NUIG.)

consciousness which this conveys is certainly an underlying concern in several of Joyce's stories in *Dubliners*, a book that is extremely sensitive to nuances of class differential among the lower-middle classes; but it is not a theme at this point in 'The Sisters'. Rather, the priest's harangue against 'commonness' in McGahern's version of Joyce's story is perhaps indebted not so much to the example of Joyce as it is to that of W. B. Yeats – perhaps as an intentional or unintentional echo of a line from his late poem 'The Gyres': 'Conduct and work grow coarse, and coarse the soul . . .'[10] The ghostly presence of that same line may also be detected behind the description in the short story 'Oldfashioned' of the shift in manners that takes place when emigrants from small Irish villages move to England, where after just a few weeks 'once-easy gentle manners, set free from the narrow rule of church and custom, grew loud, uncertain, coarse'.[11] Yeats was, after all, a constant touchstone in McGahern's thinking about the loss of 'ancient sanctities'[12] and the decline of manners in post-independence Ireland.

SINCLAIR, SOCIAL TRANSITION AND RADIO DRAMA

Sinclair was first broadcast on BBC Radio 3 on 16 November 1971. The first of McGahern's dramatic writings to be produced, this one-act radio play is about the fate of Southern Protestants such as the Moroneys and the Kirkwoods whom he had known in his youth. Or, to be more precise, it is about that class *at a remove*. The biographical

10. W. B. Yeats, *The Poems*, ed. Richard J. Finneran (London: Macmillan, 1983), p. 293.

11. McGahern, *High Ground*, p. 36.

12. That phrase appears in Yeats's defence of *Purgatory*, 13 August 1938; quoted in Donald T. Torchiana, *W. B. Yeats and Georgian Ireland* (1966; Washington, DC: Catholic University of America Press, 1992), p. 357.

facts and circumstances of the Moroneys as he had known them as a boy were sufficiently reinvented and re-imagined in the play to 'dislocate' them from their real-life origins and make them work as fiction.[13] The eponymous Sinclair is not even an Anglo-Irishman like Andy and Willy Moroney, but an Englishman, a relic of the age of Empire drawing a pension from the transatlantic telegraph company in Valentia Island at the westernmost point of County Kerry. Nor do his crude and masochistic ways of acting, thinking and speaking have anything in common with those of the 'gentle' Moroneys. But his fate is precisely that of members of many long-established Anglo-Irish families, and the writing is informed by McGahern's feelings about the disappearance of a culture that had first opened the world of books for him.

Sixteen years after *Sinclair* was first broadcast, McGahern remarked about the fate of Protestants in post-independence Ireland that 'They were an extraordinary interesting class. It's fascinating how they were devoured by the new Catholic state, mostly through the marriage laws.'[14] That term refers to a series of measures surrounding 'mixed' marriages encoded in ecclesiastical law in the early twentieth century. Simply put, these stated that 'each party of a mixed marriage give a written guarantee that all children born to the marriage be baptised and brought up in the Catholic Church . . . Related to this there was an obligation on the Catholic partner to strive for the conversion of the non-Catholic partner.'[15] It is to these measures for eradicating the minority Protestant religion that the

13. McGahern elaborated on this rule for successfully adapting things from one's real life into fiction in his Preface to *Creatures of the Earth: New and Selected Stories* (London: Faber and Faber, 2006), pp. vii–viii; reprinted in *Love of the World*, pp. 279–80.

14. Herbert, 'Window on the World', p. 60.

15. Louise Fuller, *Irish Catholicism since 1950: The Undoing of a Culture* (Dublin: Gill and Macmillan, 2002), p. 17.

eponymous subject of *Sinclair* refers when he remarks with obscene wit that 'it was no rush of faith led to my conversion but I was simply dragged into your barbaric Church, if you allow me to put it that way, Mr Boles, by my male member' (p. 69). But his crudely voiced resentment is not primarily directed against the Catholic Church and its representatives – notably the wonderfully drawn 'Monsignor Creedon' who would sit 'with both legs astraddle the one bar of the electric heater in the room' during the catechism lessons required to prepare him for his conversion (p. 70). Sinclair may avoid attending mass following his conversion, seeing it – like the characters in McGahern's final novel *That They May Face the Rising Sun* (2002), or like Paul in *The Power of Darkness*, who can talk of 'marrying for the old performance' without any thought of moral or religious obligation (p. 269) – purely as a matter of appearance and pretence; but the brunt of his bitterness and resentment is directed against his own sexual needs. As Boles relays in one of the mocking acts of mimicry of Sinclair's outrageous sayings that make up much of the play, Sinclair and his new Catholic wife had soon after their union grown to see the occasional 'fluttering sensations . . . panting and sweating' in the marital bed as an 'overrated pastime' (p. 71), a conclusion that makes the initial effort at conversion for the specific attainment of that goal all the more absurd.

Such distorted attitudes towards physical intimacy are not confined to converted country squires and Englishmen like Sinclair. They are a regular feature especially in McGahern's early work from the 1960s and 1970s. One of the two bachelors in the same play shows a comparable attitude. Gillespie's physical relationship with his dog is not so dissimilar to that between Sinclair and his long-suffering wife. Gillespie may kick his dog for no apparent reason other than the pleasure that his dominance seems to afford him, but this cruel and unmotivated act is immediately followed by a stroke accompanied by the comment that is it 'Strange how soothing a dog's coat is to flesh. Flesh gets hungry for flesh or hair as much as the belly for food' (p. 64). There is, in this world of *Sinclair*, a genuine yearning for physical contact, but this yearning is distorted by an equally urgent awareness that a physical need or reliance on another leaves one open to exploitation – or even by a twisted belief that any action that gives physical pleasure to another must be balanced by an equal but opposite act of cruelty.

*

The destruction and disappearance of the landed Protestant gentry is a recurring subject in McGahern's work. There are occasional glimpses of this world in his first novel, *The Barracks*, from 1963, and these were retained in the radio adaptation written nearly a decade later. In the penultimate scene, Guard Mullins, laboriously reading the patriotic inscription on an elaborate tombstone, is able to place the occupant of the plot as one of the 'Anglo-Irish fucking exploiters' whose number and influence have been severely reduced after the revolution: 'Their house has burned down and the woods and the walls fallen and it gives me sweet joy to look on the ruin. May their souls be damned in hell' (p. 145). But more time had to pass before he found a form suitable for dealing with the fallen world of the Moroneys and their kind in a more sustained and thoughtful way.

McGahern's first published comprehensive treatment of the disappearance of a Protestant character from a rural Irish community was the short story 'Why We're Here', first published in *The Review* in April 1968 and later collected in *Nightlines* (1970). This story was then adapted into the radio play *Sinclair* in 1971. Like a number of McGahern's works, 'Why We're Here' and *Sinclair* are about the marginalisation and disappearance of Southern Protestantism. When he returned to that same subject more than a decade later in the triptych of short stories comprising 'Eddie Mac', 'The Conversion of William Kirkwood' and 'Oldfashioned', all published in *High Ground and Other Stories* (1985), and then in some of the autobiographical prose from the 1990s and 2000s, McGahern would write about his memories of the decline of Anglo-Ireland in the 1940s and 1950s with a tone of sentimental pastoral nostalgia much indebted to that of Oliver Goldsmith's *The Deserted Village* (a poem that is referenced in his screenplay for *The Rockingham Shoot*, which belongs to the same phase of his career). But the tone and structure of 'Why We're Here' and *Sinclair* are very different from these later treatments of the same material. When, as a young writer in the late 1960s, McGahern first came to search for an appropriate model for reimagining the material connected with his early acquaintance with the two dishevelled old gentlemen in whose house he had found both domestic squalor and a tradition of leisure, learning and scholarship, he was perhaps naturally drawn to the example of *All That Fall*, Samuel Beckett's 1957 radio play about the final days of an elderly Protestant couple in reduced physical and economic circumstances in the Catholic Free State, in which the wonderfully eccentric Mrs Rooney shares memories and gossip with neighbours and local characters as she makes her way to the railway station.[16]

As a devoted admirer of Beckett's work, McGahern probably heard the first broadcast of *All That Fall* on the BBC Third Programme in 1957, and he certainly read it soon afterwards when the text was published by Faber and Faber. In later years, he would cite *All That Fall* as his

16. McGahern may have drawn on *All That Fall*'s Mrs Rooney again when he came to adapt *The Barracks* for radio the following year. The incessant chattering interspersed with '*roaring*' and '*convulsive laughter*' of Mrs Casey, particularly in the passage where she reminisces about her girlhood courtship (pp. 101–2), may draw on the vocal energies of Maddy Rooney.

favourite of Beckett's works.[17] The stamp of that play – at once comic and sometimes mocking of old pieties, and intensely moving – is evident throughout 'Why We're Here', and it is even further amplified in the expanded version of the same material in *Sinclair*.[18] This is not to say that McGahern's decision to adapt 'Why We're Here' into a radio play was motivated only by a desire to emulate *All That Fall*. Rather, he found the material particularly suitable for that medium – as we know from a letter McGahern wrote to Susanna Capon at the BBC Radio drama department:

The story 'Why We're Here' first began as a play I never finished. I think I could make interesting radio of it, using it simply as a base.[19]

The generic journey of the material that found its final shape in *Sinclair* – from abandoned stage play, to short story, and finally to radio drama – is worth reflecting upon a little further.

Its dramatic origins can still be seen in the short story, which is really a one-act play trapped in the pages of a book. With its reliance on dialogue, 'Why We're Here' is essentially dramatic in nature. There is no real difference in structure between the short story 'Why We're Here' and the radio play *Sinclair*. The latter is an extended version of the former. It includes some additional elements, like the story about the 'exceedingly peculiar' Lord Oxford, which is a superb send-up of upper-class extravagance (p. 74),

17. Stanley van der Ziel, 'An Interview with John McGahern', in *John McGahern: Authority and Vision*, ed. Željka Doljanin and Máire Doyle (Manchester: Manchester University Press, 2017), pp. 195–212, at p. 203.

18. See also Stanley van der Ziel, *John McGahern and the Imagination of Tradition* (Cork: Cork University Press, 2016), pp. 230–32.

19. John McGahern, letter to Susanna Capon, 2 October 1970. BBC Written Archives Centre, Caversham Park, Reading: RCont 17. (Hereafter BBC WAC.)

but both pieces are essentially a record of two voices exchanging gossip and memories and mimicking – with varying levels of success – the English voice and accent of a third, the eponymous Sinclair who was last seen with an empty shopping bag outside Amiens Street Station. (In this alertness to the condition of tramphood, McGahern is in tune with the concerns of contemporaries like Beckett and Harold Pinter. For all these authors, vagrants were appealing subjects both because they represented a socio-economic reality that existed on the fringes of mainstream society, and because they symbolised a metaphysical state of uncertainty, uprootedness and in-betweenness that existed more widely in the psychic landscape of the post-war period. That theme is also introduced in McGahern's play through the absent title character's questions about the reasons and meaning of existence – the 'why we're here' that gives the prose version its title.)

Where the play *Sinclair* surpasses the story 'Why We're Here' is in the performances of its two distinguished actors. For a first-time playwright, albeit one who had already a certain degree of notoriety as a novelist, McGahern was extraordinarily lucky with the casting of *Sinclair*.[20] Norman Rodway played Gillespie, while Boles was played by Cyril Cusack. Both actors, though twenty years apart in age, had impressive résumés of theatre and moving-picture work; both had been members of the Royal Shakespeare

20. This good fortune was not always replicated for productions of subsequent dramatic works in the decade that followed. He later recalled how on one occasion he had walked into a BBC television studio in Birmingham only to find that *Swallows*, a play that was intended as 'a kind of elusive poetry', had been cast with actors from the popular British television police drama *Z-Cars*. When McGahern voiced his concern to producer Barry Hanson, the latter replied: 'If you think you'll get poetry out of these guys you'd better start thinking about transmigration of souls fast. We're going to shoot in an hour's time.' See van der Ziel, 'Interview with John McGahern', p. 201.

Company since the mid-1960s. The tapes of the original recording of *Sinclair* have since been wiped by the BBC (as have those of *The Barracks*, and of the later television films *The Sisters* and *Swallows*), but those who heard it when it was broadcast, and particularly those like John and Madeline McGahern and Susanna Capon who were present during the recording, agree that both actors were in fine form, and that the result was nothing short of majestic, a potential classic of the genre.

McGahern's intuition, voiced in that letter to Susanna Capon, that this material would make 'interesting radio' even though he had been unable to make the same material work as a stage play is just as interesting. The dramatic nature of the material may be beyond dispute, but why should it have been abandoned as a stage play and then revived for radio? What arguably made 'Why We're Here'/*Sinclair* particularly suited for production as a play for voices on radio, rather than as a stage play put on the boards, is the static nature of the action. The most important actions in the play are not those which pass in real time between the onstage protagonists, for these are minimal enough. Their squabbling over the noise of a chainsaw, punctuated only by the kicking and stroking of their dogs and the occasional fart, would hardly make for a very dynamic visual spectacle. Instead, the real action of the play is that which the listener is gradually able to piece together from the scraps of shared recollections that make up most of the dialogue. The story of the eponymous Sinclair, an English Protestant whose estate was auctioned off earlier that afternoon, is revealed through the conversation of Gillespie and Boles, as they recall his origins and mimic some of his more colourful sayings. With its purely verbal emphasis on gossip, argument and remembrance of things past, rather than on staging things as they happen in the dramatic present, *Sinclair* may be situated within the modern Irish dramatic tradition of

Beckett and Brian Friel – one that is to a significant extent dependent on 'literary' effects rather than on purely dramatic ones.[21] (It may be remembered here that Friel, like McGahern, started his career as a short-story writer before turning his attention to drama, and that Beckett was the author not only of a number of 'literary' plays but also of a series of novels that take the shape of one or more dramatic monologues.) Radio may be the medium most suited to this particular device, because by its very nature it relies on voices coming out of the dark rather than on the movements or gestures of actors. Gillespie and Boles's reminiscences and mimicry of Sinclair's habits and ways of speaking conjure a mental image of the vanished Sinclair for the play's listeners, in the same way that he is imagined by the characters now that he has disappeared into the anonymity of the big city. Radio drama by its very nature relies on the listener's ability to embellish disembodied voices with a vivid mental picture that belongs solely to their own individual imagination. In a stage version of the same play, the physical appearance of two actors could only dilute this private internal imagery. McGahern may have recognised this when he first began to think of 'Why We're Here' as 'interesting radio'.

*

The unpublished 'Fragments from a Dramatic Work' included as an Appendix at the end of this edition suggest how McGahern might have developed further in this generic direction as a dramatist after *Sinclair*. The 'Fragments' are all dramatised versions of material originating in McGahern's childhood and youth already familiar to

21. See for example the Introduction to John Drakakis, ed., *British Radio Drama* (Cambridge: Cambridge University Press, 1981), pp. 1–36 (especially pp. 27–34), as well as Richard Pine, *The Diviner: The Art of Brian Friel*, 2nd edn (Dublin: University College Dublin Press, 1999), p. 289.

readers of his early fiction and of *Memoir*. The children who arrive late for school because of 'blasting' at the quarry in the first section (p. 337), for example, are recognisable versions of those returning from school on the same or another day in the *Nightlines* story 'Coming into His Kingdom'. This material also includes a couple of recollections of the Moroneys. The 'Fragments' conclude with a monologue that draws on Willy Moroney's obsession with beekeeping, turning the old beekeeper into a stoic philosopher. The stamp of Samuel Beckett and *All That Fall* is again very clear in this. But it is another section reworking a memory of the younger of the Moroneys that is most interesting in terms of dramatic form. In *Memoir*, McGahern remembers how Andy Moroney had once 'caused great local merriment by describing himself as a "gentleman farmer"' when he appeared on the radio programme *Question Time*, because 'Everybody knew the word "farmer" and had some idea as to what constituted a "gentleman", but the conjunction of the two was thought to be hilarious.'[22] That episode, alongside the author's vivid childhood memories of listening to All-Ireland Gaelic-football finals around the same period, is cast into a dramatic form suited specifically to the nature of radio – a proper, fully-fledged '*radio* drama', rather than a 'radio *drama*' adapted for the medium from a stage play[23] – as the script intermingles the voices of Andy Moroney being interviewed on a radio programme with those of his neighbours listening to the same programme in great merriment. The same radio announcer from the 'Fragments' also makes an appearance in the radio adaptation of *The Barracks* (pp. 104–6); only there the voice is not incorporated with those of his listeners in the same fluid way.

22. McGahern, *Memoir*, p. 171.
23. This distinction was made by Peter Lewis, in the Introduction to his *Radio Drama* (London: Longman, 1981), p. 8.

But the dramatic outputs of the rest of McGahern's career followed a different path – one on which he also embarked around the turn of the 1970s when he first started adapting a nineteenth-century naturalistic melodrama by Tolstoy into 'living Irish speech'. (This project is discussed in detail in the final section of this Introduction.) All of his subsequent works for radio, television and stage were to follow the realistic or naturalistic direction, rather than the more avant-garde alternative of the play-for-voices devised specifically for the unique experience of radio that *Sinclair* and the 'Fragments' had suggested was possible.

His radio adaptation of *The Barracks* – written in Cleggan in 1970–71 out of a dislike for Hugh Leonard's popular stage adaptation,[24] and first broadcast on BBC Radio 4 on 24 January 1972 – is part of that shift, and a beautifully paced one at that. In contrast with his earliest foray into the world of radio drama, the script of *The Barracks* is not written predominantly in the past tense and made up of gossip and memories. Rather, the actions with which the play is centrally concerned – that of Elizabeth's diagnosis with breast cancer and her subsequent slow death, and that of Sergeant Reagan's struggle to leave the police force – gradually unfold in the dramatic present in a more conventional chronological manner. This is not to say that there is no scope for recollection or reminiscence. Reagan's fiercely mimicked accounts of his confrontations with Superintendent Quirke are among the most memorable parts of the play, as they had been of the novel on which it was based; but what is perhaps just as

24. See a letter to a contact at the BBC in which he wrote that 'I took a chance on its acceptance as I dislike the successful Hugh Leonard stage version of it.' John McGahern, letter to Susanna Capon, 22 June 1971. BBC WAC: RCont 17. Hugh Leonard's stage adaptation of *The Barracks* was staged for an extended two-week run at the Olympia Theatre as part of the Dublin Theatre Festival, 6–18 October 1969.

striking is how the same play also contains embedded within it a critique of retro-spectives. Mrs Casey's account of her courtship in Dublin may be part of an aesthetics of reminiscence; but the story she remembers is also a great source of embarrassment to her husband, who prefers to live in the present rather than be constantly reminded of the past. As McGahern's career progressed into the 1970s and beyond, the contrast between being capable of living fully in the present on the one hand, and of being trapped between 'Remembrance of things past and dreams of things to come' on the other, became one of the recurring themes of his fiction.[25] This same championing of the joys of the present over the claims of the past may be connected with the shift away from a certain type of modern dramatic idiom of which *Sinclair* is such an outstanding example, and towards the directness and immediacy of *The Barracks*.

WRITING FOR TELEVISION

The Sisters, broadcast on BBC2 on 17 February 1973, marks McGahern's transition from radio drama to writing for television, a medium to which he returned on several occasions during the 1970s and 1980s. The John McGahern Papers deposited in the archives at the National University of Ireland, Galway, show that he started work on a number of screenplay projects over the years. These included original works as well as adaptations – of works by others, such as Pierre Loti's novel *An Iceland Fisherman*, and of a number of his own prose works, including the *Getting Through* story 'Faith, Hope and Charity' and the 1979 novel *The Pornographer*. But only three of his screenplays made it into production; all of these produced scripts are

25. See the concluding sections of chapter 5 in van der Ziel, *John McGahern*, pp. 166–81. The quotation is from John McGahern, *That They May Face the Rising Sun* (London: Faber and Faber, 2002), p. 167.

included in this volume. (The case of *The Pornographer* is not as clear as that of these other abandoned screenplays. McGahern's adaptation of that novel was scheduled to go into production by *Rockingham Shoot* director Kieran Hickey in 1991,[26] but in the end this fell through. As a result, the *Pornographer* screenplay does not exist in a definitive produced text but only as a series of drafts in the archives at NUI Galway. For this reason it is not included in this edition of McGahern's produced dramatic writings.)

Writing for the screen was not without its own set of pitfalls and technical challenges. As a writer, McGahern was keen to understand and master the limitations imposed by the form. The novelist, accustomed to writing as a solitary activity carried out facing a blank wall in his study, soon learned the restrictions of the highly complex collaborative process of filmmaking. As he told an interviewer after he finished *The Rockingham Shoot*, whereas in a novel he could make his characters go anywhere and do almost anything (anything within the bounds of believability, that is), 'I discovered in filming that there were certain things one couldn't do, simply because the money wasn't there or because the weather was too much of a risk. It was more like life itself rather than art.'[27] There was, he said, a certain stimulation in having to write to such narrow constraints – much as a poet draws strength from having to fit within the formal constraints of, say, a sonnet.

To readers familiar with McGahern's short stories, perhaps the most obvious illustration of the changes that might

26. See Ciaran Carty, 'Sex, Ignorance and the Irish', *Sunday Tribune*, 29 September 1991, p. 27. In a letter from August of that same year to a colleague at Colgate University, where he would be spending the autumn term as a visiting professor, McGahern mentioned that 'I'll bring the screenplay of *The Porno Man*. It goes into production in October.' John McGahern, letter to Neill Joy, 20 August 1991 (private collection).

27. Carty, 'Out of the Dark', p. 18.

be required to fulfil the demands of budget and time can be found in the opening scene of the 1975 television film *Swallows*. Television has a much more modest budget than film, and *Swallows* was to be shot in a single day in November 1974 in a studio at BBC Broadcasting Centre in Birmingham.[28] The screenplay for *Swallows* was based on McGahern's own short story of the same name, first published in the *Evening Herald* in December 1971 and subsequently collected in *Getting Through* (1978). The plot and dialogue of the film largely follow that of the story, but the most striking change effected in the transition to a different medium is the new setting for the opening scene. At the start of the short story, the Sergeant and the Surveyor are measuring the evidence of a road accident on a wet, windy road in the west of Ireland. The screenplay, however, opens with the two men entering a pub. The introduction of this new setting may have allowed the author to further elaborate the comical contrast between the Sergeant's alcoholism and the Surveyor's abstemiousness, which is a feature of the original story. It may also have allowed him to introduce an additional character, the barman Michael, whose conversation about painting (of the painting-and-decorating variety, that is) first introduces, in a comical, low-key manner, the theme of amateur and professional standards in artistic pursuits that becomes a central theme later. For readers already familiar with McGahern's prose fiction, these are exciting new aspects to a familiar work. But the initial motivation for moving the opening scene to a new indoor setting was more than likely motivated not so much by McGahern's private need as a literary artist to introduce a new character and new angles to existing themes, as it was by the practical

28. The Studio Schedule on the first page of the BBC camera script for *Swallows* shows that both the camera rehearsals and the recording were completed on 7 November 1974. NUIG: P71/756.

necessity imposed upon him as a craftsman contracted by producer Barry Hanson to deliver a script that could be made on budget and within a fixed schedule.

*

In retrospect, it always seemed to McGahern that his first steps into television had been destined to end in failure. In the early 1970s, the BBC and TimeLife had approached a group of directors, playwrights and novelists to adapt each of the stories from Joyce's *Dubliners*, 'and the only thing that everybody had in common', as McGahern recalled later, 'was they knew nothing about writing or directing for television'.[29] McGahern was paired with Stephen Frears, who was beginning to make a reputation as a film director. It did not help, as he was often to summarise the arrangement with pithy symmetry in conversation in later years, that Frears knew nothing about Joyce and that he himself knew nothing about film or television. Or as he said in an interview: Frears 'told me he didn't know what he was doing, and I said I didn't know what I was doing. I was horrified when I saw what I had done.'[30] This retrospective assessment was no mere exaggeration for comic effect years after the fact. At the time, McGahern's response at the end of the preview screening consisted of a single expletive – the one that had got his second novel, *The Dark* (1965), into so much trouble when it appeared in capital letters on the first page – which 'exploded' into the quiet auditorium at the end of the credits.[31]

McGahern was soon to analyse the nature of the failure of *The Sisters*, and over the following decade he set to work refining his approach to writing for television as a craft distinct from prose fiction. If writing for radio was all

29. van der Ziel, 'Interview with John McGahern', p. 201.
30. Ibid., p. 201.
31. Madeline McGahern, conversation and email communication with the editor, June–July 2017.

about voices, then film and television work foregrounded images instead. Readers familiar with McGahern's pronouncements about the nature of his fiction might think this would be a particular advantage. In the early essay called 'The Image', which has been widely regarded as his aesthetic manifesto, he had, after all, foregrounded 'the image' as the central element of his fiction. That essay explains how McGahern conceived of his fiction as a restless and futile search for a 'lost image' that would reveal the artist's private 'vision, that still and private universe which each of us possess but which others cannot see'[32] – or as he phrased it rather more accessibly in an interview years later: the task of the artist was 'to pull the image that moves us out of the darkness'.[33] What he learned from the failure of *The Sisters*, however, was that the screenwriter's job was very different from that of a novelist or short-story writer. He talked about this difference between writing fiction and writing for the screen in interviews given to mark the release of *Swallows* in 1975, and again after *The Rockingham Shoot* in 1987:

Actually the director is the artist in a movie and the writer is a secondary person. He provides the framework. The real story is being told by the director and the actors. So it was like learning a completely new discipline, much more a trade than novel writing . . . The very function of dialogue is different in a movie. It has to do with taking a picture from A to B. There always has to be a reason for it in terms of what images the director is putting on the screen and these images are much more powerful than the words themselves.[34]

32. McGahern, *Love of the World*, pp. 5–6.
33. Arminta Wallace, 'Out of the Dark', *Irish Times*, 28 April 1990, Weekend, p. 5.
34. Carty, 'Out of the Dark', p. 18. See also Gillian Strickland, 'Birmingham Welcomes Careful Writers', *Radio Times*, 15–20 March 1975, p. 13. He also talked about writing for television in van der Ziel, 'Interview with John McGahern', pp. 201–2.

This same foregrounding of images chosen by a director over words written by a scriptwriter is also the subject – perhaps ironically – of the conclusion of the short story 'Oldfashioned', first published in 1983. In that story, the Sergeant's son grows up to be a filmmaker who returns to the native countryside to make a documentary film about the place where he grew up. The story concludes not with a record of the documentary-maker's speech to camera, but with a description of the visual imagery that accompanies his words:

The camera panned slowly away from the narrator to the house, and continued along the railings that had long lost their second whiteness, whirring steadily in the silence as it took in only what was in front of it, despite the cunning hand of the cameraman: lingering on the bright rain of cherries on the tramped grass beneath the trees, the flaked white paint of the paddock railing, the Iron Mountains smoky and blue as they stretched into the North against the rim of the sky.[35]

This paragraph has often been read as McGahern's thinly veiled comment about the importance of precise observation and authorial objectivity in realist fiction;[36] but it is impossible to not *also* recognise in the same paragraphs an acknowledgement of the things McGahern had learned about the craft of filmmaking during the shooting of *The Sisters* and *Swallows* – a lesson that he would soon put to work a final time in *The Rockingham Shoot*, the last, and most successful, of his screenplays.

It is important to recognise that the detailed description of the parsonage garden in the final paragraph of 'Oldfashioned' is an ekphrastic description of a passage from a documentary film, and not a scriptwriter's detailed set of directions intended to be

35. McGahern, *High Ground*, p. 58.
36. But see van der Ziel, *John McGahern*, p. 122, on the limitations of such a reading.

followed to the letter by the documentary's 'cunning' cameraman or director. This distinction is of utmost importance. In the doomed adaptation of *The Sisters*, McGahern had not yet realised the nature of the art form, and the script, while it reads well enough on the page, is perhaps too 'wordy' to leave room for the director to find the images that would make it work as a film. *Swallows* is more focused than its predecessor had been on images (the flashbacks of Eileen O'Neill; the room seen through the whiskey bottle), and the ratio of dialogue to directions is more weighted to the latter than *The Sisters* had been, but the script is still very much text-focused. *Swallows* shows how difficult it is for a novelist and short-story writer whose *métier* it is to pull images from the darkness of his imagination by finding the right words to move away from writing beautiful, *exact* prose, and instead write directions that are suggestive enough for a director to find his own images to put on the screen according to *his* private vision.

Only in *The Rockingham Shoot* are scenes habitually described in brief, simple directions that provide an outline or 'framework' rather than a precise, completed visual picture. Thus some scenes in the screenplay consist of only a single line, leaving director Kieran Hickey the freedom to find images that best conformed to his vision. This is particularly evident, for example, for a scene like number twenty-four. In the screenplay, this scene consists of three simple sentences – 'The boys are beating the bushes and trees. Birds fly up in the air. The shooting party fire' (p. 221) – and it is only through the combined efforts of cameraman and director that this simple 'framework' is translated into one of the most visually rich passages of the completed film. What had been a simple direction for a scene that does not contain any ideas presented novelistically through the dialogue has become a wordless passage of central importance to the development of one of the director's consistent visual ideas.[37] In Kieran Hickey's hands the sequence vividly demonstrates the contrast between the richness of sensations and experiences that may be found inside the Big House, and the comparative imaginative poverty of the rest of the countryside – that between the expanse and infinite variety of the estate, and the drab confinement of the schoolroom and the Reilly farmstead. Throughout, the director sought to introduce a visual vocabulary that reinforced the themes he found in McGahern's script. He talked about this in an interview to mark the film's first transmission:

Various images recur through the film. Hands and sticks appear as the teacher asks questions and indicates spellings, as a child acts out Goldsmith's Old Soldier, as the children practise beating for birds in the woods and as the master mounts an attack on half the class. Hickey acknowledges that these were his own ideas, 'what you work out as you prepare a script. You have to find the visual images. There must be relations and resonances going on in any film, whether the audience see it the first time or not.'[38]

The Rockingham Shoot does not contain long speeches, or even long directions, like the other two television plays. The very sparseness of some of the scenes, which arguably makes reading the screenplay of *The Rockingham Shoot* less of a complete experience, is the reason why it worked so well as a finished film. A script like that for *The Rockingham Shoot*

37. See McGahern's comment about one of the pitfalls encountered by novelists writing for the screen: 'Dialogue has a completely different function in television or the cinema than it has in the novel because it's basically to take the pictures from A to B: it's an outline of the story and it takes the pictures. If dialogue isn't moving the pictures, it has no business dealing with psychology or anything. It's all [to do] with movement, because it's the pictures that really tell the story, not the dialogue.' van der Ziel, 'Interview with John McGahern', p. 202.

38. Charles Hunter, 'The Life of O'Reilly [*sic*]', *Irish Times*, 9 September 1987, p. 12.

that is simply a 'framework' without unnecessary adornments left the director free to find the appropriate visual language.

Of all his work for television, *The Rockingham Shoot* was the one of which McGahern was proud. But for all this success, it would remain his last screenplay. There was, as he stressed in an interview, no immediate financial burden that necessitated a continuation of his career as screenwriter, and he had mastered the craft he had set out to master. After that, interest largely died.[39] Ultimately, the reason why McGahern was not drawn to do more film or television work is probably twofold. Firstly, that form precluded the use of a third-person authorial voice shrewdly observing and commenting on character and action that is such a significant part of McGahern's power as a novelist and short-story writer.[40] Secondly, working on *The Rockingham Shoot* had also confirmed that the director was the person who picked the images, and that the screenwriter only provided the 'framework' that made this possible. If the reason that compelled McGahern to write at all was to find the image that moved him and

39. van der Ziel, 'Interview with John McGahern', p. 202.

40. Such a shift *away* from a narrative voice that can both comment on the action with detachment and convey the complexities of central characters' inner lives through free indirect speech, and *towards* the exteriority of dramatic speech, is also evident in his radio adaptation of *The Barracks*. Apart from a single passage towards the end (p. 142), McGahern's script resists the obvious temptation of turning the novel's accounts of Elizabeth's inner turmoil into a series of monologues or soliloquies – a decision that is particularly striking since some passages in the novel, despite being mediated through the free indirect speech of the third-person narrator, resembled dramatic soliloqies to begin with, as one early reviewer pointed out (see John D. Sheridan, 'Classic Tragedy in the Barracks', *Irish Independent*, 16 March 1963, p. 10). Instead, the radio version of *The Barracks* is a remarkable exercise in translating the interiority of the novel into the exteriority of a play.

draw it out of the darkness, then writing for television did not fulfil this purpose.

THE ROCKINGHAM SHOOT:
NATIONALISM, FANATICISM AND MAGIC

McGahern often remarked that his works usually originated with an image 'that stays in the mind and will not go away until it is written down'.[41] Two such persistent images that came to preoccupy his imagination in the early 1980s originated in his early life and are connected with the Rockingham estate and Rockingham House, the mansion overlooking Lough Key that had been built in the neoclassical style by the renowned English architect John Nash and in which, according to the north Roscommon folklore of McGahern's childhood, there was one window for every day of the year.[42]

The first of these images is that of its destruction. Rockingham House was destroyed in a fire on the night of 10 September 1957. (The first broadcast of *The Rockingham Shoot* on BBC2 Northern Ireland on 10 September 1987 coincided exactly with the thirtieth anniversary of that event.) The description of the house, its burning, and the sad spectacle of 'the magnificent shell and portals, now full of sky and dangerous in high winds' that remained on the shores of Lough Key afterwards, are described in a key paragraph in the story 'Oldfashioned'.[43] The historical fact of the burning of Rockingham is not, of course, a direct

41. McGahern, *Love of the World*, p. 9.

42. Ibid., p. 23.

43. McGahern, *High Ground*, p. 51. Note, though, that the passage in question from 'Oldfashioned' may owe as much to a literary source like W. B. Yeats's *Purgatory* – a play that haunted McGahern's imagination all his life – as it does to first-hand experience. See van der Ziel, *John McGahern*, pp. 61–2 and *passim*.

presence in the screenplay of *The Rockingham Shoot*, which is set some time earlier in the 1950s; but knowledge of the house's inevitable fast-approaching fate does lend added poignancy to the story.

Another image connected with the fate of Rockingham also refused to leave McGahern's mind in the same period. This second image, less violent or dramatic in nature than the first, was the one that led directly to the writing of *The Rockingham Shoot*. It was simply that of the wall of the estate, which extended for miles across the landscape of his early life. McGahern told an interviewer that *The Rockingham Shoot* began as a draft for a short story that 'didn't work out' and was abandoned:

But the image was always in my mind and wouldn't go away. The idea of the ordinary life of a new order beginning outside the walls and in a way the old order being carried into the beginning of the new order.[44]

This 'new order' is that of the independent state that was founded in 1922. Thematically, *The Rockingham Shoot* belongs not only with the *High Ground* stories of Anglo-Irish nostalgia for the lost world of the Big House, but should also be read alongside *Amongst Women*, the novel on which McGahern had been at work for some time by the time the television film was broadcast, and which was finally published three years later to almost universal acclaim as a watershed novel about post-revolutionary Ireland. Both novel and screenplay are about the disappointment that was widely felt after the foundation of the new State, when the promise for radical social reform and equality of the 1916 Proclamation was 'subverted', and Ireland turned into what McGahern

44. Carty, 'Out of the Dark', p. 18. Copies of drafts of the abandoned prose version of *The Rockingham Shoot* are held in the John McGahern Papers, NUIG: P71/757 and P71/759–61.

bluntly characterised in his essays as 'a theocracy in all but name'.[45] *The Rockingham Shoot* and *Amongst Women* are studies of different ways in which this disappointment with the way the realities of post-revolutionary society failed to match the promises of the revolutionary moment could be manifested.

Where the ex-guerrilla fighter Moran in *Amongst Women* retreats from the world into the 'little republic' of his own house and family when he sees the direction in which the country for which he has fought is moving, Reilly – who is younger and has not fought in the War of Independence – enters a position of service to the emerging new state by becoming a teacher (p. 240). In practice, though, the direction that Reilly's effort at national improvement takes does not support the lofty ideals of the 1916 Proclamation of the Irish Republic. As happened to many idealistic young men in the decades that followed independence, his original revolutionary idealism has gradually been replaced by a conservative nationalism, which in its equation of Catholicism with the indigenous population made the Free State into a *de facto* theocracy. In this atmosphere, patriotism was often confused with a fierce intolerance of all attitudes and practices that did not conform to Catholic teaching, and a blind hatred of everything British.

McGahern emphasised in an interview about *The Rockingham Shoot* that Reilly is based on a certain type of personality 'that was a mixture of sexual asceticism, blind Irishness and a particularly puritanical brand of Catholicism' which dominated Irish life in the 1940s and 1950s.[46] McGahern, a generation younger yet again than Reilly, had viewed such types with deep suspicion and embarrassment when he was a young man. As he explained about his and

45. See for example 'From a Glorious Dream to Wink and Nod' (in *Love of the World*, pp. 125–7), an essay commissioned to mark the seventy-fifth anniversary of the Easter Rising in 1991.

46. Herbert, 'Window on the World', p. 59.

his contemporaries' attitudes towards the Irish nationalist mainstream in the mid-century Ireland of his youth in an another interview from the same period: 'It was a young, insecure state without traditions . . . and there was this notion that to be Irish was good. Nobody actually took any time to understand what to be Irish was. There was this slogan and fanaticism and a lot of emotion, but there wasn't any clear idea except what you were against: you were against sexuality; you were against the English.'[47] In *The Rockingham Shoot*, this narrowly defined nationalist agenda determines the contents of Reilly's political speeches, which consist exclusively of populist anti-British sentiment and patriotic rhetoric about the 'native' Irish language, rather than offering constructive civic engagement or proposals for progressive social change. But since Reilly is more a target for hecklers than a viable electoral prospect, his political stance cannot cause any damage and remains a cause for merriment to the rest of the community, as the brilliantly funny opening scene shows.

It is much more worrying how the same nationalist obsessions also influence the contents of his classes. McGahern, who had trained and practised as a teacher when he was a young man, had been concerned with the great responsibility incumbent on those whose profession is to mould the minds of the nation's young in a novel like *The Leavetaking* (1974) and elsewhere in his earlier fiction, and *The Rockingham Shoot* further develops this concern. Every subject Reilly teaches, from the Irish language to English literature, is informed by nationalist propaganda calculated to instil suspicion and contempt for everything British in his pupils. One of his Irish lessons consists of making the children copy vocabulary describing different systems of government and their constituent parts – *An Parliméad* (parliament), *Rialtas daonfhlathach* (constitutional

47. Julia Carlson, ed., *Banned in Ireland: Censorship and the Irish Writer* (London: Routledge, 1990), p. 63.

democracy), *Ríocht* (monarchy). That exercise is intended more as a lesson in the politics of freedom and oppression than in the tricky orthography of a language that had once been used to write epics and satires and love poems. (The latter tradition remains ironically dormant in the comical night-time scene between Johnny and Mary Armstrong, in which the male lover has so little understanding of his 'native' language that he fails to understand the Irish for 'I love you' (pp. 226–7).) English literature, meanwhile, takes the form of a lesson on Oliver Goldsmith's *The Deserted Village*, which serves both to further a sentimental view of unspoilt country ways (a purpose for which that poem was routinely enlisted in Irish schools for most of the twentieth century), and to condemn the British imperial greed that had first drained the vitality of the Irish countryside and then claimed the reputation of its most significant writers as its own – a balance Reilly seeks to redress by proclaiming the old cliché that 'Most of the great playwrights in English were Irish; I'd have you remember that' (p. 207).

Reilly's original motive for becoming a teacher in the service of the new State may have been noble, but when the film opens he has long lost sight of these idealistic beginnings. Ironically, his actions have come to undermine the very republican ideals he had set out to defend as a young man – for as the Sergeant has to remind him, 'the people who set up this State were big people. *They* allowed room for everybody' (p. 237). His initial desire to make Ireland a better country has led instead to a fanatical hatred of any foreign or Protestant elements that goes against the spirit of the 1916 Proclamation of the Irish Republic, that important revolutionary announcement of social reform guided by principles of liberty and equality regardless of gender or creed. Where the dominant themes of *Amongst Women*'s treatment of post-revolutionary Ireland are disappointment, embitterment and entrenchment, *The Rockingham Shoot* is concerned with how frustrated idealism can turn to fanaticism, or even Fascism. McGahern used the latter word in an interview with Ciaran Carty in which he discussed how Reilly

gets enslaved by the nationalistic notion which he imposes out of some personal frustration on everyone else. Fascism is rooted in the way intelligent people like the teacher can get drawn into inhuman ideas. A narrow single thing – a dogma – can be more attractive, because it is easier to embrace, than actually dealing with the complicated difficult thing that experience is.[48]

The Rockingham Shoot was commissioned by Danny Boyle, the future award-winning film director who was then a producer at BBC Northern Ireland, as part of a series of one-off plays written for television. The only limitation the BBC had given Boyle was that the films should not be expressly about 'the situation' in Northern Ireland, and the brief Boyle gave to authors was that their films must be about education and young people growing up in Ireland.[49] McGahern's screenplay is set south of the border in the Republic of Ireland in the 1950s, but with its theme of fanaticism and its message about the dangers of instilling values of hatred and division through the education system, it was of course highly relevant in the context of the Troubles in contemporary Northern Ireland in the 1980s. Just how relevant that message was in the context of the time and place of its production was borne out less than two months after the film's broadcast when, in an act that made Reilly's beating of the schoolchildren in the film pale into comparative insignificance, an IRA bomb exploded on Remembrance Day 1987 in the town of Enniskillen, just north of the border from where the McGaherns lived in peaceful County Leitrim. McGahern

48. Carty, 'Out of the Dark', p. 18.
49. See Douglas Kennedy, 'Ireland of Dreams', *Radio Times*, 5–11 September 1987, p. 13; Hugh Hebert, 'Growing Pains', *The Guardian*, 11 September 1987, p. 20.

knew very well that the mentality that led to such extreme acts was not confined to the contested counties north of the border. He would later allude to the presence of the same violent impulses amid even the most serene pastoral settings in *That They May Face the Rising Sun*, in which it is hinted that one of the inhabitants of the sleepy town near the lake where most of the characters live in peaceful harmony with each other and their surroundings may have been involved in the Enniskillen bombing.

*

But *The Rockingham Shoot* is not just a record of fanaticism, intolerance, hatred and violence. At the conclusion, a travelling entertainer arrives at the school to perform a magic show. McGahern talked about the importance of this kind of travelling entertainer in the landscape of his youth, when the countryside was not only materially but imaginatively impoverished:

Those itinerant magicians were a permanent feature of the countryside in the forties. They were probably down-and-out actors coming to the schools to earn some drink money. They used to learn a bit of Irish to get by and infuriated the teachers with all their grammatical errors. But to us they were glamorous figures.[50]

The world of magic, music and stories to which the children are introduced through the magician's show offers an antidote to such destructive attitudes as are perpetuated by the kind of teaching offered in Reilly's lessons. As the magic show goes on, the children become animated, happy and bold: a complete transformation from the oppressed, unimaginative learners by rote they had been under the influence of Reilly.

The contrast between the drab, authoritarian attitude that dominated Irish life in the mid-century – when 'the

50. Carty, 'Out of the Dark', p. 18.

stolidity of a long empty grave face was thought to be the height of decorum and profundity', as McGahern wrote in the essay 'The Solitary Reader'[51] – and the possibilities offered by things like magic, poetry and music is an important recurring idea in a number of McGahern's dramatic works. Elsewhere in *The Rockingham Shoot*, the same contrast is also highlighted through the introduction of Canon Glynn, the lover of poetry who, like Keats, talks of beauty and truth (p. 244), and whose life is made richer and more complex by his intimate familiarity with Shakespeare and John Donne. Reilly may be able to complete the line from Shakespeare's Sonnet 60 which eludes the Canon's fading memory (which is ironic, since the subject of that poem is the great Shakespearean theme of the transience of all living things), but he does so 'insensitively' (pp. 245–6). For Reilly, as for many teachers in McGahern's experience, poetry was merely something to be learned by rote in order to pass an exam. True to this utilitarian mentality towards the arts, the content of Reilly's lesson on *The Deserted Village* is based on what he thinks is most likely to come up in this year's exam, rather than on a true didactic impulse for enlightening and deepening his pupils' pleasure and understanding of the poem or its language. Reciting a poem for pleasure would be regarded as 'showing off', as the Canon had been shocked to discover when he was young (p. 244).[52] For the Canon, on the other hand, a lifelong proximity to

51. McGahern, *Love of the World*, p. 87.
52. The passage in which *The Rockingham Shoot*'s Canon Glynn recalls his youthful discovery of the hostility that exists towards poetry in much of society replicates one of the narrator's mother's formative memories in *The Leavetaking*: 'For years now she'd kept her love of poetry a secret, as defence against the laughter and ridicule it provoked . . . [She] still shivered as she remembered the derision in Kathleen's laughter when she finished [reciting a poem], the singsong that was a vicious mimicry of the poem, "Ah yes, Kate McLaughlin showing off again that she got the gold medal

great poems has cultivated values of patience and tolerance, as contrasted with the pursuit of unbending and absolute 'ideals' against which he warns Reilly in the same scene. These make him something of a 'moral voice' of the film, in the way that the drunken Paddy fulfils that function in *The Power of Darkness* (see p. 259).

In *Swallows*, the focus is on the transformative power of music – as well as, in the opening scene unique to the film version, that of painting, as the barman Michael seems to derive immense satisfaction as he patiently sits and paints the walls of the pub. A rural Garda Sergeant is reminded of his youthful love of music through a chance meeting with a Surveyor who, unlike the Sergeant, has not given up playing the violin and turned to whiskey 'to hurry the hours' instead (p. 192). If following an artistic vocation is risky because it can lead to penury or even to becoming a social outcast (the 'unorthodox' life of Paganini, as recounted by the Surveyor, is analogous to McGahern's own run-in with the Catholic hierarchy in the mid-1960s), then on the other hand music is also a powerful antidote to the boredom and bitterness of living in isolation. Of course, this is not a new idea. McGahern was well aware that the idea that music has the potential to change human nature for the better has a long theatrical provenance stretching

for English in the Carysford Finals."' John McGahern, *The Leavetaking* (London: Faber and Faber, 1974), pp. 37–8. Both of these recollections by secondary characters in his works are probably fictionalised accounts of the kind of attitudes McGahern himself encountered in the anti-intellectual climate of mid-century Ireland, and perhaps specifically that of St Patrick's College, Drumcondra, where he trained to be a teacher in the 1950s. In St Pat's, students were liable to be 'biffed' on the back of the head by one of the priests who ran that institution if they were found reading any book that was not on the curriculum. See Carlson, ed., *Banned in Ireland*, p. 66; see also Denis Sampson, *Young John McGahern: Becoming a Novelist* (Oxford: Oxford University Press, 2012), p. 23.

back through Shakespeare all the way to ancient Greece. This tradition is acknowledged on at least one occasion in the script. When the Surveyor tries to persuade the Sergeant to take up the violin again, he gives that advice weight by grappling for a distant memory of a literary quotation: 'You should take up the violin again. Music, how does it go, soothes the savage breast. You should take it up again' (p. 195) – a misquotation of the famous opening line of William Congreve's 1697 tragedy *The Mourning Bride*:

> Musick has Charms to sooth a savage Breast,
> To soften Rocks, or bend a knotted Oak.[53]

But the situation in *Swallows* is not just a development of an idea encountered in literary sources; it also has a more immediate biographical origin in the author's early life. In an interview published in the *Radio Times* to promote the broadcast of *Swallows*, McGahern situated the origins of a story about a visiting violinist in a remote Garda barracks in a specific childhood memory. The kernel of this is essentially the same as that of the itinerant magicians who were such glamorous figures in his youth:

My father was the head of [a police barracks in Ireland]. And I remember someone rather like the violinist in the play coming there. The hurt he left behind him was palpable for days.[54]

The feeling of emptiness left behind by the real-life violinist when he departed from Sergeant McGahern's barracks only goes to demonstrate the need for imaginative stimulation that was felt by much of the countryside during the repressed middle decades of the twentieth century.

53. *The Complete Plays of William Congreve*, ed. Herbert Davis (Chicago: University of Chicago Press, 1967), p. 326.
54. Strickland, 'Birmingham Welcomes Careful Writers', p. 13.

STAGING DARKNESS

If *The Rockingham Shoot* and *Sinclair* are about the tragic fate of Protestant Anglo-Ireland, then McGahern's only stage play is about the other side of the social and political divide. *The Power of Darkness* was adapted from Leo Tolstoy's drama about the moral squalor of Russian peasants in the nineteenth century, in which McGahern recognised a world 'uncannily close to the moral climate in which I grew up', as he wrote in his Programme Note for the 1991 Abbey Theatre production (printed subsequently as an Introduction in the Faber and Faber edition of the play text). McGahern's version is transposed to rural Ireland in the 1950s, and it dramatises what he called the 'Famine mentality' of late-nineteenth- and twentieth-century Ireland. By this he meant not just the fear of the poorhouse which determines the behaviour of many of the father figures in his fiction, from Mahoney in *The Dark* to Moran in *Amongst Women*, and which causes Peter King in the play to repeatedly vocalise his fear that all he has worked for in his lifetime will be 'scattered' after he is gone. McGahern used the term 'Famine mentality' more narrowly to refer to a specific kind of behaviour motivated by what he described in an essay as 'a blind rancour against neighbours coupled with an equally blind grasping after even useless advantages'.[55] This way of thinking is the subject of the Magician's comical allegory on 'envy' at the end of *The Rockingham Shoot*, and in *Sinclair* the same grasping for 'useless' advantage may account for Gillespie's compulsion to withhold from his neighbour the information that he has bought a second-hand chainsaw at a local auction.

In *The Power of Darkness*, the advantages are not useless, and all the characters seem to be out to exploit and

55. McGahern, *Love of the World*, p. 155.

manipulate the others. This exploitation and manipulation
is economic as well as sexual in nature, and often the two
are inseparably interconnected. If, as McGahern often
said, the Catholic Church in Ireland had 'caused most
serious damage in the area of sexuality',[56] then *The Power
of Darkness* elaborates on how this was so. As McGahern
explained in his Introduction, the play is interested in how
the 'confusion and guilt and plain ignorance that surrounded sex' in the repressive and morally censorious climate of
Catholic Ireland turns men and women into 'exploiters
and adversaries' rather than helpmates or companions
(p. 255n.). Thus an old farmer, Peter King, has used his
position of economic security to attract a vivacious young
wife, Eileen, who is unfulfilled in her life of drudgery and
seeks sensual pleasures in the arms of their young
workman; Paul exploits his attractiveness to obtain sex
from Rosie, Eileen and even, after he becomes master of
the farm by marrying Eileen, from his wife's stepdaughter
Maggie, and he has no compunction discarding these
women when their attentions no longer suit him. But the
women are equally manipulative. They are not above using
their sexuality to manipulate the men into giving them
what *they* want: the security and social prestige of
marriage. Maggie's unwanted pregnancy may well threaten
her marital prospects with a respectable family, but others,
as Baby (the most ruthless manipulator of all) hints, have
used the same condition to secure themselves a husband.
(This same manipulative practice playing on feelings of
social and religious propriety is also an important plot
element in McGahern's novel *The Pornographer*.) In a
culture obsessed with sexual morality, the illegitimate
products of sin were perhaps the only fully innocent party,
but it was often they who were disposed of in a ditch in

56. Clíodhna Ní Anluain, ed., *Reading the Future: Irish Writers
in Conversation with Mike Murphy* (Dublin: Lilliput, 2000),
pp. 137–55, at p. 140.

order to preserve a family's 'good name'. And so in the 'dark' world of *The Power of Darkness* a newborn child is not a clichéd metonymic bundle of joy, but is reduced, rather, to a chillingly literal 'bundle of sheets'. McGahern had found all these plot elements in Tolstoy's original, and knew that they translated perfectly to the Irish reality that was the familiar terrain of his fiction. But the translation from one context to another, and from the dramatic idioms of the nineteenth century into one that was suitable for the second half of the twentieth, would prove an altogether more difficult task.

*

McGahern first started work on an adaptation of Tolstoy's 1888 drama sometime during the late 1960s. Over the next three and a half decades, he returned to the play on a number of occasions, and between 1972 and 2005 his approach evolved significantly. McGahern first started on a straightforward 'translation' of the pre-war English idioms of Louise and Aylmer Maude's Oxford World's Classics edition that was his source text[57] into 'living Irish speech', but he eventually ended up with a much looser adaptation that reimagined some of the plot elements and even the dramatic form and structure of Tolstoy's original. It is probably useful to take stock here of how these different incarnations of *The Power of Darkness* evolved into the final version, completed in July 2005, which is printed in this volume.

Contrary to what he would recall in his 1991 Introduction (see p. 255), it is highly unlikely that McGahern was only made aware of the existence of Tolstoy's plays when he was commissioned by the BBC to adapt *The Power of*

57. Leo Tolstoy, *Plays*, translated by Louise and Aylmer Maude (London: Oxford University Press, 1923). This edition is identified as the one from which McGahern worked in a note held in the BBC WAC: RCont 17.

Darkness into Irish speech for radio in the early 1970s. Even if he had not read Tolstoy's plays when he systematically read through his novels and stories in the late 1950s[58] – which seems unlikely, given that as a young man he had a habit of reading everything an author had written once he found one book by a writer he liked[59] – he must surely have been introduced to Tolstoy the dramatist after 1965 under the influence of his first wife, the Finnish theatre director Annikki Laaksi, who had worked for the Moscow Art Theatre and who translated nineteenth-century Russian plays by such writers as Alexander Ostrovsky.[60]

Contrary also to his recollections in the 1991 Introduction, McGahern originally conceived of his translation of *The Power of Darkness* as a stage play, eventually submitting it to the Abbey Theatre, where it was rejected in September 1972 for reasons discussed a little later. It was only after he had started working on it as a stage play that McGahern began to consider that the play might *also* transfer to the medium of radio. This happened early in its gestation, and was possibly motivated by the promise of an additional income stream. The earliest indication of the play's possible transition from stage to radio can be found in a letter from McGahern to Susanna Capon at the BBC which significantly predates the rejection letter from the Abbey, in which he points out how, 'As it is the most difficult form of translating outside verse – rhythmically it needs to be deadly exact to avoid parody – I would need to be very well paid for it.'[61] The version of *The Power of*

58. John McGahern, letter to Michael McLaverty, 22 August 1959, in *Dear Mr McLaverty: The Literary Correspondence of John McGahern and Michael McLaverty*, ed. John Killen (Belfast: Linen Hall Library, 2006), p. 18.

59. See van der Ziel, 'Interview with John McGahern', p. 207.

60. Ibid., p. 200.

61. John McGahern, letter to Susanna Capon, 28 June 1971. BBC WAC: RCont 17.

Darkness that was eventually produced and broadcast to favourable reception on BBC Radio 3 on 15 October 1972 was essentially identical to the stage play that had been rejected by the Abbey in September of that year.[62] Only minimal changes were made – either by McGahern himself or by producer Denys Hawthorne[63] – to facilitate the transition to this different medium, as was customary for much of the BBC's radio drama output during this period.

As McGahern pointed out in his Introduction, 'Generally when a play is produced or a novel published it frees the writer from the material. This did not happen with *The Power of Darkness*. Over the years I kept returning to Tolstoy's melodrama' (see p. 255). In 1987–88 he submitted a revised version to the Field Day Theatre Company. Over time, he had come to dislike the language – 'too Synge-like and too colourful'[64] – with which he had overlaid Tolstoy's plot, and this was gradually toned down in subsequent revisions. But in other respects the version he submitted to Field Day in the 1980s stayed very close to the Abbey/BBC version from the early 1970s. The shape of the play and the size of the production do not seem to have

62. The assessment of the radio adaptation by the BBC's internal Radio Weekly Review Board contrasts sharply with that of the Abbey Theatre's rejection letter of the stage play. Extracts from the minutes of the Board are quoted in a letter from Ronald Mason (who had produced *Sinclair* the previous year): 'The action had translated into an Irish environment successfully and naturally . . . Ch.Asst. R.3 [Chief Assistant, Radio 3] said he had been completely gripped by the play. It was only afterwards that he had asked himself whether this could really happen in modern Ireland. A.H.D.R. [Assistant Head of Drama, Radio] said the translation had been so accomplished and the dialogue so authentic that while listening one accepted that it could.' Ronald Mason, letter to John McGahern, 2 November 1972. BBC WAC: NI 25/30/1.

63. I am indebted for this information to Susanna Capon, email communication, June 2017.

64. Carty, 'Sex, Ignorance and the Irish', p. 27.

altered significantly between 1972 and 1988. After long delay, Field Day finally passed on the play. In the rejection letter written in his capacity as a director of Field Day, Brian Friel expressed his admiration for McGahern's 'brilliantly realised adaptation', but he was also very clear about why the company could not take it on:

But there is absolutely no possibility of Field Day doing any play with 13+ characters. The touring costs alone would absorb all our grants for five years. Only an institution – the Abbey, the British National Theatre, the Royal Shakespeare Company – can take on a project of this size but I'm sure you understand all this.[65]

It was only following the advice of another Field Day board member, McGahern's friend the playwright Thomas Kilroy, that the list of characters was reduced[66] and the Tolstoy play began to take on the leaner form that we now recognise as the McGahern version.

Kilroy, in fact, took a detailed interest in McGahern's latest attempt at revising *The Power of Darkness*. Their surviving correspondence from this period paints a fascinating picture of the direction in which the play was, for a brief while at least, moving, before McGahern finally settled on the shape that was produced at the Abbey in 1991 and published by Faber and Faber in the same year, and which was in broad essence retained in his final attempt to rewrite the play in the years immediately preceding his final illness and death in 2006. This period between 1988 and 1991 was the one in which the play most drastically

65. Brian Friel, letter to John McGahern, 20 April 1988. NUIG: P71/1183.
66. See a letter to McGahern: 'I think I'm talking about four or five big scenes. In terms of characters it means a reduction to: Peter, Eileen, Maggie, Paul, Oliver, Baby and *possibly* old Paddy. Something like this is the scaling down that we talked about.' Thomas Kilroy, letter to John McGahern, 24 August 1988. NUIG: P71/1184.

changed. In a letter from August 1988, Kilroy urged that 'I still think the central material needs to be "framed" in some way, in a contemporary theatrical style, for it to be accessible.'[67] McGahern spent the next year grappling with such a 'framing' device, and in August 1989 he wrote to Kilroy:

I'm ½ way through the play. The hard part was to get it started. It's strange how the framing device has changed the whole play. I begin with a priest at Maggie's hospital bed. End it with Maggie visiting Paul's cell. I think it has taken much of the melodrama out and it have [sic] given me more control.[68]

Kilroy only partially concurred. After reading this version of the play with its new 'framing' structure, he advised that the prologue should be retained but shortened to a 'monologue . . . of the kind that offers a narrative which tells only enough to whet the audience's appetite', while the epilogue should be omitted altogether so that the play ends with Paul's confession.[69] McGahern, however, after spending a year on this revised version of the play in the 'contemporary theatrical style', did not take Kilroy's advice and omitted the 'framing' device completely, returning to a more conventional naturalistic dramatic structure that moves chronologically from Peter King's sickbed in Act One to Paul's confession of his crimes at the end of Act Five. This was the version of the play that was finally staged as the Abbey Theatre's contribution to the Dublin Theatre Festival in October 1991.

In the period between the play's rejection by Field Day in 1988 and its performance at the Abbey Theatre in 1991, McGahern made crucial changes not just to the structure but also to the plot. Not all of these were a result of Friel's

67. Ibid.

68. John McGahern, letter to Thomas Kilroy, 23 August 1989. NUIG: P103/446(9).

69. Thomas Kilroy, rough draft of a letter to John McGahern, n.d. NUIG: P103/488(3).

or Kilroy's suggestions. Both the 1972 BBC radio version and the Field Day submission from 1987–88 stayed very close to the plot of Tolstoy's original. But the later versions take more liberties with the actions of the characters. One change to the plot in particular is worth dwelling on. In Tolstoy's original, Akulina's (called Maggie in McGahern's version) child is born alive and must be killed by Nikita (Paul) before he can bury it in the cellar. The script of McGahern's 1972 version preserved this plot line in all its gruesome detail, as Eileen and Paul each graphically report on how the child's bones 'crunched' when it was smothered under a board;[70] and so, judging from Kilroy's reference to 'the killing of the infant' in his letter from August 1988, did the version he submitted to Field Day.[71] By the time it was staged at the Abbey Theatre in 1991, however, the child is prematurely stillborn (most probably with a helping hand from Baby, the townland's illicit pharmacist who had earlier supplied the 'tablets' that dispatched Peter King). This was a crucial change, and we shall return to its significance shortly.

*

One thing that had changed between the time when McGahern first started working on Tolstoy's play shortly after the banning of *The Dark* in 1965, and 1991, when Garry Hynes chose the new version of *The Power of Darkness* as the Abbey Theatre's contribution to the Dublin Theatre Festival, was the public's attitude to the Catholic Church and its increasing openness in accepting the reality

70. Tolstoy, *Plays*, pp. 91–3; John McGahern, '*The Power of Darkness*: A modern version of Leo Tolstoy's play in living Irish speech', produced by Denys Hawthorne, BBC Radio 3, 15 October 1972. Microfilm script. BBC WAC: Play Library (Radio) (pp. 81–4).

71. Thomas Kilroy, letter to John McGahern, 24 August 1988. NUIG: P71/1184.

of the 'dark' things that had happened – and were happening still – in Ireland in the name of Catholic morality. In 1972, Lelia Doolan, in her capacity as Artistic Director of the Abbey, had concluded that McGahern's translation of Tolstoy's play was 'not . . . acceptable for production here' because 'The melodramatic theme of the play does not translate sufficiently well to the Irish situation.'[72] The rejection letter also quotes extracts from the report of their reader, who complained that 'The grim and primitive life of the Russian peasant in the mid-nineteenth century, the ignorance and superstition does not at all translate to Ireland at any time.'[73] The Abbey's defensive response to McGahern's play about young girls marrying old farmers, lust, adultery, murder and infanticide echoed not only the reception of *The Dark* following its banning by the Censorship of Publications Board in 1965 (an *Irish Independent* editorial which found the novel 'unreal . . . in its picture of provincial Ireland today' was not untypical);[74] but also the outraged responses of Dublin theatregoers to Synge's portrayal of sexual frustration, lust and ambiguous moral standards in the Irish countryside in *The Playboy of the Western World* more than half a century earlier. Official opinion for most of the twentieth century was unchanging in its insistence that *such things did not happen in Ireland.*

This mood was beginning to change by the turn of the 1990s, when Garry Hynes, the Galwegian with a reputation for mounting controversial productions of classic plays who had just been appointed as the Abbey's new Artistic Director,[75] chose to direct *The Power of Darkness*

72. Lelia Doolan, letter to John McGahern, 28 September 1972. BBC WAC: RCont 14.

73. Ibid.

74. 'Banned', *Irish Independent*, 3 June 1965, p. 12.

75. See for example Richard Pine, 'Garry Hynes: A Year at the Abbey', *Irish Literary Supplement*, vol. 11, no. 2 (autumn 1992), p. 11.

as the Irish national theatre's contribution to the 1991 Dublin Theatre Festival. Though many maintained the traditional defensive stance and made the case of unreality or untruth – the *Irish Independent*'s drama critic petulantly referred to 'the broken, soulless world [which] it *purports* to portray'[76] – audiences in the new Ireland of Mary Robinson were gradually beginning to seek out exposés of the dark things that had gone on in Ireland during the twentieth century. McGahern synthesised the advent of this turnaround in the climate in a paragraph from the story 'Oldfashioned'. The description of the Sergeant's son's career as a documentary filmmaker near the end of that story is really a thinly veiled comment on the history of McGahern's own reception over the years:

> . . . he made a series of documentary films about the darker aspects of Irish life. As they were controversial, they won him a sort of fame: some thought they were serious, well made, and compulsive viewing, bringing things to light that were in bad need of light; but others maintained that they were humourless, morbid, and restricted to a narrow view that was more revealing of private obsessions than any truths about life or Irish life in general.[77]

The Abbey Theatre may have rejected McGahern's first, large-cast translation of *The Power of Darkness* in 1972 because it was untrue to the reality of Irish life, but in 1991 Hynes set out to use the same author's new version of the same play expressly to make a point about the existence of the 'darker aspects of Irish life' which her distant predecessor had so matter-of-factly denied.

To an extent, McGahern cooperated with this agenda, alluding in his Programme Note to the fact that the sort of things portrayed in the play were not fanciful imaginings but a brutal reality. To lend weight to this point, he

76. Desmond Rushe, 'No Good Points in the Murk', *Irish Independent*, 17 October 1991, p. 10 (emphasis added).

77. McGahern, *High Ground*, p. 55.

referred to the Kerry Babies case, one of the darkest chapters in recent Irish social history.[78]

But author and director sharply disagreed on the way in which these newly revealed truths about Irish life should properly be staged. The main bone of contention during rehearsals was Hynes's attempt to exploit the play for maximum shock value. Specifically, she wanted the 'bundle of sheets' containing Maggie's stillborn child which is carried on by Baby in Act Five to be dripping with blood and as realistic a match for a real dead baby as possible – arguably in an effort to stir up painful recent national memories of the gruesome find of the body of a baby stabbed to death in the Kerry Babies case. McGahern's preference was exactly the opposite; he wanted the bundle of sheets to be just that – a bundle of sheets, clean and only suggestive of its gruesome contents. In the radical revisions he had just made to the play in 1988–89, he had got rid of the graphic descriptions of 'the killing of the infant' that carried over directly from Tolstoy's original plot, and replaced these with a tactful reference to a premature birth that could not possibly sustain life. As Baby says, 'How could it be alive the way it came into the world?' (p. 321). What interested McGahern was not the shock of an

78. This referred to the case of a Kerry woman called Joanne Hayes who was already bringing up one illegitimate child when she became pregnant with a married man with whom she was having an affair. The baby died at birth, and the woman's family buried its body on the family farm. Soon after, the body of another baby was found stabbed to death on a nearby beach. Hayes was accused of also giving birth to this second child, killing it and hiding the body. The investigation that followed turned into a latter-day witch-hunt demonising evil women who lived outside the norm established and policed by the teachings of the all-powerful Catholic Church. The Kerry Babies Tribunal subsequently became a feminist *cause célèbre*, and has been cited as the last stand of traditional patriarchal attitudes. See Tom Inglis, *Truth, Power and Lies: Irish Society and the Case of the Kerry Babies* (Dublin: University College Dublin Press, 2003).

audience being confronted with something that had all the appearance of a genuine dead body, as they might have been in an Elizabethan or Jacobean revenge-tragedy,[79] in a Martin McDonagh play, or indeed in a Victorian melodrama. Like a Greek tragedian, McGahern was more interested in the *idea* that ordinary people could be driven by the social and religious pressures brought to bear by their environment to do dreadful things (the 'darkness' of the title) than in shocking graphic representations of the bloody outcomes of such moral turpitude. At the heart of *The Power of Darkness* is McGahern's concern with demonstrating how the repressive religious climate that he had known in his youth had been the cause of the kinds of violence and manipulation and mistrust that transpire throughout the play. Gratuitous bloody spectacles of the kind that Garry Hynes sought to introduce would be a distraction from this core idea.

It seems, then, that even as the 1991 production of the play was advertised as a 'melodrama' and widely criticised for the use of an exaggerated acting style that played up emotions in the old-fashioned melodramatic style, and even as the reference to that generic origin was maintained on the title page of the published text, McGahern was, as he had explicitly indicated in his August 1989 letter to Kilroy, purposefully reducing – if not altogether removing – much of the melodramatic quality of Tolstoy's original play. The plot still retains quintessentially melodramatic devices, like the poisoning of Peter King. But even if the way he is

79. This is not to say, of course, that McGahern was not interested in that genre. He was particularly fond of Webster's *The White Devil* and *The Duchess of Malfi*. According to Madeline McGahern, he probably first read these and others as a young man in Dublin, but his appreciation of Jacobean theatre was no doubt further deepened by conversations with Professor Donald Gordon during his stint as a research fellow at the University of Reading between 1968 and 1971.

dispatched through the agency of a blackly drawn melodramatic villain (Baby) belongs more properly on the
Victorian stage than on a real-life Irish farm in the mid-
twentieth century, the feelings of entrapment and frustration
that drive a young woman like Eileen, who has married a
prosperous but much older man because of the economic
realities of her society, to commit that drastic deed are very
real. Much the same feelings are, after all, documented in a
very different key in Patrick Kavanagh's *The Great Hunger*,
a poem widely acknowledged as one of the most acute
indictments of the social ills that were crippling the Irish
countryside in the century following the Great Famine.

This move away from the shocking, the sensational and
the sentimental that had existed in earlier versions of the
play is even further sharpened in McGahern's final revision
of the text, completed less than a year before his death.
This final revision – the text included in this edition – was
produced for RTÉ Radio in 2005, but it is clear from the
text that McGahern did not conceive of it specifically as a
radio play. Like the script of the 1972 BBC Radio
production that is filed in the Play Library at the BBC
Written Archives Centre in Reading, the 2005 recording
script is full of specifically 'stagey' references to the actors'
expressions, gestures and movements across the stage.
This edition, therefore, presents McGahern's last revision
of *The Power of Darkness* as the stage play for which it
was conceived.

In this final version, even more of the crucial action
takes place off the stage. In Tolstoy's original and in
McGahern's translation from the 1970s, the play had
ended with Paul's melodramatic confession of his sins to
the assembled wedding guests and to the audience. In the
1991 Abbey text, Paul still delivers his final confession
'*fac[ing] the audience*',[80] but the last word is given to Paddy,

80. John McGahern, *The Power of Darkness* (London: Faber
and Faber, 1991), pp. 51–2.

the drunk labourer who wakes up in the straw at the end of Paul's confession and delivers a monologue that has no equivalent in the source play by Tolstoy but which is wholly original to this late evolution of the McGahern version. In the definitive 2005 version, this move is taken even further. Paul now leaves the stage before his confession, which is only overheard in the distance as it is delivered offstage to the wedding guests. Paddy is now the sole occupant of the stage before the final curtain, and his final speech is extended from the 1991 version. Dramaturgically, this final speech has much in common with a chorus in a Greek tragedy, but the drunk casual labourer is a very strange chorus indeed. Paddy may commentate on the action and on the fate of the characters after the play, as befits the duties of a Greek chorus; but it is not so clear how he fulfils the other choral function of expressing the common moral, religious and social attitudes of his society. Instead of confirming the principles of Catholic morality, Paddy's speech roundly mocks the hypocrisy and opportunism that prevail in Irish society when he remarks of the gathered neighbours and wedding guests that 'They are all for God when God is on their side' (p. 335) – a line whose syntax replicates that of McGahern's misquotation of James Joyce's dig at that other holy cow, nationalism: 'They are all for the country, when they know which country it is.'[81] This distancing from the predominant culture of Catholic morality and respectability – both by making the confession less central and through Paddy's exposure of hypocrisy and self-interest – points to a crucial difference between Tolstoy's vision in the original play and that of McGahern in his adaptation. Because, as Nicholas Grene first pointed

81. McGahern, *Love of the World*, p. 200. Joyce had actually written: 'They love their country when they are quite sure which country it is.' James Joyce, *Giacomo Joyce*, ed. Richard Ellmann (London: Faber and Faber, 1968), p. 9. McGahern quotes this correct version in a book review: see *Love of the World*, p. 316.

out, while for the pious post-conversion Tolstoy, Christian faith was the remedy that could finally lift the 'darkness' of human sinfulness, for McGahern the structures of Catholic morality and belief were themselves at the root of a darkness of ignorance and repression.[82]

*

Moving Paul's confession off the stage, like the removal of the killing of the infant from the plot, is part of a move away from melodrama's exploitation of 'violent effect and emotional opportunism'.[83] But this is not to say that McGahern was trying to turn *The Power of Darkness* into a pure drama, or even a tragedy in the Greek mould. Despite his efforts (as he wrote to Kilroy) to take 'much of the melodrama out',[84] the play remains at its core a melodrama – but one that contains many deliberate references and allusions to well-known Greek and Elizabethan tragedies with which it shares crucial thematic concerns of greed, ambition and lust. The universality of the plot is made clear when Baby remarks, 'There is many a funeral that's followed by a fine wedding' (pp. 274–5), a statement that is both a justification of her amoral actions and a paraphrase of a line from the first Act of *Hamlet*.[85] From *Macbeth* it borrows the murder of a king (the low-born horsedealer Peter King, rather than gracious King Duncan), the debilitating guilt felt by his murderers, and even the gruesome presence of a 'birth-strangled babe, | Ditch-

82. See Nicholas Grene, 'John McGahern's *The Power of Darkness*', *Krino*, no. 13 (1992), pp. 52–60, at pp. 56–8.

83. M. H. Abrams, *A Glossary of Literary Terms*, 6th edn (Fort Worth: Harcourt Brace, 1993), p. 110.

84. John McGahern, letter to Thomas Kilroy, 23 August 1989. NUIG: P103/446(9).

85. That about how 'The funeral baked meats | Did coldly furnish forth the marriage tables.' William Shakespeare, *Hamlet*, ed. T. J. B. Spencer (Harmondsworth: Penguin, 1996), I.ii.180–81.

delivered by a drab';[86] while the characterisation of Baby owes as much to the ambitious and manipulative Lady Macbeth as to Tolstoy's Matrëna. There are also a number of comically scaled-down instances of mock-tragedy. The constant sound of 'knocking' on ceilings and doors echoes the ominous knocking on the gate that spells the murderer's doom in *Macbeth*, and Eileen's sarcastic advice that if Paul wants to avoid the terrible fate he fears he should simply 'stay away from trees' (p. 271) plays off one of the apparitions' ambiguous assurances of the hero's safety in the same play.[87] The constant references to blindness and the gouging of eyes, meanwhile, are a clear homage to the most famous tragic plot of all – that of Sophocles' *Oedipus Rex*. All these underpin the point that the object of these common characters' ambitions may not be of the same magnitude as those of an Oedipus or a Macbeth, nor the play in which they act as lofty in diction, but that their motivations spring from similar impulses and their suffering can be just as deep.

So while *The Power of Darkness* is serious in its intent to expose some of the 'dark' truths about human nature, and about Irish society, the means by which the author chose to convey these important truths are not those of a serious, 'high' form like a tragedy or a naturalistic drama. Denis Sampson has drawn attention to McGahern's habitual 'manner of placing and undercutting that high drama of murderous violence and abject victimisation'.[88] In *The Power of Darkness*, this 'undercutting' is achieved not only by the way in which some of the key action is underplayed, or even moved off the stage, but also through the choice of genre and register for this play about the 'dark'

86. William Shakespeare, *Macbeth*, ed. G. K. Hunter (Harmondsworth: Penguin, 1995), IV.i.30–31.

87. Ibid., IV.i.91–3.

88. Denis Sampson, 'The Common Condition', *Irish Literary Supplement*, vol. 11, no. 2 (Autumn 1992), 11–12, at p. 12.

side of Irish life in the twentieth century. A number of the reviews of the 1991 Garry Hynes production complained about the laughter which the acting and dialogue elicited from the audience. The drama critics of the *Irish Times* and the *Irish Independent* both found that the play degenerated into 'unintentional farce'.[89] The thought that one might *laugh* at a play about murder and moral 'darkness' was clearly considered distasteful, so the natural assumption seemed to be that any laughter it provoked must be 'unintentional'; surely, these critics seemed to be saying, this should be the stuff of tragedy, not of farce!

Contrary to what these reviewers assumed, however, the play most certainly did not fall from high seriousness by accident. *Farce* was one of McGahern's favourite words, and throughout his career he regularly harnessed the powers of that genre. In *The Power of Darkness*, as in certain passages in his prose fiction, he cannily uses the exaggerated, absurd registers of melodrama and farce to good effect. (Think for example of the out-of-proportion self-pity of both father and son in *The Dark*, or of Reagan in *The Barracks*; and of the farcical figure those same men cut when they act on that self-pity, often in theatrical ways.[90]) As Eric Bentley wrote in his influential book on *The Life of the Drama*, writers who use these genres 'may be said not to tumble into absurdity by accident, but to revel in it on purpose . . . The exaggerations will be foolish only if they are empty of feeling.'[91] Far from killing the play's serious intentions with 'unintentional farce', McGahern

---

89. Gerry Colgan, 'Sadly Risible Drama Debut for Author', *Irish Times*, 17 October 1991, p. 9; Rushe, 'No Good Points', p. 10. For more on the reception of the Abbey production, and on the character of these reviewers, see Christopher Murray, 'The "Fallen World" of *The Power of Darkness*', *John McGahern Yearbook*, vol. 2 (2011), pp. 78–91.

90. See van der Ziel, *John McGahern*, pp. 35–52.

91. Eric Bentley, *The Life of the Drama* (London: Methuen, 1965), pp. 203–4.

had always envisaged *The Power of Darkness* as 'harshly comic as well as violent', and shortly before the premiere he reported to a journalist that after attending a run-through he had been pleased to find the play was 'very black and funny, and the acting looks as if it's going to be very powerful'.[92] Despite the dismissal by the reviewers from the two main Irish dailies, some spectators recognised this intention and applauded its execution. In a letter to the *Irish Times* defending *The Power of Darkness* against the misapprehensions of its reviewers, Nicholas Grene, Professor of English at Trinity College Dublin and an authority on Irish and English drama, wrote that 'neither of them had told me the play was funny. Not "sadly risible" (Colgan), but savagely, devastatingly, intentionally funny.'[93]

Nor was this the first time that McGahern had dealt with the very themes that are at the heart of *The Power of Darkness* in a way that deliberately shied away from the seriousness of tragedy or naturalistic drama or social realism. In its attention to the damage done to the natural relationships between men and women by racial memories of famine and the moral teachings of the Catholic Church, *The Power of Darkness* is closest to *The Pornographer* (1979). Of all McGahern's novels, *The Pornographer* has traditionally enjoyed the least esteem, and the reason for this comparative critical neglect – like that for the critics' dismissal of *The Power of Darkness* – is probably connected with the author's choice of genre. *The Pornographer* is a satirical farce, and some of the most devastatingly critical

92. Carty, 'Sex, Ignorance and the Irish', p. 27.

93. Nicholas Grene, 'McGahern's Play', *Irish Times*, 9 November 1991, p. 11. In an essay published the following year, Grene further elaborated on how McGahern's adaptation deliberately transformed the 'black comic vein' that already existed in Tolstoy's original into a full-blown 'comedy of the grotesque'. Grene, 'John McGahern's *The Power of Darkness*', pp. 55–6.

passages are also the most grotesquely farcical. Think, for example, of Maloney's outrageous suggestion that nobody would notice if one wheeled a baby around in a coffin, 'But show them a man and a woman making love – and worst of all enjoying it – and the streets are full of "Fathers of eleven", "Disgusted" and all the rest of them'; and perhaps above all of the hilarious pornographic short story about a debauched river cruise on the Shannon written by the title character which is really a study in the repercussions of sexual repression.[94] This generic choice was further sharpened in McGahern's screenplay adaptations of the novel – a project to which he returned on several occasions, but which never came to fruition despite attempts to start production by Kieran Hickey and others. By all accounts, the *Pornographer* screenplay became increasingly farcical as the drafts evolved, but it never lost sight of the original intent of the novel as a critique of the unhappiness and suffering that resulted from repressive attitudes towards sex and marriage rooted in religious belief and material deprivation. McGahern's reliance on 'low' genres like melodrama and farce in dealing with these subjects closest to his heart shows a desire not to make light of the problems he observed in late-twentieth-century Ireland, but rather to engage with them in a manner that defied the possibility of sentimentality, judgement and 'self-expression' that can so easily draw in other artists and commentators engaging with the same subjects.

*

The six plays collected in this edition represent an important, though up to now generally overlooked, aspect of

94. John McGahern, *The Pornographer* (London: Faber and Faber, 1979), pp. 249, 153–63. See also Stanley van der Ziel, 'John McGahern, Post-Revival Literature and Irish Cultural Criticism', *New Hibernia Review*, vol. 21, no. 1 (Spring 2017), pp. 121–42, at pp. 128–30.

John McGahern's identity as a writer. Making the texts of all of his produced dramatic writings available in this volume, in most cases for the first time, expands the fictional landscape with which readers have become more familiar with each new published novel and collection of short stories. But this volume will also allow readers to form a more complete picture of McGahern's interests in different forms and genres. His ventures into dramatic writings for the various media represented in this volume (radio, television and stage) are manifestations of the same need for 'contant experiment' that defined the trajectory of his career as a novelist whose subject matter continuously re-circled the same territory, but whose approach to that material changed, sometimes radically, with each new work. As a dramatist, the 'constant experiment' of form and tone and genre is at the root of his lifelong struggle with *The Power of Darkness*, and the way in which that work was repeatedly repositioned generically. Equally, the technical possibilities – and limitations – of writing for radio and television appealed to McGahern's curiosity as a writer, even if he did not further pursue those forms once he was satisfied that he had mastered their specific formal or technical demands; that kind of ceaseless reinvention and refinement was ultimately confined to his work as a writer of fiction.

STANLEY VAN DER ZIEL
AUGUST 2017

Acknowledgements

In preparing this edition, I am indebted to many individuals and institutions.

For helping me obtain copies of the various scripts, I am grateful to Fergus Fahey and Barry Houlihan at the John Hardiman Library, NUI Galway; Els Boonen and Hazel Simpson at the BBC Written Archives Centre; and Kate Manning and Orna Somerville at the UCD Archives; and to Richard Pierce and Patrick O'Byrne. Susanna Capon, James Runcie and especially Sharon Terry at the BBC all went to much effort to track down a copy of a script previously presumed lost. Kevin Reynolds at RTÉ generously provided both a copy of the script and an audio recording of his 2005 production of *The Power of Darkness*. Mary Conefrey at Leitrim County Library very kindly sent me a DVD of *The Rockingham Shoot*, which was essential for establishing the final text of the screenplay.

I wish to thank Madeline McGahern and Susanna Capon for sharing memories of McGahern's life as a dramatist, Frank Shovlin for his comments on a draft of the introduction and for allowing me to consult a copy of a McGahern letter in his possession, and Siobhan McNamara for checking McGahern's spelling and usage of Irish-language words and phrases throughout. At Faber and Faber, I am grateful to Dinah Wood and Kate Ward, who have guided every aspect of production with impeccable good humour and professionalism, and to Simon Trussler and Jill Burrows for meticulous copyediting and proofreading. Finally, my most comprehensive debt, as always, is to my wife Jana, who offered practical as well as moral support throughout.

SvdZ

SINCLAIR

Sinclair was broadcast on BBC Radio 3 on 16 November 1971. The cast was as follows::

BOLES Cyril Cusack
GILLESPIE Norman Rodway

Produced by Ronald Mason

A roar of chainsaw through timber. Whine of saw running free. Saw splutters to a stop. Sound of heavy breathing.

GILLESPIE Terror the amount of timber it runs through in a half-hour. (*Pause. Heavy breathing.*) Two men with a crosscut wouldn't do it in a week in the old days, and all the sweat and toiling and moiling. Knew the old bastard was too lazy to give it much wear and tear. But when I bid seventeen-ten my heart was in my mouth till Beirne brought down the blasted hammer. Would have disimbursed myself with the quandary whether to bid higher if he hadn't brought it down and it's as good as the hundred it costs new, isn't that right, Shep? (*Dog barks uncertainly. Reads*) 'Manufactured in the US, McCullough Company Inc., the best to be got for money.'

Tries to start the chainsaw again. It starts but splutters and comes to a stop.

That's peculiar. Maybe flooded. (*Anxiously*) Takes time to get your hand in.

Tries to start saw again. It starts easily. Shouts excitedly at dog above roar of saw:

It's better than new, I told you. Better than bloody new. You should always go by your instinct. Better than bloody new it is. Always trust to your instinct when it comes to the pinch.

Turns off chainsaw. Heavy breathing. Silence.

Knew he didn't give it much wear and tear. *Encyclopaedia Britannica* more in his line. A burden to himself and everybody connected. (*Farts. Long silence.*) Great release that into the evening, thank God. Takes four good pints of porter to give any fart its proper aroma. Those four pints relaxed me no end after the bloody excitement of the auction. My chainsaw tucked under my oxter by that time safe as a house on fire, a solid pint in my fist. (*Pause.*) Terror the amount of sawdust a half-hour's sawing leaves on the grass. Get rid of the evidence, that's it. (*Noise of boot scattering the sawdust into the grass. Voice grows fierce*) For it'll not be long till he's up with his nose smelling unless I'm far out, for he'll hear the noise, and curiosity would hang that bloody old Boles if there was a law, hung he'd be long ago by the no time, and if he spotted the dust he'd hit on a chainsaw, and that'd make him wiser than myself, and that'd never do, much better for him to die standing than to be killed by the fall. (*Speaks fiercely to dog*) Isn't that right, Shep? Isn't that right, Shep? Come here, old man, isn't that right?

Takes kick at dog. Dog's squeal of pain fades slowly to whimpering.

Got you that time, old fellow. Came too close. Never trust to get near man or beast. My safe motto. That'll be a lesson for you. (*Voice grows tender*) Ah, but you're hurt, I meant only to give you a warning, not hurt you, old man, for what would I do without you? I'd be lost, lost without you, and I didn't mean to hurt you, it was on the spur of the moment when I saw you close, couldn't resist, but you know I didn't mean it, and I'd be lost without you, don't you know that, old man, don't you know that? (*Pause.*) Strange how soothing a dog's coat is to flesh. Flesh gets hungry for flesh or hair as much as the belly for food. (*Pause. Voice hardens*) We have nothing to do now but wait for him to arrive with his nose smelling unless I'm far out.

Country noises. Birds. Lonely barking of dogs in distance. Rattle of feeding bucket. Noise of car closing, passing, fading away. Distant sharp cry of 'Moses, heel' above roar of another car.

It's him. I knew he couldn't resist coming up smelling. Calling heel to that fool of a dog Moses who'll get under a car too many, believe me, before long.

Noise of dogs barking after car fades. Growls of dog very close.

Easy, Shep, old man, let them stew in their own juice.

Sharp blow of cane on road in distance. Sharp voice: 'I said once and for all heel, Moses.'

Let them stew in their own juice, is what I say.

Slow dragging feet come closer. The dragging punctuated by tapping of cane.

Taking a bit of a constitutional, Mr Boles?

Three slow dragging steps with stick.

BOLES The usual forty steps before the night.

GILLESPIE Go away with you now, lepping out of your skin, you are, Mr Boles. No holding the young ones these days.

BOLES Ah no. The clock can't be put back. The old works winding down, you know, no matter what.

GILLESPIE No future in that way of thinking and you're good for ten Bechers yet if you ask me. (*Noise of dog snarling.*) The one thing about dogs is they go straight for what counts, without any beating around the bush, none of the shuffling or cafuffling the humans indulge in.

BOLES (*sarcastically*) Humans. (*Pause.*) I thought there was some demarcation line, humans were humans and dogs were dogs. (*Pause.*) Ah, but no matter. (*Playfully*) Are you at much this weather?

GILLESPIE Oh, the usual fooling around. Went to the auction.

BOLES See anything there?

GILLESPIE The Ferguson was the star attraction. It went for a hundred and it wouldn't pull you out of your bed in a week of Sundays.

BOLES Second-hand stuff is not the thing, a risk, no guarantee. I never had use for auctions.

GILLESPIE I couldn't agree less. I've got stuff as good as new at auctions, real bargains.

BOLES Sooner or later you scorch your fingers.

Silence. Lonely howling of a sheepdog in distance. Much nearer and very loud a donkey starts to bray.

Always gives me a feeling of great contentment, an ass braying. You feel somehow that God's in his heaven, you know, and all's right in the world.

GILLESPIE Just Jackson's bloody old ass braying to me, I'm sorry to have to admit.

BOLES (*carefully*) Did I hear an engine running up here a short time ago?

GILLESPIE None that I know of.

BOLES I'd swear there was an engine between here and the house – a light, whining sort of engine.

GILLESPIE The country's full of engines these days, can't believe your ears where they come from.

BOLES Strange . . . Strange . . . I'd swear . . .

GILLESPIE Sure the whole world is strange if you had the time to look at it close enough.

Long embarrassed pause.

BOLES Has there been any news of Sinclair lately?

GILLESPIE Odd now that you mention it, yes. The crowd up for the Croke Park semi-final saw him outside Amiens Street Station with an empty shopping bag. They said he looked shook. Booked close enough to the jump.

BOLES He never was very extra healthy.

Donkey starts to bray again.

GILLESPIE Looks as if Jackson's bloody old ass is intent on providing you with all the contentment you need for this evening.

BOLES I knew Sinclair well. (*Starts to mimic rather gently an English accent*) 'The ignorance and boredom of the people of this part of the country is appalling, simply appalling' – that's how he used to begin.

GILLESPIE Oh, that'll be his first spake to Peter at the Gate, all right.

BOLES A strange person.

GILLESPIE Touched. That's all. If you ask me. I got to know his form well, the summer I bought this place from him and was waiting for him to shunt off, but he was no fool, believe you me, he'd always the excuse that the people hadn't vacated yet the house he'd bought in Dublin, and he'd got it written into the deeds, and all I could do was put a straight face on it and sit tight. And when I was mowing between the apple trees there with the scythe, they were hot days, and he'd stand with his hands behind his back spouting to the end of the world till he nearly had me driven half-demented in the head. The ignorance and the boredom but nothing about his own. Bad manners and the rain. Speaking as one intelligent man, if you don't mind, to another, *O Saecular O Saeculorum* world without end amen the Lord deliver us. He even tried . . . (*said with fierce indignation*) tried to show me how to put an edge on the scythe.

BOLES I knew him for the whole fifteen years that he was here.

GILLESPIE Fifteen too long, I'd safely warrant.

BOLES No, not at all. He was a strange person. He suffered from the melancholy.

GILLESPIE What had that josser to be melancholy about? He had a pension, hadn't he, from that cable they laid out from Valentia? A radio officer's pension at that.

BOLES It wasn't money. (*Chuckles and starts to mimic English accent*) 'No reason why we exist, Mr Boles, why we were born. What do we know? Nothing, Mr Boles. Simply nothing. Scratching our arses, refining our ignorance. Trying to see some make or shape on the nothing we do know.'

GILLESPIE That was his style all right, no mistaking it, nature of the beast. The way he used to treat that wife of his was nobody's business.

BOLES In Valentia he met her, when he was on the cable, girl in the post office.

GILLESPIE She'd have been as well off to have met her own funeral coming back that week instead of yon looney. I remember he used to cut firewood in the plantation. And when he'd enough cut he'd blow a whistle. She'd come running with the rope the minute she heard the whistle. Believe me, it was a fair sight to see her come staggering up the meadow there and him strolling elegant and cool as you please behind, golfing at the daisies with the old green Bushman he had, shouting 'Fore' as he swivelled. Poor soft bitch, I knew a few who'd give him fore all right, and the cut of him in those plus-fours. He should have stayed where he belonged.

BOLES (*mimics*) 'I am reduced to the final ambition of wanting to go back to look on the green of the billiard table in the Prince of Wales on Edward Road. They may have taken it away, though. Sign of a misspent youth, proficiency at billiards.'

GILLESPIE As this place is halfway between the two churches, he used to tell the Cootehalls he'd gone to Mass in Boyle and the Boyles that he'd gone to Mass in Cootehall. He thought he was pulling wool over everybody's eyes, when the whole world knew it was gall and wormwood for him to darken any church door.

BOLES He'd explain that without trouble. (*Laughs slowly as he begins to mimic*) 'You have to pretend to observe appearances, simply for your own safety, Mr Boles. They'd tear out your entrails – in some accepted fashion, of course – if you didn't pretend to observe appearances. And since appearances are a pretence, a pretence at pretence is one better. To be quite frank, Mr Boles, it was no rush of faith led to my conversion but I was simply dragged into your barbaric Church, if you allow me to put it that way, Mr Boles, by my male member.'

GILLESPIE The disgusting blackguard, never any respect. When he should have went down on his bended knee and thanked his God that any Church would have him.

BOLES (*mimics again*) 'Bessie, you see, was religious
when she worked in the post office and I burned for
Bessie in the manner St Paul refers to in his famous
tract. My burning dragged me via Bessie to Monsignor
Creedon. For how many hours, Mr Boles, did I sit in the
front room of the presbytery, my balls, if you'd forgive
this rather unfortunately appropriate phrase, practically
frozen off, the Monsignor sitting with both legs astraddle
the one bar of the electric heater in the room? No danger
of him allowing *his* balls to freeze, I assure you, while
I got off by rote all your shalls and shall-nots, heaven is
a place or state of happiness, hell is where the wicked
grunt and groan, God made the world for man's use and
benefit, that I thought such a huge joke that I nearly
swallowed my moustache every time I had to trot it out,
and of course all those unrevealed truths and mysteries
our weakened natures cannot comprehend, which part,
to me, had always been perfectly obvious. And then a
wet Sunday afternoon, after I had satisfied them that I
had all the answers correct, they doused my thirty-four-
year-old head over their stone font with what felt like
water from the Arctic Ocean, some of it running down
the back of my neck, with the result of a wet shirt all
afternoon, which led to me getting practically double
pneumonia. And for all that huffing and puffing I was
allowed into Bessie's bed where for some years my male
member, after much sweaty exertion, had three or four
pleasurable fluttering sensations a week within Bessie's
dear old whatever-you-call-it, which is nature's way of
saying: "Thanks, Mr Boles, this is your toffee, you'll
get the same toffee every time you participate in the
dear act." (*Shouts*) "Good chap, you've done your
duty, pat on the head for you, old boy." (*Pause.*)
My balls frozen off watching the red electric bar between
the Monsignor's thighs, getting practically double
pneumonia the wet Sunday afternoon of my baptism,

and for all that my male member gets three or four
fluttering sensations a week, panting and sweating, until
Bessie and myself, fortunately simultaneously so that
there was no anguish, came to the conclusion that it was
an overrated pastime, and that was that.'

GILLESPIE On the same tack to me in the orchard. A
strange coot. Luther's idea about women. The bed and the
sink. (*Tries to mimic an English accent but unsuccessfully
and coarsely*) 'As good to engage a pig in serious
conversation as a woman. All words for them lead to
the one thing, prayer, Gillespie, prayer before the twin
altars of their vanity and vaginas.' I'll not forget in a
hurry how he came out with that spiff.

BOLES He had a curious blend of language sometimes.

GILLESPIE And he ends up after all that guff being seen
by the crowd up for the semi-final outside Amiens Street
Station with an empty shopping bag. There's your lesson.

BOLES I liked him, though. (*Silence while car passes.*)
A great smell of apples in the evening?

GILLESPIE Rotting on the ground. Wouldn't pay you
to pick except to gather the windfalls on the ground for
Breffni Blossom. The factory doesn't mind the bruises.

BOLES Better than wasting in the grass. Those
headlamps'd cut the eyes out of your head. (*Sharply hits
ground with cane.*) Here, Moses. That dog of mine needs
watching like a hawk. Surprisin' he's not been run over
long ago.

*Rattle and roar of approaching diesel train, and as it
fades:*

That row of lighted windows roaring through the night.
If we didn't know it was just the nine-twenty to Sligo it

might drive us out of our minds, a prehistoric monster surfacing out of some of the fearsome ages of our forefathers.

GILLESPIE And I suppose it's empty as usual, subsidised by us the unfortunate ratepayers, and the guards and ticket collectors with their feet up in the first class, putting the world in order.

BOLES In the summer it's full, though. The tourists.

GILLESPIE Oh yes. More tourists than people soon.

Ass braying.

That bloody old ass of Jackson's must surely have something on its mind to continue braying like that after dark.

BOLES (*tiredly absent*) Christ rode into Jerusalem on an ass.

Car passes. Dog howling.

GILLESPIE (*aggressively*) Wasn't on Jackson's ass, that's sure fire.

BOLES Moses! (*Crack of stick on ground.*) Time to be moving in the general direction of the bed.

GILLESPIE What hurry's on you? We'll all be long enough lying down in the finish. How's the eczema?

BOLES Stays quiet enough as long as I don't go near timber, and I have the blue ointment to keep the midges off.

GILLESPIE If everything was right sure we'd appreciate nothing.

Night flutter of birds in branches overhead. Silence. Car goes past very fast, roar.

BOLES Hellbent to nowhere. (*Increase of exasperation*)
Do you know I'd swear I heard an engine – a peculiar,
whining engine – running up here today?

GILLESPIE Must have been from elsewhere. What the
wind can do with sounds is no joke.

BOLES There was hardly a puff of wind today.

GILLESPIE Oh every little helps, as the woman said
when she pissed in the sea. (*Laughs aggressively. Snarling
of dogs close.*)

BOLES I was quite certain, but . . . (*Tap of cane on
ground*) here, Moses. It's time to go.

GILLESPIE No use detaining you so if you have, though
it's young, the night yet, and there's even a slice of moon
thrown into the bargain.

BOLES Of course, the moon. The moon's not the same
since those eejits clambered about on it. (*Mimics Sinclair*)
'Nature of the human animal is that if you lock your
door against him he'll want to break it down while if
you open the same door and ask him in he'll either laugh
at you for a fool and look upon you with contempt or
he'll be so scared as to take to his heels. They all want to
go to the moon or Everest but nobody wants to give you
a lift to town, which'd be of some use to a man. It's all
running and racing and everybody gets everywhere
which is the same as nobody gets nowhere and you're all
back in the finish where you started, your arse up in the
air like Lester Piggott's.'

   Donkey brays loudly.

GILLESPIE I'd say that ass of Jackson's had lost a foal
if it was a *she* instead of a *he*. It won't give us a wink of
sleep never mind your contentment if it goes on the like
of this for the whole of the night.

BOLES To go back to Sinclair . . .

GILLESPIE Between Jackson's ass and Sinclair we're
between the devil and a foul sea if you don't heed my
contribution to the evening.

BOLES (*mimics*) 'To return to human idiocy and the
previous Lord Oxford. An exceedingly peculiar family
the Oxfords, you must have heard of them, Mr Boles.'
Well, if I hadn't heard before I soon heard. (*Mimics*)
'Trains were hideously crowded during the war but Lord
Oxford still wanted his private carriage. He was of
hideous aspect and immediately the train pulled in he
boarded the first carriage, and anyone who approached
that carriage from then until departure time was invited
aboard with open arms and hideous aspect wreathed in
smiles, so of course no one dared to enter. So in some of
the most crowded trains between Oxford and
Paddington in the history of England, Lord Oxford
generally succeeded in still having his private carriage.
After the war he got artistic ambitions and had a piano
installed in his Rolls-Royce: Johann Sebastian Bach at
Lancaster Gate, Beethoven at Marble Arch, Mozart at
Piccadilly Circus, Lord Oxford in the middle of the rush
hour in the traffic diddling away on the piano in the
back of the Rolls. Making little artistic progress, he
eventually partook himself to a psychiatrist, a Harley
Street gentleman, as eccentric as himself, who told him:
"After careful examination of your cranium and long
deliberation with my own I have eventually come to the
conclusion, my Lord, that you have a dead bird in your
chimney." And haven't we all, Mr Boles, dead birds in
our chimneys!' Sinclair used to fold up laughing.

GILLESPIE A disgusting and perverted view of the
world, he was even against progress, look at the
moonmen, and a lot of progress he made to wind up

after all that guff with an empty shopping bag outside Amiens Street Station.

BOLES I liked him and sometimes he made more sense than most. Are you sure you weren't using a mechanical saw or something up this way today?

GILLESPIE A mechanical saw? You must be joking. Where would I get the readies for a mechanical saw? By the Lord God, that's a fresh one. Mechanical saw.

BOLES I'd have sworn, but time to go. (*Sharp rap of cane.*) Moses. (*Pause. Awkward*) Night then.

GILLESPIE Good night, Mr Boles.

Tap of cane to drag-drag of feet. Car. Sharp tap of cane. 'Heel, Moses!' As car fades, slow drag-drag-tap very slowly fades.

Here, Shep. (*To dog*) Don't go straying. I told you he'd be up with his nose smelling, didn't I? No point, is there, making someone wise as yourself, him and his bloody old fool Sinclair, and his poetry-book remarks about Jackson's jackass. (*Farts.*) A great need of a good fart after listening to that fool's guff. (*Sniffs loudly.*) Not much scent of the porter left that I drank to calm the old nerves after the auction. Like ourselves it weakens, farted away, and suddenly gone. (*Long pause. To the dog, fiercely, almost sexually*) And we'll start the McCullough again tomorrow. Louder than ever we'll saw. And he'll be up smelling. Sure as there's a foot on a duck. Smelling. A lot of good it'll do him. Not if he smelled till Doomsday will we tell him. We'll give him, we'll give him, we'll give him, we'll give him something to think about. (*Dog's yelp of pain.*) Got you again. A right boot in the knackers. Never learn not to come too close, never learn.

75

Dog's yelp of pain dies. Loud braying of donkey.
Lonely cry of dog, fading.

THE BARRACKS

The Barracks was first broadcast on BBC Radio 4 on
24 January 1972. The cast was as follows:

SERGEANT REAGAN Kevin Flood
ELIZABETH REAGAN Kate Binchy
GUARD CASEY Kevin McHugh
GUARD MULLINS J. J. Murphy
MRS CASEY Catherine Gibson
SUPERINTENDENT QUIRKE Patrick Brannigan
SHEILA ⎤
UNA   ⎥ Fionnuala Rolston
WILLIE ⎦ Anne McCartney
OTHER PARTS Wolsey Gracey

Produced by John Scotney

Noise of wind and rain on windows. Click of knitting needles. Crackle of burning wood.

WILLIE (*suddenly*) Is it time to light the lamp yet, Elizabeth?

ELIZABETH Oh Willie, you gave me a fright. It's almost dark. Can you read what time it is? I never felt the night come.

WILLIE It's ten past six, Elizabeth.

ELIZABETH Light the lamp then so.

UNA I'll have my blind down first tonight, Sheila.

SHEILA I'll have my blind.

WILLIE None of yous can move till I shout the lamp is lit . . . Watch, watch, outa me way!

ELIZABETH Be careful, Willie, with that blazing paper.

WILLIE (*shouts*) The lamp is lit!

Noise of girls running for blinds. Blinds being pulled down.

SHEILA My blind was down the first.

UNA No, no, my blind was down the first. Wasn't my blind down the first, Elizabeth?

ELIZABETH What does it matter what blind was down first or not down? Can you not give me a little peace for once? Don't you know I've been to the doctor in town today and can't you try to make it a little easier for this once? Why is it, why, after every day I'm away and I leave you for Mrs Casey to mind it gets like bedlam here in the evening?

Long pause.

SHEILA Our mother used to go to the doctor too in town, Elizabeth. Then he started coming to the house and then she went away and never came back. Will you be going away, Elizabeth?

ELIZABETH (*carefully*) I may have to go away for a few days.

SHEILA Won't you come back though?

ELIZABETH Yes, I'll come back.

SHEILA (*chanting*) That's good, Elizabeth. For if you didn't come back, Daddy would have to marry somebody else. And *my* blind was down the first.

UNA No, no. My blind was down the first. Wasn't my blind down the first, Elizabeth?

ELIZABETH I think it was a draw tonight. Both blinds came down at the same time. What do you think, Willie?

WILLIE I think it was a draw, Elizabeth.

GIRLS It was a draw so.

Wind and rain.

WILLIE Daddy will be wet tonight.

ELIZABETH What do you think I'm airing the clothes for? Do you hear what it's like outside?

GIRLS He might shelter and come home when it fairs.

ELIZABETH It has no sound of fairing to me. Only getting heavier and heavier. Will you hold the rope for me while I get his clothes off the horse?

WILLIE You think he'll be late, Elizabeth?

ELIZABETH He's late already. You never know what trouble or hold-up he may run into. Or he might have taken shelter in some house. I don't know why he should have to go out at all on a night like this. Never join the Guards when you grow up, Willie.

WILLIE I'll not.

ELIZABETH And what will you be?

WILLIE (*cautiously*) I'll not be a Guard.

ELIZABETH (*laughing*) Well you better do your homework so. If your father sees the last rush for the books at night there'll be trouble.

Sound of pencils and schoolbooks. Footsteps on boards in distance. Door. Rattle of bucket.

(*Tiredly*) That's Guard Casey going out for turf.

UNA Will I be going up to Mrs Casey's to sleep tonight?

ELIZABETH I don't know. Your nightdress is ready in the press if you are.

UNA Guard Casey said this evening that I would.

ELIZABETH You'll likely have to go up so. You'll not know for certain till your father comes home. (*Absently*) That woman will never learn that everybody lives alone.

Silence. Rustle of schoolbooks. Noise of bicycle tyres on gravel in wind and rain.

WILLIE Daddy's home.

Noise of outside door. Then door of room out of wind and rain.

REAGAN Wet to the bloody skin. A terrible night to have to cycle about in like a fool.

ELIZABETH All the clothes are aired. You better change quick.

Noises of somebody being given clothes and changing.

REAGAN A terrible night. Not fit for a dog to be out in.

ELIZABETH In what direction were you in?

REAGAN Round by Derrada . . . And you'd never guess who I met?

ELIZABETH Who?

REAGAN The bastard Quirke.

ELIZABETH You mean the Superintendent? What had him out, do you think?

REAGAN He was looking for a chance he didn't get, you can be sure. (*Dramatises encounter*) He stopped in front of me and pulled down the window and asked: 'Is that you, Reagan?' 'That's me, Sir,' says I. 'And is there some trouble?' says he. 'No, Sir,' says I. 'And what has you out on a night like this?' 'I'm out on patrol, Sir,' says I. 'But are you mad, Sergeant? Are you stone mad? No man in his senses would be out cycling on a night like this without grave reason. Good God, Sergeant, don't you realise that all rules and regulations yield at a certain point to human discretion? Do you want to get your death, man, cycling about on a night like this?' 'Aye, aye, Sir,' says I. 'But I'll not get the sack, Sir.' (*Laughs fiendishly.*) That shook him. That's what took the wind out of his sails. That's what shut him up, believe you me. (*Fiendishly caricatures pompous voice*)

'Even regulations, Sergeant, must yield at a certain point to human discretion. Even the law – even the law, Sergeant! – must yield at a certain point to human discretion.'

ELIZABETH You're only causing annoyance and trouble for yourself. That'll bring him the more down on you. For the sake of a few words couldn't you let it go with him?

REAGAN (*with aggressive caution*) You mean it'll be all the same in the end and that we'll all be nice and agreeable when we're dead and gone? Is that it?

Long silence. Distant noise of somebody poking a fire. Sound of the schoolbooks.

(*Aggressively*) What did ye learn at school today?

WILLIE (*hesitantly*) English, Irish, sums, Daddy.

REAGAN (*laughs*) That tells me nothing. Did ye learn anything new? Did ye learn anything ye didn't know yesterday? (*Silence.*) Can the lassies tell me anything when this great fool of ours only goes to school to recreate himself? (*Silence.*) By the look of it you might as well be stopping at home and giving Elizabeth here a hand about the house. Do you know why you go to school at all?

WILLIE To learn.

REAGAN To learn what?

WILLIE Lessons.

REAGAN (*laughing*) You'll never get wit, Willie. Did I never tell you that you go to school to learn to think for yourself and not to give two twopenny curses for what anybody else is thinking?

ELIZABETH (*tiredly*) And a lot of good that will do them.

REAGAN (*laughing*) A lot of good it did any of us. We might as well have been learning our facts and figures and have come out in every other way just as God sent us in as long as we learned how to bow the knee and kiss the ring. And we'd have all got on like hayricks on fire, isn't that right, Elizabeth?

ELIZABETH (*laughing gently*) That's perfectly right. (*Silence.*) There's something for you to eat.

Distant steps on boards. Door opens. Approaching boots up concrete hallway. Knock on door of room.

REAGAN Come in.

CASEY God bless you all.

MUMBLED CHORUS And you too, Guard Casey.

CASEY Don't trouble to move yourself, Sergeant, I'll work my way in all right to the fire, don't you worry. I just thought that if I carted up the book it'd save you the trouble of coming down to sign.

REAGAN That's powerful. It's a bad night away from the fire.

CASEY And God's truth, I was glad enough of the excuse to come up with the same book. I was getting the willies down there on my own looking at the same old wonders in the fire and expecting to be lifted out of my standing any minute by that phone in the wall. And it is a bad night. I stuffed a few old coats against the butt of the door but the draughts still go creeping up the legs of your britches like wet rats. I nearly got drowned when I ran out of turf and had to go out. (*Changes*) Did you meet anything strange or startling on your travels, Sergeant?

REAGAN I met something all right. Whether you can call it strange or startling is another matter.

CASEY What did you meet with, Sergeant?

REAGAN (*viciously*) Did you ever hear of John James Quirke, did you?

CASEY Jay, you never met the Super, did you? And what was him doing out on an evening the like of this?

Break of silence for Reagan recounting the story, ending it more violently than the first time with:

REAGAN '. . . But I'll not get the sack, Sir.' That shook him. That's what took the wind out of his sails, believe you me.

CASEY Bejay, Sergeant, you'll have him night and day lyin' in wait for us round this place, if you're not careful.

REAGAN What do I care and what the hell do I care?

Embarrassed silence.

CASEY Maybe you'd like to write in the old book?

Reagan takes the book.

(*To the children while Reagan writes*) You've finished the old lessons?

CHORUS OF CHILDREN All's finished.

CASEY And ye have them all off?

CHORUS Yes, Guard Casey.

CASEY Well, that's the way to be, be able to puzzle the schoolmaster.

ELIZABETH I wouldn't be sure they're that well known.

CASEY Well, you get nothing without the learning these days. Pass the exams, that's what gets people on, that and swindling. I didn't do much of either meself, more's the pity, and signs are on it.

REAGAN I have this nearly finished, except I'm not sure from what direction the wind was blowing?

CASEY It was coming from Moran's bay at a howling rate when I was out for the turf. The southwest seems about the only direction it knows how to blow from, this weather.

REAGAN (*repeats as he writes*) Wind from the southwest.

CASEY (*mock pompous voice to the children*) Where does the southwest come from, William Reagan?

WILLIE From the Atlantic Ocean.

CASEY Very good, young Reagan. And can you tell me now what it gathers on its long journey across the oceans?

WILLIE (*giggling*) Gathers moisture, Guard Casey.

CASEY (*same mock pompous tone*) Very right, my boy. I see you are one boy who comes to school to learn something other than villainy and rascality. And then as I have repeated day in day out while the hairs of my head turn grey it strikes against the mountains, rises to a great height and pisses down on the poor unfortunates who earn their daily bread by the sweat of their brows in this holy Catholic and apostolic country of Ireland.

ELIZABETH (*mid general laughter*) You're a terrible man, Ned.

CASEY It's the God's truth, Elizabeth. And you know Cromwell's words: get roasted alive in hell or drowned in Connaught. (*Pause before he asks tentatively*) The missus was wondering if it'd be all right for Una to come up with me when I go for the supper . . . for her to stop the night?

REAGAN Sure, but that's the women's territory.

ELIZABETH Of course. Her nightdress is ready in the press.

CASEY I don't like troubling you all the time for Una but that woman of mine will go off her head if she'd to stop the night alone up in that house.

ELIZABETH It's no trouble and it's no wonder she'd be afraid at night alone there. She didn't think of trouble when she minded them all day.

CASEY She loves minding them. It takes her out of herself. (*Cautiously*) It was all right in town, Elizabeth, I hope?

ELIZABETH (*tensely*) Thanks, it was all right.

Pause.

CASEY Why don't we have a game of cards? It's ages since we've had a game.

Sounds of the beginning of card game. Fade. Loud opening of door. Unsteady, heavy steps. Loud knock.

REAGAN Come in.

MULLINS (*in tipsy voice*) A wild night and it seems I'm the last of the Mohicans.

CASEY But the last should be first, remember?

MULLINS (*resentfully*) Aye, and the first might be last.

ELIZABETH Don't be standing there, John. There's a cup of tea and it's not who's first or last counts.

MULLINS It seems I made it on the eleventh hour all right, and you were out on patrol, Sergeant.

REAGAN I was and I met the Super. (*Fade as before. Very violently*) '. . . Even regulations must yield at a certain point to human discretion. Even the law, Reagan, even the law.'

MULLINS They can't ride roughshod over us these days. Them days are gone. They can try it on but that's all, thanks Jesus.

CASEY You'd be surprised what they can do. Things don't change that quick. And if you cross them they'll find ways and means. Who do you think the Chief Super will stand up for if it goes to the test? Power, let me tell you, always stands up for power.

REAGAN What do I care, what the hell do I care?

CASEY What does young Willie think of this? Will he join the Force when he grows up?

REAGAN Not if he has any sense in his skull.

CASEY Will he have the measurements, though?

MULLINS We'll have to put a stone on his head with the way he's growing. But I fear he'll never be thick enough. Thirty-six inches across the chest and a yard thick with solid ignorance, five feet nine inches against the wall in your stocking feet and you're right for the Force.

CASEY Some of the old drill Sergeants were a terror in the depot. Do you remember By Garrup?

MULLINS Oh Jasus, as if a mortal could forget. (*Mimics*) 'By Garrup, look at the creel of turf on Mullins' back. You're not on the bog now, Mullins, by Garrup. Head to the front, right wheel, chest out, you're not carrying your dying grandmother up the stairs on your backs now, by Garrup. Mark time, lift the knees, by Garrup.'

CASEY Do you mind Spats at the law classes?

MULLINS (*mimics a cultured accent*) 'A legal masterpiece, gentlemen of the jury, is the proper distribution of the proper quantity of ink in the right places on white paper. That, gentlemen, is simply, solely and singularly the constitution of any masterpiece.'

CASEY But wasn't he a BA and a barrister?

MULLINS What's a barrister? A barrister. A chancer of the first water. Argue & Fibbs of Sligo. Argue & Fibbs. Only properly named law firm I know of.

CASEY Isn't it strange that with all the men that went in to the depot no one was exactly six feet?

MULLINS That's right. No man ever born was exactly six feet. It's because Jesus Christ was exactly six feet and nobody born since could be the same.

CASEY It's like the Blessed Virgin and Original Sin. (*Quotes*) 'The Blessed Virgin Mary, by a singular privilege of grace, was preserved free from Original Sin, and that privilege is called her Immaculate Conception.'

ELIZABETH I think there's some gap in that logic.

MULLINS (*loudly*) Six feet is the ideal height for a man. Anything bigger is getting too big, while anything smaller is getting too small. It's the ideal height for a man.

REAGAN (*bored*) What about 'Kelly the Boy from Killann'?

MULLINS (*starts to sing*)

Seven feet was his height with some inches to spare
And he looked like a king in command.

CASEY (*rising*) Kelly or no Kelly won't be of much use if I keep that woman of mine waiting any longer.

MULLINS (*amid general rising*) It's time for us all to be making ourselves scarce.

ELIZABETH Here's your nightdress and goodnight, Una.

General exit. Silence.

REAGAN It's a good cursèd job that those don't decide to come up many nights.

ELIZABETH Oh what harm and the nights are often long enough?

REAGAN Suffering duck, but were you listening to that rubbish? Jesus Christ and six feet and By Garrup and Spats and the Immaculate Conception.

ELIZABETH It's only a saying that he was six feet, and what was it only talk? Did you not hear it before?

REAGAN Of course I heard it. I'm not deaf, unfortunately. (*Then gently*) Sure you're not getting like the rest of them, girl?

Turns on the radio. Music. Voice:

RADIO ANNOUNCER So now before you sleep, make up your mind to buy a sweepstake ticket and the first prize of fifty thousand pounds out of a total of two hundred thousand pounds in prizes and this year's Grand National may be yours.

REAGAN (*abruptly switching off radio*) The news is long over. It's time we said the prayers and went to bed.

Noise of beads and rustle of newspaper.

REAGAN Thou, O Lord, will open my lips.

CHORUS And my tongue shall announce Thy praise.

CHANT I believe in God, the Father Almighty, Creator of heaven and earth . . .

Fade.

REAGAN That's another day put down. Now off to bed. Rush. You'll be asleep in school all day tomorrow if you don't rush.

Distant steps on stairs.

Guard Casey's even takin' down his bed from upstairs.

CHILDREN Goodnight, Elizabeth. Goodnight, Daddy.

CASEY (*hearty voice to children in distance*) You're off to your warm beds now.

CHILDREN Goodnight, Guard Casey.

CASEY Goodnight. Sleep tight and mind the fleas don't bite.

REAGAN Are you all right, Elizabeth? You look tired.

ELIZABETH I feel tired. It's the cycling, I suppose.

REAGAN What did the doctor say? I'm sorry I got no chance to ask till now, with that crew up here all the night.

ELIZABETH Oh that's all right. He said more or less what I knew he'd say. He'll have to send me for a biopsy.

REAGAN What's a biopsy, Elizabeth?

ELIZABETH A small operation on the breast. You see there's this lump. I discovered it as long ago as last summer, an evening I went with the children to Malone's island, when I was drying myself after the swimming. I should have gone to the doctor then but I kept putting it off, you know the way. Nothing may be wrong. Maybe just a harmless growth.

REAGAN Why didn't you tell me, Elizabeth?

93

ELIZABETH I didn't want to needlessly worry you.

REAGAN But we're married, Elizabeth. We are for giving each other that kind of help.

ELIZABETH Don't you notice that we hardly ever talk now? Hardly ever talk, and when the small talk stops it gets impossible to say the big things. (*Laughs.*) You know the catechism, 'He that contemneth the small things.' But it is not your fault, it happens to everybody.

REAGAN But we're married, Elizabeth.

ELIZABETH Yes, and I love you and you've given me great help, especially with the children, when I came a stranger.

REAGAN When will you have to go away, Elizabeth?

ELIZABETH The doctor said he'd ring when there was a vacant bed and don't worry it may be nothing. (*Pause.*) Look, I'm not worried.

REAGAN You gave me a fright. I suppose we'd better go to bed now. Are the hens shut in? Is there anything you want me to go out for?

ELIZABETH No, there's nothing wanting.

REAGAN You look tired out. You're killing yourself working. (*Pause.*) Take it easy, especially until we hear that it's all clear.

ELIZABETH I don't feel killed. It's tiredness after the cycling, no more.

REAGAN Maybe it's a holiday you need. You could go up to Dublin and stay at thirty-six for a change.

ELIZABETH No, no, no. I hate holidays.

Noise of Casey on the stairs.

REAGAN Casey is taking a hell of an amount of pounding up and down to make up his bed beside that bloody phone. Don't stay up long, Elizabeth. Come to bed now.

Steps on concrete and later on hollow stairs.

ELIZABETH When I rake the fire.

*

Noise of alarm. Getting-up sounds. Feet on stairs.

WILLIE Daddy's off to court today, Elizabeth.

ELIZABETH He is.

SHEILA Can I go up to call him?

ELIZABETH Do it quietly then.

WILLIE I'll quench the lamp, Elizabeth. There's enough light now without the lamp. It's all white with frost outside. We'll be able to slide on Cassidy's pond soon if it keeps up.

Pause.

SHEILA Daddy, it's time to get up. (*Pause.*) It's the day of the court, Daddy. It's time to get up, Daddy.

REAGAN (*waking*) It's you, Sheila. What day is it today?

SHEILA Thursday, Daddy. It's the day of the court.

REAGAN (*rising*) Christ, it left my head. Another blasted day in town.

Feet on stairs. Feet on concrete. Door.

Is the shaving water ready, Elizabeth?

ELIZABETH It's there on the fire.

Shaving noises. Pounding of feet on stairs.

REAGAN You'd think it was a stone-crusher we had in the house with that Casey leaving his few blankets and mattress back up the stairs. Next he'll be banging at the fire with that poker and pounding down to the ashpit with his ashes.

Banging of poker on iron. Slamming of doors in distance.

Oh my sainted aunt. There's no need for prophets around here.

Loud feet on cement. Knock on door.

ELIZABETH Good morning, Guard Mullins.

MULLINS Dondered up to see what time the Sergeant's going to court?

REAGAN At half nine after the mail car comes in.

MULLINS Right then, Sergeant. Bit of a head this morning, Elizabeth. These pints I had did me no good last night. A fierce matter of dehydration this morning. That's a powerful smell, the frying, Elizabeth, on a frosty morning. Freeze the arse of a brass monkey, this morning would. A terror it was to get out of the bed.

ELIZABETH Six days of frost we've had now.

MULLINS Six days, but anything's better than the wet. We're all off for the court today. Casey will be holding the fort on his own. I suppose I'd better make a move and start shining myself up.

Departing feet on concrete. Pause. Approaching feet. Knock.

CASEY I'm leaving the door open so the phone can be heard if it rings while I go up to get some breakfast and bring Una down from that woman of mine.

Household noises. Noises of children. Departing feet on concrete.

ELIZABETH Are there many cases today?

REAGAN (*aggressively*) Not many.

ELIZABETH I just wanted to know if you'd be home for dinner or not.

REAGAN There's only one big case. Last month's crash at the quarry. It'll depend on when it's called. We might be out in an hour and we might be there till night. If we're not home before two you'll know we'll probably be late.

ELIZABETH Will you call for me at the doctor's and see if he has any word from the hospital?

REAGAN I'll get the doctor to come out, that's what I'll do.

ELIZABETH No. There's no need. Besides it's a useless waste of money.

REAGAN We're not paupers.

ELIZABETH It makes no sense to bring him out. It's only to wait for a bed.

REAGAN You wouldn't think of going to thirty-six in Dublin for that holiday while you're waiting? They always like to see you there. It'd take you out of yourself. A change is as good as a rest.

ELIZABETH Look at the cost, the train fare . . . (*Laughing*) Those shop windows that I'd never get past without spending every penny that we have.

REAGAN If the money's wanted it'll be always found.

WILLIE Why don't you go, Elizabeth, if you get the chance?

ELIZABETH Who'd look after the place while I was away, Willie?

REAGAN That's a poor excuse. There's no fear of the old barracks taking flight while you're away, and more's the pity.

WILLIE I think you should go, Elizabeth. I'd definitely go if I was in your place.

ELIZABETH Who can wash and bake and sew?

WILLIE We would, Elizabeth. We'd stop from school in turn, we'd buy loaves.

ELIZABETH You only think you could. It's not as simple as you imagine, Willie.

WILLIE We'd manage, Elizabeth. I think it'd be foolish to miss Dublin. Not many people ever get to Dublin. We'd manage. Sure, Elizabeth, didn't we manage for ages before you ever came after our own mother went away?

Pause before Reagan shouts at the boy:

REAGAN Now you see what you've done? You've gone and upset Elizabeth. Will you never get it into your thick skull that you have to be careful what you say to women? (*Mutters*) Now I'll have to go upstairs after her and it a court morning to boot.

Feet on concrete. Climbing stairs. Creak of door carefully opened.

Elizabeth, I came to see if you're all right, Elizabeth.

ELIZABETH I'm all right now. I had to be on my own. I'm sorry I broke down but I got a shock. I had to come up to think. I'm all right now. Of course you know you can be done without, that nobody really needs anybody all that much, that we'll all be done without and replaced and life will go on as indifferently as before, but to hear it out of the blue it is like a blow.

REAGAN Of course you're needed. Everybody knows how you've changed this house, but that scatterbrain of a Willie never thinks twice and comes out with the first thing that enters his head.

ELIZABETH It's not his fault, and what he said was true, only it was a shock to hear with that suddenness.

REAGAN Of course it's not true. It's just careless child's talk.

ELIZABETH I'm perfectly all right now and I'll come down to get you ready for the court.

Fade. Steps downstairs.

*

Knock on door.

ELIZABETH It's you, Mrs Casey. I never heard your steps come up the hallway.

MRS CASEY They're gone to court today. Ned's on his own today. (*Sitting down*) Isn't it strange you never smoke, Elizabeth? Nearly all doctors and nurses smoke. They say it's antiseptic or something, and isn't it strange you never started when you were nursing in London? Did you see the three Murphys at the rails last Sunday? They must have got early holidays from the civil service. They were all clever, weren't they? They flew through their exams, but I think Mary has failed. Irene is the prettiest now – she was dressed in all lavender, that lovely white lace in her hair, and it said in *Woman* last month that lavender is all the rage in Paris now.

Loud scrape of kettle.

ELIZABETH (*in whispered aside*) Oh my God, is this to go on all morning?

MRS CASEY Do you think it's true Irene's the prettiest now?

ELIZABETH She is a very pretty girl.

MRS CASEY (*changes into a kind of reflection*) Do you never regret marrying, Elizabeth? You even had to give up your nursing.

ELIZABETH No, I don't regret.

MRS CASEY Sometimes when I'm up in that house on my own I often feel you could be no lonelier single.

ELIZABETH Yes, but you'd think differently if you really were single.

MRS CASEY You think so, Elizabeth?

ELIZABETH There was a Sister Murphy who worked with me in hospital. One day she said to me, 'I lit three candles today in St Anne's before the Virgin.' 'Are you praying for something special or is there something worrying you, Brigid?' I asked her. 'You won't mention what it is to anybody if I tell you?' she said. 'No, of course not. But why tell me if you're afraid?' Then she told me that she was praying for a man, praying to the Virgin to send her some nice decent person for a husband and she was all of sixty years, a wisp of a little woman. I wanted to laugh it was so funny, as a kind of defence, I suppose; but then I grew scared, that I would grow old in the hospital as laughably longing as the poor Sister.

MRS CASEY I suppose there is that side to it too. At least if you burn your fingers you're not wondering what the fire's like, but sometimes I feel as if I was never married, up in that house, on my own.

ELIZABETH Wouldn't it be nice to have a cup of tea and we can call Guard Casey up?

MRS CASEY Well it's not overwork will detain him. He's down in that dayroom, having measured the rainfall, with his feet up like Lord Muck, reading the paper. But it's a lot of trouble for you to go to.

ELIZABETH It's no trouble. Call him up. It's practically ready.

MRS CASEY (*shouts*) You're wanted, Ned.

Noise of door. Feet on concrete.

CASEY The wanted man is here. Bad as being in *Fogra Tora*. I'm the most important man in the house today, sole guardian of the fortress, and the phone never rang, not to talk of anybody coming. The only time anybody seems to come is to sign for the dole or with a dead fox fit to stink you out of the place.

ELIZABETH You can sit down and you can have tea with us. You preferred it, I think, in Skerries.

CASEY The tea is a great man, but it's a lot of trouble. The east coast is good, there was great life there, near the city: the market gardening, places you couldn't throw a stone without breaking glass, the fishing boats and the tourists in summer. Too busy we were at times, but not too busy that I couldn't meet my Waterloo.

MRS CASEY You hear him now but it wasn't always that tune. The first night he left me home from the dance, I remember.

CASEY Aren't we a bit past it now for that class of reminiscing?

MRS CASEY We were dancing in the Pavilion, Elizabeth, and he got so hot that nothing would do him but to get me out of it before it was over. (*Mimics*) 'It's too hot in here and we can't dance with the floor crowded, Teresa.' So he brought me down by the harbour and put me up against Joe May's gable. You could still hear the music from the Pavilion, and it was coming across the bay from the dancing in Red Island too. Mike Delahunty playing there that night. There was a big moon over the masts of the fishing fleet. (*Embarrassed laughter.*) I knew he was mad for a court. And just as he was kissing me, and he had his arms around me (*more laughter*) and to tell you the truth he had the breath squeezed out of my body for he was feeling amorous as the devil, I pulled back my head of a sudden and I said, 'Do you see the moon, Ned?' You'd laugh till your dying day if you saw the cut of his face as he searched for the moon above the fishing fleet. And you know what he said when he found it? (*Convulsive laughter.*)

ELIZABETH What?

CASEY Oh my God!

MRS CASEY He said the moon was beautiful. (*Roar of laughter.*) He said the moon was beautiful, and I nearly burst.

CASEY That's a nice story to tell on anybody.

MRS CASEY I might never have married ya only for you were eejit enough to say the moon was beautiful. And if you'd had to wait for another few years, you'd be as bald as an egg, the way you are now, and you'd have got nobody.

CASEY After that story, Elizabeth, it's time for a man to beat a hasty retreat. Thanks for the tea. You won't mind if I come up later to listen to the soccer match? That's more in my line than the moon.

MRS CASEY Go now before you hear more about yourself.

Steps. Domestic noises.

Can I help you to wash up or anything? You've not been looking yourself, you know, lately.

ELIZABETH I feel well.

MRS CASEY Was it to Dr Ryan or Dr Walsh you went that day? I hadn't time to ask you when you came back, there was such a rush on.

ELIZABETH Just to Dr Walsh, the police doctor.

MRS CASEY Ned swears by Dr Walsh, but I don't like his manner and I go to Dr Ryan who has always a joke or a smile. (*Chattering*) I'd better be slipping off now. There's Mrs Lynch cycling up the road to ring the Angelus, twenty minutes late, no more than usual, and I've got to make sandwiches to bring down to Ned, as it's not likely they'll be early enough home from the court to release him from that phone on the wall for his meal, and thanks for your tea, Elizabeth.

ELIZABETH Goodbye, Mrs Casey.

Steps. Bang of door.

*

Steps on concrete. Knock on door.

CASEY Came up for the soccer match, Elizabeth. I'll borrow this chair to leave against the door in case I'd not hear the phone in the excitement if it rang. Heavy I feel after those beef sandwiches she brought me down. But now for the match, if that won't be too much annoyance. And I brought you up the paper in case you'd like to have a look, except I'll remove the sports page, for that would be no interest to you anyhow.

Rustle of paper.

ELIZABETH Thanks, Guard Casey. Was there anything strange in the paper today?

CASEY No, nothing strange. Same old disasters. But you read them all the same, as if they were always new. (*Laughs.*) Glad, I suppose, they're not your own disaster. The sports page though is more in my line. That's fairly cut and dry.

ELIZABETH Had you any callers since this morning?

CASEY Only a Peter Mulligan. He wanted a licence to cut trees.

Radio turned on. Sleepy waltz.

ELIZABETH Is it difficult to get a licence to cut trees?

CASEY What are licences for only for getting? Who's to stop him except myself? And why should I want to stop anybody from cutting something that's no concern of mine?

ELIZABETH There'll be no trees soon.

CASEY There'll be no country soon, never mind trees, if you ask me. But I suppose there'll always be some eejit left to sound the last post. We'd be all on our uppers long ago if we weren't sure there would always be some eejit left to sound the last post.

Announcement of soccer commentary. Scrape of chair.

The match at last, Elizabeth. If Wolves win this replay they'll be in with a great chance for the Double, and there's three Irishmen playing.

Excited commentary on game.

It's a fireworks start, Elizabeth. It's a goal! Now the fat is in the fire if Wolves want to bring off the Double.

There's three Irishmen playing, to boot. (*Loud slap on knee.*) This is the stuff to bring a man to life, Elizabeth.

Heavy noise of river boat into radio.

ELIZABETH I'll go out to watch the river boat, maybe see some of the spring flowers.

CASEY There's three or four boats a day now bringing the timber down.

Fade. Close of soccer commentary. Casey's loud sigh of relief.

Listening to that was like walking a tightrope.

ELIZABETH (*coming in from outside*) Was it a good match, Ned?

CASEY A real humdinger, Elizabeth, but the suspense of the last quarter was terrible to endure, and Wolves are in with a great chance for the Final. And there's three Irishmen on the team. I wish you'd call me Ned more often instead of that Guard Casey. I've never been able to fathom out who Guard Casey is.

ELIZABETH (*carefully*) It's because of the children. I don't like to show them too much familiarity. You fall into a habit.

CASEY Respect is taking a back seat in the world, with the way it's going. And talking of respect wasn't that a terrible story that woman of mine told about me and the moon today? I'll take the chair away from the door and leave you in peace. I see you have daffodils. That woman of mine is daft on flowers. Trees are more in my line.

ELIZABETH The soccer season will be over soon.

CASEY In four weeks' time, with the Cup Final, and then it will be cricket. And after that it will be our own stalwarts of the GAA on Sundays with Michael O'Hehir.

(*Mimics*) '*Bail ó Dhia oraibh go léir a chairde Gael ó Pháirc an Chrócaigh*. Hello everyone from Croke Park and this is Michael O'Hehir.' (*Loud laughter.*)

ELIZABETH You'd better go back to the dayroom before you say too much. If the children aren't home soon I'll have to go to the Quay. I told them they could play on the Quay after school.

CASEY I'll take the chair away from the door before I go, Elizabeth. They'll be soon back from the court anyhow.

Steps on concrete. Voices of children. Doors.

CHORUS Daddy's home from the court, Elizabeth.

Feet and doors in distance.

ELIZABETH You shouldn't have stayed so long on the Quay.

WILLIE We never thought of the time, Elizabeth, till we saw the blue uniforms come on the bicycles round by the lake.

ELIZABETH It'd be nice if you came sometime when I told you. You better get at your exercises before your father comes up and sees you've been playing the whole evening.

Loud footsteps. Loud opening of door.

CHORUS Welcome home, Daddy.

REAGAN Oh yes, I've brought you the sweets. Silver Mints with the polar bear on the wrapping. Catch!

Noise of children fighting for the sweets.

ELIZABETH I've your tea ready. You've had a long day.

REAGAN The crash didn't come up till three; hanging around all day with our two hands as long as each other.

ELIZABETH Did you have any lunch?

REAGAN At the Bridge Café. Herded at tables like cattle, we were.

ELIZABETH And the case? How did the case go?

REAGAN A fine, and a suspended sentence for dangerous driving. The drunken driving charge was dismissed. He had a good solicitor, a good background, a university education, a good position that might be endangered by a conviction for drunken driving. What more could you ask?

Long silence. Sound of knives and forks on plate.

ELIZABETH Did you see the Superintendent?

REAGAN How could I miss but see him?

ELIZABETH Was it all right?

REAGAN Oh of course it was all right, as all right as the last time and as all right as the time before and as all right as the time was before that again. Two labourers home from England were up for drunken brawling and you should have heard bloody old Justice O'Donovan. (*Mimics*) 'Labourers home from England who behave between jobs like writers between books can't expect to get the same admiring treatment.' Apparently Brendan Behan was up for brawling last week in Dublin, which was the whole point of the joke; and you should have heard them laughing as if they were laughing for their lives. If anybody had the misfortune to let out an honest shout of laughter he'd have had him up for contempt. And of course nothing would do Quirke but come up to me and ask (*mimics viciously*) 'Don't you think, Sergeant, Justice O'Donovan has a wonderful sense of humour?' 'Yes, Sir,' says I. 'He has a very fine sense of humour. He could make his living in a circus, Sir.'

'A circus, Sergeant, a circus? I find it rather difficult to imagine Justice O'Donovan in a circus, Sergeant.' But you should have seen the look on his face. He'll get on, make no mistake. He led the laughing at every vomiting crack O'Donovan made. It's the legal system of arselicking. They lick the arse above them, and to keep their minds easy about their own arselicking the bugger below them must lick their arses for what his life is worth. And it goes like a house on fire down to the bottom of the ladder where the last arse is firmly licked by perishing mud. I am sick of it, sick of saying yes, 'Yes Sir, no Sir, it looks so Sir, what do you think Sir, I think it might be the best way to do that Sir.' As I get older I get sicker and sicker, I can't take much more of it. That's certain. I don't want to come just because someone shouts 'Come' and go away when he doesn't even take the trouble to tell me to go but turns to someone else and leaves me standing there like the bloody agnostic that died and was all dressed up and had nowhere to go. Oh I'm sick of being pushed around and I'll not stand much more of it but I'm telling you I'll take one or two of those bastards with me before I go. I'm telling you that now.

Long, heavy silence.

ELIZABETH Did Guard Mullins come home?

REAGAN If you listen long enough you'll probably hear him holding forth about the exciting day to Casey down in the dayroom. We had just two drinks after the court, a round each, and he came with me. I suppose it's a bit too near the end of the month for him to go on a tatter.

GIRLS Can we go out, Daddy?

REAGAN What do you want to go out for?

GIRLS To put water on the slide, Daddy.

REAGAN And probably to cause some misfortunate to break his neck in the dark.

GIRLS It's on the river path.

REAGAN Oh go then while you have the chance, if that will give us some peace. If I could squeeze a bit more out of the turf-cutting this summer, for I've already got the contract for the nuns and the convent laundry, with what I've already saved we'd be able to buy and stock a fair-sized farm. It'd be tough at first, pay wouldn't be coming in every month, but we'd be answerable only to ourselves and I'd be able to give that bastard of a Superintendent Quirke something to remember me by before I left. I'll gut that bastard before I finish.

ELIZABETH I'll go anywhere with you. Wouldn't it be as easy to go quietly and ignore him?

REAGAN He didn't ignore me and I'm telling you I'll savage that bastard's teeth in once I'm ready to go.

ELIZABETH Did you remember to call on the doctor today?

REAGAN I'm sorry, I delayed telling you because of the children. He said he was still waiting for the bed but he'd press them and if he had news he'd ring this evening. Do you think it'll be all right, Elizabeth?

ELIZABETH It'll be all right. Don't worry.

Pause.

REAGAN I'll call the children and get the prayers said so that we can have an early evening. (*Calling*) The Rosary, the Rosary, the Rosary, time to say the Rosary!

Fade.

*

REAGAN It's nice to have the court and day over and to be in bed.

ELIZABETH I had the Caseys today. Mrs Casey embarrassed poor Ned by telling how he said the moon was beautiful when they were courting.

REAGAN I wouldn't be surprised what either of that pair might say.

ELIZABETH Do you remember when we first met? I came to the barracks to get those papers put in order. I was just getting over that terrible time of nursing through the Blitz. Do you know what you said to me that day?

REAGAN What did I say?

ELIZABETH (*laughs lowly*) You have no need to be afraid, it was nothing romantic. You said when you handed me back the papers, 'It must have been a terror in London during the bombing.' And then we met again at the Pioneer concert.

REAGAN You don't regret marrying me?

ELIZABETH No, that I do not regret.

REAGAN I feel tired, Elizabeth. Good night now.

ELIZABETH Good night. Sleep well.

*

Boots on concrete. Door.

ELIZABETH I've been waiting for you this past hour. The doctor has rung.

REAGAN I'm sorry, Elizabeth. I was out on patrol. I couldn't get back till now. (*Pause. Afraid*) When have you to go then, Elizabeth?

ELIZABETH On Wednesday. I have to go to Dublin. The doctor will phone on Wednesday. (*Pause.*) Do you think the hospital expenses will interfere with your plans for the farm and for getting out of the police?

REAGAN Don't worry, Elizabeth. It doesn't matter about the farm or the police if you are sick, Elizabeth. (*Vehemently*) Money doesn't matter if you are sick. We'll get you better, Elizabeth. Don't you know that we love you, Elizabeth? (*Pause.*) Even if we don't say it often, Elizabeth.

Steps on concrete. Knock on door.

MULLINS I'm off for the old supper. I'll leave the doors open so that you'll hear the phone.

REAGAN Did Casey come in off patrol yet?

MULLINS No, Sergeant. Something must have held him up.

REAGAN Leave the key on the sill.

MULLINS I've left it on the sill, Sergeant.

Fierce mating cry of foxes in distance.

That crying of the foxes mating in the brushwoods up the river gives me the shivers. And it'll get worse before it gets better, a terror to get to sleep with them in the night.

Cry of foxes.

I better be making a move for the supper so.

Loud feet on concrete, on boards. Banging of doors.

REAGAN (*sarcastically*) It's better they're making them these days. (*Softly*) I'm sorry to be late but don't worry. I'll take the day off and go up with you, Elizabeth. We'll go on the train.

ELIZABETH Isn't that a lot of trouble when I can easily go on my own?

REAGAN You'll not go on your own. And don't worry. All the money you want you'll have. I'll stay in uniform till the pension if it's necessary to get you better. So don't worry, don't worry. We'll go together on the train on Wednesday.

ELIZABETH It may be nothing. I may be home in no time but thanks, thanks, thanks. I'm so glad you're coming with me on Wednesday.

*

Scrape of feet on gravel. Stacking of boxes. Voice of anxious passenger:

PASSENGER When will you open to give us the tickets? The train will be in any minute.

TRUCULENT OFFICIAL I have to stack these crates that were rushed in at the last minute. And don't worry about your tickets. I'll give you your tickets soon enough. And the train won't go without you unless I tell it.

ELIZABETH It's cold for April.

REAGAN It's better to have it cold now than bad in summer, Elizabeth. But the amount of turf we cut we need all the good weather we can get this summer, and then to look around for a farm and kick Quirke's teeth down his throat.

ELIZABETH There's not many travelling.

REAGAN No, never many in the morning, except on Thursday when there's the cheap excursion ticket. But the three twenty-five will be crowded like a cattle train and them all for the night boat to Holyhead.

ELIZABETH There'll be soon nobody left in the country.

REAGAN In four minutes it's due. I think I can hear it in the distance. There's the signal.

Scrape of feet on gravel. Click of signal.

ELIZABETH Is the watch going well?

REAGAN It hasn't broken for five years. It's more than twice my age. There are no parts for it any more. It costs a fortune if it breaks. (*Reads*) 'Elgin', pure gold, white face, hands of blue steel, passed to me from my father when he died. It was bought in New York. I suppose it will pass to Willie when I go.

Roar of approaching train. Clanks to a stop. Official's voice above roar:

OFFICIAL I told ya, yous would have plenty of time, and it'll not go without yous unless I tell it. (*Calls*) Dublin train, train to Dublin!

Rest of conversation takes place in moving train:

ELIZABETH I remember how I used love coming home from London on the train, especially at Christmas, my cases full of presents, coloured bulbs in the station, Christmas tree, whiskey on people's breath, and how I used hate the train when the home holidays were over. Then there was that summer that I met you (*flirtatiously*) and I didn't take the train back. It was a hot summer's day, wasn't it, that day we met? I'd come to the barracks for some form. There was a cart of hay coming through the village, I remember, and Johnny Mulhern half tipsy on top, a stalk between his teeth, and he shouted down to me, 'Powerful weather we're having.' And then at the Pioneer concert you asked me if I'd go with you to the Regatta. Do you remember?

REAGAN There was hardly a bad day that summer, Elizabeth.

ELIZABETH Except the day of the Regatta. It rained so much that instead of watching the boats we went to the Bush Hotel and we talked. We hardly ever talk now.

REAGAN That happens to everyone, Elizabeth.

ELIZABETH I'm sorry. (*Pause.*) It sometimes seems to me that life's all arranged wrong. After struggling you achieve a little security, you begin to learn something of what's going on about you, so that all seems in some way wonderful or interesting. And you become of some use to yourself and the people around you, and then your hair and teeth fall out or you get cancer or you lose your reason; it seems all wrong.

REAGAN Don't worry, Elizabeth. You think too deep, that's your trouble, and there's others that goes round and thinking of nothing except when next they'll fill their belly and they're happy. There's probably very little the matter with you, Elizabeth, except that you're worrying about it; and you'll be home to us in a week or so, as right as rain.

ELIZABETH I hope so, Jim, but I don't know. (*Pause.*) Mullingar. Fifty miles to Dublin. We're halfway.

REAGAN In another hour we'll be there. It's dreary-weary country through the Bog of Allen.

Fade.

*

Steady noise of train. Station and city noises.

ELIZABETH We're coming into the city already. Will we get a bus to the hospital?

REAGAN No, we'll get a taxi from the station. When you're not well I don't believe in skimping.

Station noises. Banging of taxi door.

To St Luke's Hospital.

ELIZABETH You don't mind if I take your hand? I'm a bit afraid. I hate to bother you like this. I know it's foolish.

REAGAN No, no, don't worry. It's hard for me to say but it was a lucky day for me the day I met you.

ELIZABETH Yes, yes. No matter what happens we have that. We've had all that much; nothing can take that away from us.

Taxi pulling up.

It's the hospital. After I get admitted how will you manage to pass the day till the evening train goes?

REAGAN Don't worry about that. In fact I was thinking of taking a ramble up to have a look at the depot in the Park where I was trained for the bloody old police years ago.

*

Noise of heavy traffic.

REAGAN Excuse me, Inspector, but what would be the best bus to take for the police depot in the Park?

BUS INSPECTOR The number ten over there. It'll drop you at the park gates, it's only a few minutes from there.

REAGAN Thanks.

Noise of bus. People leaving bus at terminus. Reagan's steps.

Yes, this is the road all right. They used to march us down this road to Mass on Sundays. We had to be shining.

Reagan's steps. Sudden drilling shouts. Wheeling and marching of boots. Police recruits drilling on the square.

By Jesus, it's as if nothing had changed. Poor bastards being drilled for their lives, though they probably think it's the bee's knees; but they're young. The clocks, the tricolour, the square, the grey stone, the sentries at guard house saluting. The canteen over there where they used to dish us out that slop. (*Chuckles harshly*) Lemonade on Sundays.

SENTRY Would you be one of the Force?

REAGAN I might be now. (*Sharply*) How did you come to that conclusion now?

SENTRY Even in plain clothes (*laughs*) a policeman has always a certain stamp by which you can tell. A kind of suspicious look and the way he stands. Is it down the country you're stationed?

REAGAN I'm up for the day. I thought I'd come out and have a look.

SENTRY It's not changed very much, has it, though the young fellows have it easier than in our day. It's not as strict. Treated, they are, more like humans, and a change for the civilised better I say.

Stamp of drilling feet. Drill shouts.

REAGAN Doesn't seem all that changed to me.

SENTRY (*affably*) I was in the class of 1924. I'd think you couldn't be much before or after me.

REAGAN I was in the spring class of 1922.

SENTRY Wasn't the Assistant Chief in the spring class of 1922? I think there's men I know who were in the spring class of 1922.

REAGAN There were many of us in the spring class of 1922, our heads in the clouds.

SENTRY Do you ever regret joining the old Force or not?

REAGAN Every minute of it. It was the worst move of my life.

SENTRY Is it because you didn't get any promotion?

REAGAN (*sharply*) I was a Sergeant after six months and that's what I still am today. The system of arselicking came in after that. If you didn't lick the arses above you, they closed ranks, especially if they thought you dangerous. It was as if we had fought for nothing all the years on the run. We just changed the colour of the uniform and that was all. We should have gone on fighting.

SENTRY Well, it's farther than I got. I was up for the Sergeant exam three times but that's as far as it got me. Have you been stationed in many parts of the country or what part might you be in now?

*

Voices of birds in the evening. Whine of sawmill in distance. Dogs. Suction of pumping. Spray falling on leaves.

CASEY That's what will keep the blight away, Sergeant.

REAGAN It's time, too, Casey. The edges of some of the leaves are burned.

CASEY Go to God, I never imagined the old blight would be so soon. It's high time so I sprayed my own few ridges. I wonder if I could borrow the can and barrel as soon as you're finished? For if Mullins hears of the blight he'll be in a rush to spray.

REAGAN Course you can borrow. I'm hoping to be finished before the night.

Noise of spray, sucking of pump. Birds. Sawmill.

CASEY It's three weeks now since Elizabeth's gone. I was reminded 'cause the wife had a note from her today. It seems she's mending as well as can be expected.

REAGAN I wanted to go up to see her Thursday but she wrote for me not to bother, that I'd need all my free days for the turf, that she'd be home soon.

CASEY It'll be great to see her home. She'll get a surprise when she hears you've bought that farm of Mullany's.

REAGAN (*coldly*) She knows I bought the farm.

CASEY She must be delighted so, must be as good as a tonic. As the wife says you're one man that's paving the way for a secure retirement, except you're showing the rest of us up, and that's a terrible rake of turf you have cut for sale this year.

REAGAN (*embarrassed, aggressive*) I'll get out as soon as I can afford. I've had my bellyful of the police.

Noise of approaching car into the whining saw and the birds. Both stiffen into silence.

I wonder who the hell that could be. (*Pause.*) It'd be just like that bastard to pay us an inspection the evening he wasn't wanted.

CASEY My God, there's it round the bridge, it's the Super's car all right. I'll be making for the dayroom, Sergeant.

REAGAN Jasus Christ tonight, and it's only four days since that bastard was out.

Noise of car coming to a stop. Slam of door. Steps on gravel.

QUIRKE Good day, Sergeant.

REAGAN Good day, Sir.

QUIRKE I see you are doing some spraying.

REAGAN That's right, Sir. It's the weather for blight.

QUIRKE Is there any news of Mrs Reagan?

REAGAN She's hoping to be home soon.

QUIRKE I'm glad to hear that, I'm very glad. Marvellous what hospitals can do these days. Well, as I was just passing I said I would drop in and sign the books.

REAGAN Very good, Sir.

Departing feet on gravel. Door.

QUIRKE (*in distance*) Good day, Guard Casey.

REAGAN (*spraying savagely*) The bastard will find me signed out on patrol in the book. He'll get his chance this time but soon he'll dance to a bloody different tune.

Sound of Quirke's admonishing voice in distance.

He's giving Casey the once-over now.

Silence. Birds. Scream of saw. Door. Steps on gravel.

QUIRKE Excuse me, Sergeant.

REAGAN Yes, Sir.

QUIRKE I noticed in the book that you are still supposed to be out on patrol, Sergeant.

REAGAN It was three before I got back, Sir, and it'd slipped my mind I was supposed to go out on patrol again, Sir. I was in such a rush to get this barrel out.

QUIRKE It's understandable perhaps this time but don't let it happen again, Sergeant. In your position it gives a bad example. If you and I, Sergeant, in positions of authority don't do our work properly, how can we expect our inferiors to do theirs?

REAGAN I'm sorry it slipped my mind, Sir.

QUIRKE We have a fine reputation to uphold and if we don't uphold that reputation for ourselves, nobody else will do it for us. In the years ahead we'll be seeking professional status and if we look upon ourselves as a depressed and irresponsible section of the service how will others look upon us? We must have pride in ourselves and in our work, and it is up to people, like you and me, Sergeant, in positions of responsibility to set the tone. At inspection the other day I asked a certain member of the Force – in kindness we'll leave him nameless – what he knew of the Dangerous Drugs Act. He looked at me in such a way as to suggest that I had asked him the way to the moon. Then I inquired if he knew of any dangerous drug, if for instance he could name me one; and you wouldn't credit the answer I got, Sergeant.

REAGAN No, Sir.

QUIRKE Mrs Cullen's Powders. He stood there in his blue uniform and informed me that Mrs Cullen's Powders was a dangerous drug. What kind of respect can a man like that have for himself or for his work? And that man would be the first to have his hand out when it comes to an increase of salary. And I say unless we raise the efficiency and morale of the Force how can we expect to raise its status?

REAGAN (*ironically*) There's not many men in the country realise that as you do, Sir.

QUIRKE I've been saying it for years. We must raise our status first ourselves before we can hope to get anywhere. But none of them seem to realise it, Sergeant.

REAGAN That's right, Sir.

QUIRKE I'm very glad to hear that Mrs Reagan will be home soon. I'll leave you to your spraying now. And don't forget to put those books right.

REAGAN No, Sir.

QUIRKE Goodbye then, Sergeant.

REAGAN Goodbye, Sir.

Departing steps on gravel. Departing car. Door. Steps on gravel.

(*Hisses*) A good bloody riddance. But soon, soon I'll make the bastard dance to a different tune.

CASEY He stayed a long time talking, Sergeant.

REAGAN Aye, and me with the can on my back like an eejit. (*With mocking sarcasm*) Do you know, Casey, that you're my subordinate? Do you know that I should set a good example for you gentry to follow? Did he tell you that the Sergeant had signed himself out on patrol when he was spraying his potatoes in the front of the barrack garden?

CASEY No. I saw him examine the book but he said nothing.

REAGAN (*jeering viciously*) That's the way to behave. Never undermine an officer's position before one of his men. We in authority must give a good example. We in positions of responsibility must set the tone. That's it, Casey.

CASEY All he was on to me about was that my buttons weren't shone enough.

REAGAN Oh my God, Casey. Will you go for your tea before something happens?

CASEY Thanks, Sergeant.

Pumping and spraying. Sawmill comes to a stop in distance.

REAGAN (*as he sprays*) Only a fool acts when he's caught out on the wrong foot. Play them at their own game. That's the way. Wait easy for your chance. And, Jesus, when I get the chance that bastard had better watch out for himself. I'll put his teeth down his throat. There's going to be more than one day to this job.

Spraying. Pumping. Lowing of cows. Rattle of a feeding bucket.

*

Cries of curlew on the bog. Wind in leaves. Creak of cartwheels.

WILLIE (*calling*) Daddy, the ass is sunk!

REAGAN (*running*) Keep him from going over on the shafts. A great bloody nuisance. Twice he's gone down today. Unhook the tacklings.

Noise of chains rattling. Panting of donkey.

Here, lift the shafts. That's it. Up, up you get. (*Sound of kick.*) Come on, I'll make you get up. That's it. Pull the shafts, Willie. I'll spoke the wheels out on the firm ground. We'll have to throw more branches and heather on that part of the pass.

Noise of cart being moved.

We'll be able to tackle him in here on the firm ground. It's last night's rain caused the old pass to cut up like that. Pray God it stays dry tonight.

WILLIE Must be near time to quit, Daddy?

REAGAN If we could just knock another hour out of it. If we could get four more loads out. We were probably too greedy and loaded the cart too much that time. If we could get four more loads before the night. We have to have ten lorryloads on the road by next week for the laundry and most of Thursday will be gone waste, for Elizabeth's coming home on Thursday.

WILLIE After four loads we can quit then?

REAGAN If we can get at least four loads out. You won't have any trouble between this and the road. We'll not put so much on the cart next time. I'll be getting back to see how the girls are at the clamping.

Rattle of cartwheels. Sound of blow on donkey.

Gee-up!

Lonely cry of curlews. Wind in leaves. Cow lowing in distance. Rocking of cart in ruts.

REAGAN You lassies are getting on like houses on fire.

SHEILA It started to get cold, Daddy, and Una says she's shivering. Will it be soon time for quitting?

REAGAN If we could just knock another hour out of it. Time for Willie to get out four more loads. And you've done great work today. Elizabeth will be proud of you when she comes on Thursday. And I'll be buying the whole lot of you lemonade and gingersnaps in Henry's on our way home this evening.

Night cries of dog. Rattle of cart.

We'll have a race to see who'll be first up with the next
clamp. (*Maniacally to himself*) It'll be a long hard
summer but it'll be worth it. We'll have enough to stock
the farm after this summer and we'll be able to go free
without cowing or bowing to anybody. We'll be able to
go free. (*Fiercely*) Quirke will dance to my tune before
this year is out. (*To the girls*) We'll have our own farm
and cattle and sheep and be free and owe nothing to
anybody. We mayn't have much but we can hold our
heads high. Won't that be something? Without cowing
or bowing to anybody.

SHEILA It's getting bitter cold though, Daddy.

REAGAN We'll stick it out for a short time. We'll warm
ourselves to see who has the clamp built first. And
there'll be lemonade and gingersnaps waiting for you in
Henry's on the way home.

*

Busy scuffling of gravel with spade.

MULLINS (*singing*)

> Said the Bishop of old Killaloe,
> 'I am bored, I have nothing to do.'
> So he climbed on his steeple
> An' pissed on his people,
> Singing tooralaye – ooralaye – oo.

You caught me singing, Elizabeth. It's a nice way for a
bishop to behave, isn't it, Elizabeth? Behaving like that
to his poor flock.

Elizabeth laughs.

It must be great to be back in the barracks after that
operation on a day the likes of this. It's a powerful
day.

ELIZABETH It is great to be back. I'm going to pick blackcurrants in the garden.

MULLINS You can't beat blackcurrant jam.

Sharp stroke of spade on stones.

I'm doing a bit of an old scuffling as you can see. Quirke was complaining last week about the weeds in the gravel. (*Mimics*) 'We must take pride in the appearance of our stations. If we don't take pride in ourselves no one else will.' (*Sarcastically*) And very full the same pride will fill our bellies. (*Changes*) But this station was the tidiest station in the country first. It won a prize. There was a fellow by the name of Joyce here then. A quiet sort of strange fellow from Galway, and he used to keep this place like the bee's britches, just lovely. He was mad about flowers and, strange as it may sound, dirty jokes; but you could get him interested in nothing else and he was a walking encyclopaedia on both. But he'd never turn up for inspection or patrols or anything. He nearly drove Sergeant Jennings that was the Sergeant here at the time out of his mind until he eventually managed to get him shifted up to one of the penal stations in the Donegal mountains at the back of beyond somewhere where he could flower away to his heart's content. (*Pause.*) When you see a stray lily like that over there in the wild grass you can be sure it was Joyce's doing.

ELIZABETH I've often wondered about those flowers in the wildness.

MULLINS That's twenty-one years ago. I'll be here twenty-one years the sixteenth of September coming, a month married then.

ELIZABETH It's odd they never transferred you in all that length of time.

MULLINS They must have forgotten about me up in the depot, Elizabeth. My name astray in some drawer or thrown into some of their wastepaper baskets. For would you believe it, I was never reprimanded for as they say dereliction of duty in all that time, not to talk of ever being commended and my name appearing in the box in the *Garda Review*. (*A few energetic scuffles.*) Only the pay comes the first of every month. If they forgot to send the pay, it'd be the last catastrophe.

Noise of motor van.

There's Broderick's bread van across the bridge. Two royal events of the day, Broderick's bread van and the mail car.

Noise of bread van stopping and starting up again. A few scuffles. Pause. Stop of scuffling.

It's moved from McDermott's to Murphy's. Believe me, that old dry stick didn't delay them long talking. (*Mimics a managing woman's voice*) 'Here's your order and give me the bread and go in the name of the Lord and don't disturb me further for I'm killed for want of business and the terrible times that are in it, my good man.' (*Changes*) They'll not get away so handy from Murphy's. Big Mick will want to know what happened in every dance hall in the county and outside. Oh, the big fat lazy bastard, his arse planked above on the counter, the best of rump steak from the town under his belt, nothing in his head but football and women, hot curiosity without benefit of cooling experience. But isn't the smell of fresh loaves wonderful, Elizabeth?

ELIZABETH It is. I remember once walking in Whitechapel and there was a van with open doors outside a pastry shop. It was a day I had off from the hospital, and I got the smell of loaves, and suddenly

I could see Broderick's van outside the chapel wall with its doors open and a bread rake thrown on top of the loaves. Smell of fresh loves, and I was sick for home.

MULLINS You probably wish to get away now? Back to a great place like London for a change.

ELIZABETH No, I'm glad to be home. I better start on the blackcurrants or they'll be back from the bog.

MULLINS They're always on the bog these days. Terror the amount of money the Sergeant will make when he sells that turf. Yous will be millionaires soon.

ELIZABETH (*laughs gently*) I doubt it. It's just that he's anxious to get enough money to be able to leave the Force.

MULLINS Wouldn't we all be anxious to leave the Force if we had the finances? (*Bitterness turns to joking*) As the father said to the son when he took the girl he wanted to marry home, 'It's all right having the financé (*pronounced 'fineancy'*) but where's the finances?'

ELIZABETH You're a terrible man and I better be going before you delay me longer.

Sound of bread van starting up.

MULLINS (*indignantly*) Didn't I tell you how long Big Mick would keep the bread men? The lazy old bollocks must have got enough information by this to keep his swamp of a mind employed for another few days. Some of the bread-van men and the travellers would want to be sexual encyclopaedias to satisfy some of the people in this village.

ELIZABETH You're too hard on people. I better be going.

MULLINS Sex is a bit overrated anyhow but when it's confined to talking and imagining it's surprising how worked up people can get.

Bread van stops.

It's at Glin's now. They'll have to satisfy her curiosity too. (*Mimics*) 'Jesus Christ, tonight, and you wouldn't be telling me that now, would you?' In her man's voice and her legs spread far enough apart to drive a fair-sized tractor through.

ELIZABETH (*laughs*) I'm going.

MULLINS (*hums*) And I'm going with you.

Loud scuffling. Noises of summer's day. Silence. Bees. Feet swishing through grass. Hollow sound of berries dropping in tin. Van.

ELIZABETH (*softly amid picking noises*) You only realise the heaven that's all about you when you lose it, like in hospital. To feel simply no pain. These rough green leaves, the silken skin of the currants, to make jam tomorrow in the kitchen, rows of washed jamjars on the table so that they seem made of light – shining glass till you pour in the black jam.

Busy scuffling of gravel grows louder, then stops. Mullins's footsteps draw nearer.

MULLINS Elizabeth, do you know where I'd like to be now?

ELIZABETH (*in affectionate exasperation*) Where?

MULLINS In one of those pubs along the Liffey, the White Horse or the Scotch House, and a good pint of stout in my fist. It's strange that the pint of stout is never as good outside Dublin. They say that travelling sours it. (*Changes*) Do you ever think, Elizabeth, that getting married and having a steady job like the police takes a lot of the ginger out of life, all more or less settled and finished with? The only missing information is the old age put on the name plate of the coffin.

ELIZABETH I don't know. I suppose what's distant is always tempting, but I don't know. For me to be out of hospital picking blackcurrants for jam on a day like this is enough.

MULLINS Oh the old hospital is a terrible place. That's right, Elizabeth. We don't half of the time realise our luck when we have it. You're the only person makes much sense around here. You're the only person a man can have a good talk with.

ELIZABETH Go away with you now and don't be trying to flatter me.

MULLINS I'm not but I can see when I'm not wanted. (*Sings*) 'I know where I'm going and I know who's going with me.'

ELIZABETH Nobody's driving you away.

MULLINS (*jauntily*) Oh I know when I'm not wanted.

Steps fading. Energetic scuffling of gravel. Noises of hot summer's day. Mullins's voice rising in distance as he sings again, 'Said the Bishop of old Killaloe', etc., fading.

*

WILLIE (*insistently*) Is it time to light the lamp yet, Elizabeth?

GIRLS Can we draw the blinds, Elizabeth?

ELIZABETH I don't think there's need to light the lamp at all this evening. Listen, you can hear somebody still mowing. (*Noise of mowing machine in distance.*) There's even light enough to mow.

WILLIE (*disappointedly*) They might be using their headlamps.

ELIZABETH No, I don't think there's need to light the lamp. It's nicer in the half light, unless of course you want to do your lessons.

WILLIE No, it's Saturday tomorrow.

GIRLS There's no school.

WILLIE But there's the bog.

ELIZABETH Look how dirty your legs are after the bog this evening. While there's light why don't you run down to the river and wash your legs? You can't get into clean sheets with legs that black.

CHILDREN All right, we'll race to the river.

> *Exit children. Banging doors. Silence except for small domestic noises. Singing of corncrakes. Steps on concrete. Door.*

REAGAN Where's the children, Elizabeth?

ELIZABETH They're gone to the river to wash their legs.

REAGAN Oh I'm tired out, Elizabeth!

ELIZABETH That's no wonder. You're driving yourself too hard on the bog and you're driving those children too hard. They're worn out at night now. They're not able to stand it. They'll not grow natural.

REAGAN Turf isn't heavy work. If they had to dig or something it'd be a different story.

ELIZABETH They're worn out at night and it can't be good.

REAGAN I never saw hard work do harm. Laziness and idleness was all I ever saw do harm. And they get oranges and lemonade. And I've promised to take them to Duffy's Circus when it comes to Boyle in August.

ELIZABETH That's only replacing the stick with the carrot.

REAGAN It'll do them no harm. You can take my word. And anyhow I can't do it all myself with that bastard Quirke all the time hanging around. He knows I'm at the turf. He doesn't like it. (*Mimics viciously*) 'It's not professional.' And he's out to get me.

ELIZABETH If you have to drive yourself and the children that hard, wouldn't you be better to stay on another year in the Force?

REAGAN (*violently*) To stay one day more than I have to under that bastard would stick like a fish bone in my throat. (*Changes*) Oh I'm tired, Elizabeth. Would you make us a cup of tea? I wonder if we'll get to sleep at all tonight with that bloody old corncrake craking away. These corncrakes are the worst of the bloody old summer.

*

Loud ringing of telephone.

CASEY Damn me, Sergeant, but if it didn't ring at last . . . Hello? (*Whispers*) Superintendent, Sergeant. He wants to talk to you.

REAGAN Yes, Sir. That's all right, Sir. I'll see you at that time then, Sir. (*Hangs up. In quiet voice to Casey*) Can you go quietly round to the pubs, Casey, and tell them to have everybody out by eleven tonight? Quirke is coming out. He's going to raid the pubs with me and Mullins. Say nothing about it to Mullins.

CASEY Why will I not say anything to him, Sergeant?

REAGAN You know him as well as I do. What he doesn't know won't trouble him.

CASEY Will I be going now then, Sergeant?

REAGAN Do. I'll stay here till you get back. Just tell them quietly.

CASEY I'll do that, Sergeant.

Departing footsteps on boards. Fade.

*

QUIRKE Goodnight, Sergeant. Goodnight, Guard Mullins.

REAGAN Goodnight, Sir.

MULLINS Goodnight, Sir.

QUIRKE We're ready then. From the reports I have we're likely to occasion a few surprises.

Steps. Loud knocking at door. Shuffles inside.

SENTRY Who's there?

REAGAN The law.

Unlocking of door.

SENTRY Yous can look around. You'll find nobody here.

QUIRKE Yes, there does seem to be nobody here. (*In suspicious voice*) This surprises me.

Repeat inspection at two other pubs.

REAGAN That's all the three pubs in this village, Sir. They seem to be keeping lawful hours, Sir.

QUIRKE (*exasperated, suspicious*) This surprises me.

It goes against all the information I had. And there's a man over there who doesn't appear to have left the pub that long, urinating, if I don't mistake, against the chapel wall.

MULLINS (*shouts*) Get out, get out of it!

MAN Aw, eff off with yourself and mind your own effin' business.

MULLINS Get out of it, have you no shame, against the chapel wall, and young girls passing every day this way to Mass?

MAN You wouldn't mind handling those same fillies closer than ever my pissing will get to them, you narrow-minded old bastard.

MULLINS What did you say to me, what did you say to me? Do you know that you're talking to the law, do you?

MAN No . . . I'm sorry. I didn't know, I'm sorry.

MULLINS It's never too late in the day to be sorry. That wasn't your tune a minute ago. It's never too late in the day to be sorry, is it?

REAGAN Take it easy. (*To the man*) What's your name?

MAN Jimmy Moran, the sawyer, Sergeant.

REAGAN That's no way to behave or talk. Go now before you find yourself in court.

Steps. Night noises.

QUIRKE I didn't want to interfere with your exercise of authority, Sergeant, but it's my opinion that that gentleman should have found himself in court.

MULLINS A disgrace, such language, against the chapel wall, and young girls passing.

REAGAN They don't pass this time of night. He's a decent working man. He just had a drink or two too many.

QUIRKE What bothers me about your area, Sergeant, is the tone, a certain lack of respect. And it was my information that the pubs in this village keep open hours.

REAGAN They seemed to have kept lawful enough hours tonight, Sir.

QUIRKE It's not my information, and I want to tell you that I'm far from satisfied, Sergeant.

Banging of car door. Starting of engine.

REAGAN *and* MULLINS Goodnight, Sir.

Car moves off. Steps in the night.

MULLINS It's cold, Sergeant.

REAGAN (*angrily*) What the hell did you make that fuss over old Jimmy Moran for? Was it trying to impress the bastarding Super you were?

MULLINS (*defensively*) It's me job, isn't it?

Firm steps in the night.

REAGAN It's your job, I suppose. (*Exasperated*) Some job.

*

Doors. Climbing of stairs. Door.

ELIZABETH Is that you, Jim?

REAGAN I'm sorry to be so late, Elizabeth. We had to do the pubs with Quirke.

ELIZABETH Was it all right?

REAGAN (*viciously*) Of course it was all right. I made sure it was all right. I had them warned beforehand.

(*Mimics*) 'What bothers me about your area, Sergeant, is the tone, a certain lack of respect.' And Mullins, in order to impress the bastard, made as much fuss as a Reverend Mother over Jimmy Moran pissing against the chapel wall.

ELIZABETH Wouldn't it be easier on you to let them go with it?

REAGAN That's all right but they won't let you go with it, they won't let you go with it, and before very long I'll give that Quirke something to remember me by till his dying day.

ELIZABETH I'm tired, Jim. I'm sorry. It's late. Why don't you come to sleep?

REAGAN I'm sorry, Elizabeth. It's late.

*

Ringing of alarm clock. Creak of bed springs.

ELIZABETH I'm not well, Jim. I've had a bad night. I'm not able to get up today. You'll have to get the doctor for me.

REAGAN You've been doing far too much work about the house since you've come from the hospital. I've been wanting you to go to Strandhill, to the sea for a holiday. You've been straining yourself too much.

ELIZABETH It's not that. Just get me the doctor.

Noise of Reagan rising.

REAGAN I'll go down to the dayroom and ring him up this minute.

Steps on boards. Fade.

*

Feet on gravel.

REAGAN Is she all right, Doctor?

Pause. Rattle of cart. Bees. Birds.

DOCTOR I'm afraid Mrs Reagan is very ill, Sergeant. There are some prescriptions that I want you to get immediately from town. There should be always somebody in the room with her, Sergeant.

REAGAN (*quietly*) Is it that bad, Doctor?

DOCTOR I'm afraid it is, Sergeant. I'll come out again this evening to see how she is. Get those prescriptions immediately.

REAGAN I'll get them at once.

Fade.

*

MRS CASEY I'll just dust a bit, Elizabeth. Tidy up the bed so that everything will be nice for the doctor when he comes.

ELIZABETH I don't know how to thank you. You've done so much for us, even managed the children since I got sick.

MRS CASEY Not at all. Work, I say, never killed anybody. When I'm on my own up in that joint of ours with Ned doing BO or out on patrol it's worst when I've nothing to do, stare at four walls. When you've nothing to do you start brooding and then your nerves get bad and everything frightens you. Since I've started helping here in the barracks I've never felt better. I think I could even sleep on my own these nights. Now that's more or less tidy. We won't be disgraced if the doctor comes now. Do you think you're feeling any better today?

ELIZABETH I don't think I'm too bad. I hope you won't mind if I don't talk. I'm so tired.

MRS CASEY No, no, of course I don't mind. A little sleep now would do you a world of good. I'll be going downstairs to put on the lunch so that it will be ready for the children when they come from school. If you need anything, knock, won't you, Elizabeth?

ELIZABETH Thanks, Mrs Casey.

Steps going downstairs. Fade.

*

Steps. Knock on door. Opening of door.

CASEY Are you awake, Elizabeth?

ELIZABETH That's Guard Casey, is it?

CASEY The one and only, Elizabeth. You're looking improved today. With the weather we're having you'll be on your feet and out and about in no time.

ELIZABETH I wonder if the weather counts for all that much?

CASEY Are you joking, Elizabeth? Of course the weather counts and I brought you the paper.

ELIZABETH Is there anything strange in it today?

CASEY There's never anything strange. But you buy them all the same, don't you? If you didn't you'd feel you might be missing something and the day wouldn't be the same. I think I hear that woman of mine moving about downstairs. I better be going before she comes up. She'll be complaining that I'm tiring you out with my foolish old chatting.

ELIZABETH Thanks for the paper and for coming up to see me.

CASEY For nothing, Elizabeth, for nothing. We'll not be easy till we have you better and up and about in this good weather.

Footsteps on stairs. Fading.

*

Steps approaching. Knock.

MULLINS You're awake, Elizabeth?

ELIZABETH Guard Mullins . . . Come in.

MULLINS Just dropped up for a minute, Elizabeth, to see how you were. I've left up the bed. It's a question of a bit of a dehydration today. Had a few over the top last night.

ELIZABETH Are you at much this weather?

MULLINS The usual fooling. Out on patrols. The bog. We'll kill the pig at the end of the week. We're giving him windfall apples in the hope it'll sweeten the bacon. We'll have black pudding for you next week. That's what'll help you to your feet. If you don't feed the inner man you might as well throw your hat at it. Empty bags can't stand.

ELIZABETH It was very good of you to think of the black pudding and to come to see me.

MULLINS For nothing, Elizabeth, for nothing. Haven't I been always tellin' them that you're the only woman I've ever met that a man can have a good conversation with? The only thing the wife likes less than that is the pints I have in the evening. But she says she'd love to come over and help in the house now that you're out of action. Except Mrs Casey wouldn't probably welcome that because since you took ill she's a kind of queen and parliament downstairs.

ELIZABETH Tell Mrs Mullins that I'm thankful, that I hope I'll see her soon.

MULLINS I'll be going now. You'll have to get better soon so that we can have another good few gosters or two before the summer's over. Do you remember the Bishop of old Killaloe? (*Hums the first line.*)

ELIZABETH Thanks for coming to see me, Guard Mullins.

MULLINS For nothing, Elizabeth. I'll bring you the black pudding when the pig is killed. I won't be tiring you out with my old talk. (*Very softly*) Goodbye now, Elizabeth.

Careful departing feet on stairs.

*

Steps up stairs. Knock on door. Opening of door.

REAGAN Are you awake, Elizabeth?

ELIZABETH It's you, Jim? Come nearer.

REAGAN Just got back from the bog. Are you feeling anything better today?

ELIZABETH Guard Casey and Guard Mullins came to see me.

REAGAN That was hardly much comfort. I too ran into the Super. He was complaining that I was lowering the standards of the police by going into the turf business. I told him in a careful way what I thought of him and the police.

ELIZABETH Oh Jim, is it worth bothering with?

REAGAN It is, but not, thanks be to Jesus, for much longer. We'll leave this barracks in September, Elizabeth. They say spring's the best time to move, but that's only old prejudice. You can have lovely weather often in the autumn.

ELIZABETH Can you draw a little nearer? Sit on the bed's edge. (*Pause.*) Somehow, Jim, I don't feel I'll be moving from the barracks in September. I've been happy in the barracks. Not till I left London and we married did I come to know my life and myself, how can I say it now, in some fullness; to know them for the rich gifts that they were.

REAGAN That's no way to talk. You'll never get better with that way of talking. You'll probably be better by September. And it'll be quieter for you in the farm than in this bloody barracks. And sure if you're not better itself in September I'll be able to carry you in my arms upstairs in the farm house, and with the relief of moving from this cursèd barracks you'll be out and about and on your feet in no time. We'll all be happy and we'll have a new life together.

ELIZABETH If that happens it'll be more than I'll ask for.

REAGAN Course it'll happen. In four days we'll be finished on the bog. The profit will be fiercer than I thought. I'm keeping them home from school tomorrow, except I'll leave Una in the house with you so that she can run for anything you want to Mrs Casey downstairs. The doctor will be coming in the morning too. You don't mind that we go to the bog, Elizabeth? In three or four days the whole shoot will be over, and then as I promised I'll be taking them to Duffy's Circus. You don't mind that we all go to the bog except Una tomorrow, Elizabeth? Three or four days more and it'll be all finished.

ELIZABETH I'll be glad when it's finished. It was a brutal summer and I wasn't much help.

REAGAN What would we have done without you, Elizabeth? We'll carry you upstairs if you're not all right by September. But it's a long time until September and you'll be better in no time then. They're tired out from this day on the bog and I better be saying the prayers with them and get them to bed. Mrs Casey is probably anxious to be off home by now. I don't want to troop them all up around your bed, but would you like me to leave your door open so that you can hear or follow?

ELIZABETH Leave the door open then.

Steps downstairs. In the distance, Reagan and the children say, 'Goodnight, Mrs Casey.' Reagan bolting the door. Pause.

REAGAN Thou O Lord shalt open my lips.

CHILDREN And my tongue shall announce Thy praise.

Fade. Rest of the Rosary in distance:

REAGAN Mystical Rose.

CHILDREN Pray for us.

REAGAN Tower of David.

CHILDREN Pray for us.

REAGAN Tower of Ivory.

CHILDREN Pray for us.

REAGAN House of Gold.

CHILDREN Pray for us.

REAGAN Ark of the Covenant.

CHILDREN Pray for us.

REAGAN Gate of Heaven.

CHILDREN Pray for us.

REAGAN Morning Star.

ELIZABETH (*to herself*) I have never understood people
who have hated their religion. Isn't the religion that we
are born into as much an accident as our life? I have
never understood. It was always the weather of my life
and to deny it seemed to make as little sense as denying
the actual weather; and hardly ever there are real
choices, and rain or sun what does it matter since it's
your life that the rain or sun falls on? The Rosary was
the weather of all my early evenings and I would no
more change that than I would change my own life for
another person's. Especially in London I've never
understood when they complained, but then I have never
understood; and it has always been the weather of my
life. Mystical Rose, pray for us, Gate of Heaven, pray
for us, Morning Star . . .

*

*Hot summer's day outside. Noises of summer. Bedroom.
Long silent toiling of Angelus bell in summer.*

ELIZABETH That was the bell, wasn't it?

UNA It was, Elizabeth.

ELIZABETH I wasn't sure. All day I seemed to hear
strange bells ringing in my mind, church bells. It was the
bell, wasn't it?

UNA 'Twas.

ELIZABETH Did they come from the bog yet?

UNA No, not till evening. Daddy has a day's monthly
leave. They're hoping to make a big hole in the last of

the turf. They brought bread and bottles of tea in the socks.

ELIZABETH But they were to be back to go to Devotions. It grows cold on the bog in the evenings. It was the first bell, wasn't it?

UNA No, it was the Angelus, Elizabeth.

ELIZABETH It's the bell for the Angelus.

UNA It's the bell for the Angelus. Late no more than usual. Twenty past twelve on the clock now.

ELIZABETH But why did you draw the blinds?

UNA What blinds?

ELIZABETH The blinds of the window.

UNA No, there's no blinds down. But it will not be long before it's brighter. The sun will be round to this side of the house in an hour. Listen, you can hear the birds down by the river. They've a hot day on the bog.

ELIZABETH There's no clouds.

UNA No, no.

Noise of disturbance.

(*Shrieking*) Mrs Casey, Mrs Casey, Mrs Casey! (*Noise of Una's footsteps.*) Something's happened to Elizabeth, Mrs Casey!

Doors. Steps.

MRS CASEY Oh my God, oh my God. She looks gone. Oh send for the doctor and nurse and the brown habit. Oh my God, I'll have to run for Ned. Word will have to be got to the bog.

Sound of steps. Hysterical call:

Ned, Ned, Ned! Oh my God, word will have to be got to the bog.

Doors. General commotion. Fade.

*

Slow toll of funeral bell. Noise of motor cars in low gear, stopping, jerking.

FIRST WOMAN I counted twenty-eight cars behind Elizabeth's hearse before I got tired of counting.

SECOND WOMAN Ah but sure what would you expect, isn't himself the Sergeant, and they all have to turn out?

FIRST WOMAN Must be no joke for a man for two women to die under him.

Funeral bell. Motor noises speeding.

SECOND WOMAN They'll start to go faster once they get to the bridge.

*

Noises of brilliant summer's day. Steps on grass and stone.

MULLINS I didn't want to wait to see the grave filled, Guard Casey. Though I miss poor Elizabeth something shocking about the barracks since she's gone. It's terrible that I'm glad it's such a good summer's day and that it's her that's been covered and not me. She could always laugh at a remark like that. She had a better roof to her head than most.

CASEY The woman is heartbroken but she's looking after the children back in the barracks. Don't some get a rough passage? Himself looks pretty bad but there's a look of murder in his eye that I don't like at all. A hard, cold look. When he shook hands with the Super I saw a look in his eye, it was outside the church, that'd go through you like a night of frost.

MULLINS If I was Quirke I'd be careful. But he can't be all that careful, since he's the Super, isn't he? And it's my opinion that there'll be sparks.

CASEY I suppose. And the worst will be getting used to a new Sergeant.

MULLINS Now that's interesting. Look at that for a fanciful tombstone over there, hanging chains and all. (*Reads laboriously*) 'Thomas Edward, killed in Normandy, 4th August 1944 and was buried in an orchard adjoining the churchyard of Courteil, South of Gaumont. Capt. Edward Charles, Irish Guards, killed in action 6th Nov. 1914 at Klein Billebecke near Ypres and has no known grave; greater love hath no man than this that a man lay down his life for his friends.' Easy to know who those gentlemen belong to, Guard Casey. You can be sure they weren't on speaking terms with my grandfather or yours. Anglo-Irish fucking exploiters. Their house has burned down and the woods and the walls fallen and it gives me sweet joy to look on the ruin. May their souls be damned in hell.

CASEY (*reads comically*) '*Spes tutissima coelis.*' A tourist told me once, a sort of professor eejit, that it means sure-fire hope of heaven.

MULLINS Sure fire all right, isn't that obvious? You see that stone finger under your *spes*-whatever-it-is pointing to the sky? Isn't it obvious, Guard Casey, that the finger points out what the words say? But now what I'd like to ask you, Guard Casey, is who told them heaven is in that direction anyhow? (*Belly laughter.*)

CASEY Though it is up, they're right in that, it was up Jesus Christ went on Ascension Thursday.

MULLINS But how do they know Jesus Christ went that way up? The world rotates, it does a full circle every twenty-four hours. In twelve hours' time it'll be down where Australia is now, and it'll be pointing in the direct opposite direction then.

CASEY It was to Molloy's you said we'd go to. The pubs in the village will be full. And it wouldn't be the thing to be seen drinking in the village with Elizabeth gone so soon. Molloy's will be empty, and if there's a few there they'll give us the back room all to ourselves.

MULLINS It's to Molloy's we're going, that's for certain shooting. We're safe there from Quirke. It would be too disrespectful of him to be out for this day. It's terrible hot. I'll have to unbutton this tunic. I have a fierce need for pints of cider.

CASEY As long as we don't overdo it. But what you seem to forget is that the sun goes round the earth as well as the earth goes around the sun. Now doesn't that put up a different way of seeing? We'd be all a bit banjaxed, wouldn't we be, if we couldn't decide what way was up?

MULLINS Well, up or down, we better be getting a move on, for I have a great want of pints of cider, and my *spes* is that I'll be remaining on terra firma as long as possible. Quick, march, Guard Casey; left, right.

CASEY Right, left, right.

Noises of summer's day. Fade.

*

Door. Feet on stairs. Knock on door.

REAGAN Who's there?

CASEY It's me, Guard Casey. The Super's downstairs
and he's hopping mad, Sergeant. And he wants to know
if you're reporting sick or coming down.

REAGAN So he's arrived at last, has he? (*Stir of bed.
Shouts*) Tell him I'm coming down.

CASEY Right, Sergeant.

*Noise of violent dressing. Bang of door. Stairs
pounding. Door.*

REAGAN I heard you wanted me and I am here.

QUIRKE Have you any explanation to offer?

REAGAN I have no explanation to offer to you.

QUIRKE Stand to attention, Sergeant.

REAGAN Stand to attention yourself.

QUIRKE I'll have you dismissed. Do you realise I'll have
you dismissed?

REAGAN You'll not have me dismissed. I've sent in my
resignation to headquarters a week back. If they had any
respect for you, they should have informed you.

QUIRKE You're still in the police, Sergeant. I'll see
you're disciplined. I'll see to that.

REAGAN You'll see to nothing. You think you can see
to something 'cause you wear an officer's belt over your
uniform. (*In fierce voice*) I wore the Sam Browne too in
my day and I wore it to command men in the fighting
who were killed. I wore it in the days it was dangerous
to wear it in this balls of a country. I never wore it to
motor around to see if a few poor harmless policemen

would lick my arse while I shit day and night about law and order. Now get out of this dayroom before I smash you.

QUIRKE You are obviously in no condition to listen to reason but I'm telling you you will regret this.

REAGAN I'm telling you to get out. Come on, get out. I'm going to smash you if you don't get out.

Noise of feet. Bang of door.

That's taken care of that.

CASEY (*scared*) I didn't know you'd sent in your resignation, Sergeant.

REAGAN I'm sorry I didn't tell you. I forgot. We've already started to move to the farm. I'm going up to the kitchen. If you want me for anything just come up.

CASEY All right, Sergeant.

Fade. Feet on hallway. Knock on door.

REAGAN Come in.

MULLINS Jesus, Sergeant. I've never heard the beating of what happened this morning. I'd have given anything to be there. You have him humped, Sergeant. They'll have to give him an office job. This day will follow him around for the rest of his life. Apparently, several of the stations have been on the phone to Casey for the details. It's gone round like wildfire. You have him humped, Sergeant! That was a blow you struck.

REAGAN (*tiredly*) It's always easy to make a Cuchulainn out of the other fellow, isn't it, Mullins?

MULLINS What? What do you mean, Sergeant?

REAGAN Nothing. I was just talking. Don't worry about it.

WILLIE Is it time to light the lamp yet, Daddy?

REAGAN Why don't you ask Guard Mullins?

WILLIE Is it time to light the lamp, Guard Mullins?

MULLINS It's time, Willie.

WILLIE Watch, watch, out of my way . . . The lamp is lit.

Noise of girls racing for windows.

GIRLS My blind was down the first. No, my blind was down the first. Wasn't my blind down the first, Guard Mullins?

MULLINS Why don't we say it's a draw? We'll say it's a draw then.

James Joyce's

THE SISTERS

The Sisters, a television adaptation of the first story from James Joyce's *Dubliners*, was broadcast on BBC2 on 17 February 1973. The cast was as follows:

FATHER JAMES FLYNN Robert Bernal
ELIZA Marie Kean
NANNIE Sheila O'Sullivan
STEPHEN Basil King
STEPHEN'S AUNT May Ollis
STEPHEN'S UNCLE P. G. Stephens
COTTER Arthur O'Sullivan

Directed by Stephen Frears
Produced by Gavin Millar and Melvyn Bragg

Location

The small redbrick terraces of Dublin. Typical: those behind Fairview Church in north Dublin. The small rooms of one of those houses where Stephen lives with his aunt and uncle. The shop where Father Flynn lives with his sisters.

1 INTERIOR. CHURCH

*A priest brings the empty chalice to the side of the altar.
An altar boy pours wine and then water into the chalice.
The priest turns to the centre of the altar, genuflects,
raises the Host, genuflects again. The gong sounds each
time. He bends his head over the chalice then genuflects.
He raises very formally the chalice.*

2 EXTERIOR. STREET AND DRAPERY SHOP.
EVENING

*The Aunt and Stephen are on the way from Evening
Devotions. They both carry black prayer books with a
gold cross. The Aunt's prayer book is covered in leather,
Stephen's in cloth. They pause as they approach the
shop. The shop is shuttered for the night. It has an
appearance of lifelessness.*

AUNT No, we won't go in. The poor sisters have enough
bother with Father James paralysed. Oh, it'll be a release
for them all, poor things, if he went . . .

STEPHEN Hardly anybody recovers from a third attack.

AUNT Nobody knows how he's held on for so long. All
the time it looks just a matter of hours. Ah, it'll be a
release for himself and them, poor things, when he goes,
and his life so crossed all these years.

STEPHEN (*very gravely*) He's not gone yet, Auntie.
We'd see the two candles by his head on the blind of the
window if he was gone.

*Her face is solemn, almost hypocritical. Stephen walks
in her shadow, overgrown and sensitive, with a
nervousness that comes from long hours of study.
They disappear up the narrow street of redbrick
houses and iron railings.*

3 INTERIOR. STEPHEN'S BEDROOM. NIGHT

*Stephen's room. It is very bare and simple, with books.
There is a small narrow bed in the corner and in the
opposite corner a bare table and chair, and above the
table a black and white crucifix on the wall. He rises
from the table where he has been studying, tidies neatly
his books, blesses himself before the crucifix and, after a
short silent prayer at the end of work, leaves the room.*

4 INTERIOR. CORRIDOR AND STAIRS. NIGHT

*Stephen crosses a narrow corridor that leads to a small,
straight wooden stairs to the living room.*

5 INTERIOR. LIVING ROOM. NIGHT

*Old Cotter is in the living room with Stephen's Aunt and
Uncle. Cotter is an ex-distillery worker, a prejudiced old
fool. There is a natural antipathy between him and
Stephen. Cotter is smoking with Stephen's Uncle over the
fire. The Aunt chaffs Stephen affectionately as she ladles
out his stirabout, which is his usual supper after he
finishes his studies.*

STEPHEN Good evening, Mr Cotter.

COTTER It's yourself, Stephen.

AUNT Those books will drive you astray in the head.

You were up there so long I thought we'd never see you this night.

STEPHEN Thank you, Aunt Elizabeth.

COTTER Those books. I don't trust young fellows who are too much over those books. *Mens sana, in corpore sano*, I say.

UNCLE Hear, hear. I have my tongue wore out telling him the same. Enough is as good as a feast.

Cotter returns avidly to what is obviously a conversation Stephen's entrance had interrupted as the Aunt returns the saucepan of stirabout to the hob:

COTTER No, I wouldn't (*puffs his pipe with the utmost complacence*) say he was exactly . . . But there was something queer . . . there was something uncanny about him. I'll tell you my opinion . . . I have my own theory about it. I think it was one of those . . . peculiar cases . . . But it's hard to say . . . It's the two sisters I feel sorry for, having to keep him all those years after he was silenced, otherwise how'd he have stayed out of the poorhouse?

UNCLE (*notices Stephen staring at him*) Well, so your old friend is gone, you'll be sorry to hear.

STEPHEN Father Flynn?

UNCLE Yes. God rest his soul.

STEPHEN How did you hear?

UNCLE Mr Cotter here has just told us. He was passing by the house.

Stephen knows he is under observation and continues eating as if the news has no interest for him.

The youngster and he were great friends. The old chap taught him a great deal, mind you; and they say he had a great wish for him.

AUNT God have mercy on his soul.

Cotter stares at Stephen, as if examining him, looking for a chink, but Stephen will not look up from the plate. Cotter spits on the grate. The spit hisses.

COTTER I wouldn't like children of mine to have too much to say to a man like that.

AUNT What do you mean, Mr Cotter?

COTTER What I mean is, it's bad for children. My idea is: let a young lad run about and play with young lads of his own age and not be . . . Am I right, Jack?

UNCLE That's my principle, too. Let him learn to box his corner. That's what I'm always saying to that Rosicrucian there: take exercise. Why, when I was a nipper every morning of my life I had a cold bath, winter and summer. And that's what stands to me now. Education is all very fine and large . . . Mr Cotter might take a pick of that leg of mutton.

The Aunt takes dish of mutton from the safe and puts it on the table.

COTTER No, no, not for me.

AUNT But why do you think it's not good for children, Mr Cotter?

COTTER It's bad for children because their minds are so impressionable. When children see things like that, you know, it has an effect . . .

6 INTERIOR. STEPHEN'S ROOM. NIGHT

Stephen is sleeping. His dream takes place in the same room with the books, the table and chair and crucifix and narrow bed of Scene Three.

7 INTERIOR. CHURCH. NIGHT. (DREAM SEQUENCE)

Stephen comes out of the door of the sacristy on to the altar steps. It is night. The church is empty. A ghostly light comes from the blood-red sacristy lamp before the high altar. The lamp is big and silver and hangs from a chain. The blood-red light comes from the red glass glow. Stephen has the priest's collar around his neck and is robed for the confessional. Around his neck is the narrow confessional stole with tassels on its ends. He genuflects and kneels in prayer before the altar as is usual for the priest before confessing, and at the end of the prayer he raises the end of the stole to his lips. He goes to the gate in the communion rail and walks along the aisle to the confession box. He enters the place for the priest by drawing back the thick black curtains, closes them behind him and draws back the wooden shutter. As the shutter is open Father Flynn's face appears through the wire of the grilles. The face is revolting as it was in the last stages of the illness.

FATHER FLYNN Forgive me, Stephen, for I have sinned. (*The voice has a sweet caressing tone and a smile plays over the spittle of the lips.*) It was first the chalice, Stephen, the spilling of the wine that had been changed into blood, the simoniac sin . . .

> *Stephen wrenches himself out of the dream and on his lips in terror as he wakes says, 'Forgive me, Father, for I have sinned.'*

8 EXTERIOR. STREETS AND DRAPERY SHOP. DAY

It is a bright and lovely morning. Stephen is walking down a little terrace. All the windows facing east are brilliant with the sun. The shutters of the shop are up. A crape bouquet is tied to the door knocker with ribbon.

Two poor women and a telegram boy are reading the card pinned to the crape. Stephen too reads the notice:

1ST MARCH, 1895

THE REV. JAMES FLYNN (FORMERLY OF
ST CATHERINE'S CHURCH, MEATH STREET)

AGED SIXTY-FIVE YEARS

R.I.P.

He looks up at the blinded window but cannot see the candles burn behind the glass because the glass reflects the bright sun. He moves to the doorstep but withdraws and turns away.

STEPHEN (*as he turns away*) I suppose I'd be still taking him the snuff if he hadn't died.

9 INTERIOR. DRAPERY SHOP. EVENING

Flashback to Stephen entering the shop. It is open. Shutters outside are down. Eliza is behind the counter. She leaves off weighing on her brass scales.

ELIZA You're welcome, Stephen. Father James will be so pleased to see you. All morning he was asking me if I thought Stephen would be around this evening.

As she talks she lifts the leaf of the counter and unbolts the little door beneath it to let Stephen in. As soon as he's inside the counter she lets down the leaf without closing the door beneath, and opens the door that leads through the shop into the living room.

10. INTERIOR. LIVING ROOM OF DRAPERY SHOP.
EVENING

ELIZA There's a visitor to see you, Father James.

*She uses the singsong voice women use to small
children. Father Flynn is dozing in a very big armchair.
The armchair must stand out as the most distinctive
piece of furniture in the room, probably an heirloom
from the better days of the Flynn family in their
parental home at Irishtown. Father Flynn is obviously
ill and struggles out of his stupefied doze in front of
the fire. He has his overcoat on in the big chair. The
overcoat is stained a faded green from long use and
snuff stains. The red handkerchief he will use to try
to brush away the snuff he spills on his overcoat is
blackened with the snuff. Eliza withdraws almost
immediately (to tend to a customer who has entered
the shop behind Stephen), leaving the boy alone with
the waking priest.*

FATHER FLYNN It's you, Stephen, is it . . .? It's good to
see you . . . Strange, I was thinking of you just before I
nodded off . . . I was thinking how short the time I have
now in this world and that the first Stephen will know
that I'm gone is when he comes and sees the two candles
burning behind the blinds in the upstairs room.

STEPHEN (*controlling his emotion*) Aunt sent you this
packet of snuff, Father.

The priest lights at the sight of snuff.

FATHER FLYNN Your aunt is a wonderfully kind
woman. You must tell her I can't thank her enough for
her kindness.

*His shaking hands struggle to draw the black
snuffbox from his pocket. Stephen's devotion – and to*

*some extent fear – is shown by the care and tenderness
with which he pours the snuff from the packet into
the snuffbox; the contrast between the old shaking
hands holding the snuffbox and the young hands as
if they were pouring wine into a chalice. The shaking
hands spill half the snuff on the floor and when he
brings a pinch to his nose it dribbles from his fingers
to his greatcoat. He tries to brush off the snuff with
the red handkerchief. The whole scene of the snuff is
stylised. It becomes a grotesque parody of the altar
boy pouring the water and wine into the chalice in the
priest's hands in the sacrifice of the Mass. Snuff is the
water and wine. The box is the chalice. The old red
handkerchief is the white cloth the altar boy hands to
the priest after the lavabo.*

FATHER FLYNN I've always felt I might have been a
better priest, Stephen, if I'd had strong hands. My hands
were always nervous and they grew worse after they let
slip that consecrated chalice I told you of.

*Stephen listens sympathetically. He has taken the
blackened red rag from the old priest and helped to
clear the mess of snuff from the overcoat.*

STEPHEN The coat is fine now, Father.

*He hands the rag back to the priest much in the way
the altar boy would ceremoniously offer the white
linen to the priest after the lavabo.*

11 EXTERIOR. STREETS AND DRAPERY SHOP. DAY

*Shot of Stephen turning away into the sunlit day away
from the crape on the door. He walks in the gay
morning, the day and his own mood the opposite
reflection of death. He comes to the theatrical ads,*

*probably of the opera. He reads them with obvious
absorption and is longing to go to them. As he turns
away from the ads he is disturbed by his own happiness
and the loveliness of the day, and in his mind returns to
the room behind the shop with the priest in his big chair,
and now Stephen sitting in the corner.*

12 INTERIOR. LIVING ROOM OF DRAPERY SHOP.
EVENING

FATHER FLYNN I was thinking too before I nodded
what a great solace to me now is the thought that one
day you may say Mass for me, that you may lift the
chalice in anointed hands to God to ask him to have
mercy on my poor soul . . . (*He changes and brightens.*)
Do you remember all those evenings we had when I first
began to explain to you the sacred rites and mysteries of
the priesthood? (*Starts to laugh.*) Do you remember your
amazement when I told you that the fathers of the Church
had written books as thick as the post-office book and as
closely printed as the law notices in the newspapers to
guide the priest in his duties to the Eucharist and the
secrecy of the confessional. As thick as the post-office
directory, you repeated, with those eyes large as saucers.

*Father Flynn laughs and Stephen smiles silent and
embarrassed.*

Do you still think of entering the priesthood, Stephen,
when the time comes?

STEPHEN Sometimes, Father, but I feel afraid.

FATHER FLYNN Afraid of what, Stephen?

STEPHEN That I'll never have enough courage, Father.
That I'd never be worthy enough.

FATHER FLYNN No one, no one at all, is worthy enough, Stephen. Only through prayer and the Grace of God can we hope for strength for the awesome responsibility that goes with the awesome power, and even then, even then . . . (*Pauses as if attempting to puzzle over his own life. Then suddenly*) Do you know the meaning of the word simony?

STEPHEN From Simon Magus. You taught me that, Father.

FATHER FLYNN Of course. How I forget. We went over much together. That long winter we spent on the Mass till you had the Latin word perfect. It's a great consolation to me now. I've spoken about you to Father O'Rourke. I've told him my wish for you. And he'll see to it, if you still have your vocation when the time comes, that you get to Rome, to the Irish College, where he and I studied, forty years ago; for the places here I'm sorry to have to say are not fit places, football seminaries . . .

This is interrupted by Nannie, the old bent sister, coming downstairs. She nods smilingly to Stephen and points interrogatively to the bedroom, to see if Father Flynn wishes to go to bed, now that she has his room ready. The priest shakes his head.

I think I'll stay up a little longer to talk with Stephen. (*Unaware that Stephen has risen from the chair. Only when he turns does he see Stephen standing.*)

STEPHEN I'll be on my way, Father. I have some things to read yet before bed.

FATHER FLYNN Yes . . . Yes . . . Of course you have to study. I was being selfish. (*Looks at the clock.*) It's time for you, Nannie, to help Eliza put up the shutters. (*She nods and waits.*) I'll wait till you put up the shutters before going up. (*She nods her understanding. She'll*

have to help him up. Stephen takes the priest's hand.)
And don't forget to thank your Aunt for the wonderful
snuff.

STEPHEN Good night, Father James. I'll not forget.

FATHER FLYNN God bless you, Stephen. Good night, child.

*Stephen and Nannie go out into the shop. Eliza is
preparing to close the shop.*

13 INTERIOR. DRAPERY SHOP. EVENING

ELIZA It is very good of you to come so often, Stephen.
Father James gets nervous on his own. And Father
O'Rourke is too busy down at St Catherine's to come
often. And don't forget to thank your aunt for the snuff.
He lives for that snuff.

STEPHEN Good night, Miss Flynn.

ELIZA Good night, Stephen. God bless you.

The sisters start to close the shop.

14 EXTERIOR. DRAPERY SHOP. EVENING

*As Stephen leaves he glances apprehensively up at the
window, which is faintly and evenly lighted behind the
blind.*

15 INTERIOR. CHURCH. NIGHT

*Repeat the face of the priest in the dream saying through
the wire grille:*

FATHER FLYNN Forgive me, Stephen, for I have sinned.
(*The voice has a sweet caressing tone and a smile plays
over the spittle of the lips.*) It was first the chalice,

Stephen, the spilling of the wine that had been changed into blood, the simoniac sin.

16 EXTERIOR. STREETS. DAY

Shot of disturbed Stephen in the bright sunlight of the street beside the theatrical ads.

STEPHEN But then when I went back to sleep I didn't dream of him again. I dreamt and there were long velvet curtains and a swinging lamp of antique fashion. I felt that I had been very far away, in some land where the customs were strange – in Persia, I thought . . . But I . . . can't remember the end of the dream.

Looks at the ads and smiles and starts to walk calmly in the sunshine towards his home.

17 INTERIOR. LIVING ROOM. EVENING

The Aunt and Stephen dress up to pay their last respects to the sisters and the dead priest. The Aunt passes her hand over Stephen's new suit and straightens his black tie as they prepare to leave. It is the same room as with Cotter.

AUNT Well, Stephen, we'd better be making a move and pay our last respects to your old friend. It's no use taking the snuff he loved, poor thing, to him this time, God rest him.

STEPHEN (*very quietly*) I'm ready, Aunt.

18 EXTERIOR. STREETS. EVENING.

Shot of them going out and walking up the street. The rows of windows on the opposite side of the street from the

*morning are ablaze with the setting sun. The Aunt knocks
on the hall door, holding the bouquet so that the knocking
does not dislodge it. Nannie opens the door for them.*

19 INTERIOR. DRAPERY SHOP. EVENING

*As it would be unseemly to shout, they express sympathy
by shaking hands. Nannie points towards the stairs
interrogatively. The Aunt nods.*

20 INTERIOR. DRAPERY SHOP STAIRCASE AND LANDING. EVENING.

*Old bent Nannie toils up the stairs, and Stephen and his
Aunt follow. On the landing she stops and beckons him
forward encouragingly towards the open door of the
death room.*

21 INTERIOR. DEATH ROOM. EVENING

*The Aunt goes in, and the old woman seeing, Stephen
hesitate, beckons repeatedly with her hand. The evening
light is so brilliant on the blind that the candles look thin
pale flames. Shot of the arum lilies by the coffin. Shot of
the open coffin by the bed but in no detail. Nannie
kneels at the foot of the bed. They follow her. They bless
themselves. Stephen and his Aunt distracted by the loud
off-key muttering of Nannie going through the Hail
Mary. Shot of the trodden-down heels coming out from
under Nannie's clumsily hooked long skirt, shabby as the
priest's overcoat in the first scene. They wait for her to
finish and follow her in blessing and rising.*

*Full shot of the priest in the coffin, vested as for the
altar; lingering shot of the chalice loosely held in the*

dead hands, moving to the face and back again to the chalice. Shot of Stephen hurriedly blessing himself as if in self-protection. Shot of the flowers.

22 INTERIOR. DRAPERY SHOP STAIRCASE AND LANDING. EVENING

Shot of them leaving the room behind Nannie and following her down the stairs to the room of Scene Nine. They turn up the hallway to the living room that Stephen entered in Scene Ten.

23 INTERIOR. LIVING ROOM OF DRAPERY SHOP. EVENING

Eliza sits in state in the big chair before the fireplace as a close parody of the priest in Scene Ten. She has obviously assumed his position now that he is dead. Stephen gropes his way to his usual chair. The scene should exactly resemble the flashback except that the fireplace is now empty. Nannie takes a sherry bottle and wine glasses from the sideboard and sets them on the table. She invites them by gesturing to take a glass of wine and then at her sister's bidding fills the glasses. She presses cream crackers on them and looks disappointed at Stephen's refusal. Then she takes her place on the sofa behind Eliza's chair.

ELIZA (*sighs*) Ah well, he's gone to a better world.

AUNT (*nervously fingering the stem of the wine glass before sipping*) Did he . . . peacefully?

ELIZA Oh, quite peacefully, ma'am. You couldn't tell when the breath went out of him. He had a beautiful death, God be praised.

AUNT And everything . . . ?

ELIZA Father O'Rourke was in with him a Tuesday and anointed him and prepared him and all.

AUNT He knew then?

ELIZA He was quite resigned.

AUNT He looks quite resigned.

ELIZA That's what the woman we had in to wash him said. She said he just looked as if he was asleep, he looked that peaceful and resigned. No one would think he'd make such a beautiful corpse.

AUNT Yes, indeed. (*Sips again from the glass, before, platitudinously*) Well, Miss Flynn, at any rate it must be a great comfort for you to know that you did all you could for him. You were both very kind to him, I must say.

ELIZA (*smooths her dress importantly over her knees*) Ah, poor James! God knows we done all we could, as poor as we are – we wouldn't see him want anything while he was in it.

Nannie has leaned her head against the soft pillow on the sofa and seems about to fall asleep. Eliza looks at Nannie.

There's poor Nannie, look at her, she's wore out. All the work we had, she and me, getting in the woman to wash him and then laying him out and then the coffin and then arranging about the Mass in the Chapel. Only for Father O'Rourke I don't know what we'd have done at all. It was him brought us all them flowers and them two candlesticks out of the Chapel and wrote out the notice for the *Freeman's General* and took charge of all the papers for the cemetery and poor James's insurance.

AUNT Wasn't that good of him?

ELIZA (*closes her eyes and shakes her head slowly*) Ah, there's no friends like the old friends when all is said and done, no friends that a body can trust.

AUNT Indeed, that's true. And I'm sure now that he's gone to his eternal reward he won't forget you and all your kindness to him.

ELIZA Ah, poor James! He was no great trouble to us. You wouldn't hear him in the house any more than now. Still, I know he's gone and all to that . . .

AUNT It's when it's all over that you'll miss him.

ELIZA I know that. I won't be bringing him in his cup of beef tea any more, nor you, ma'am, sending him his snuff. Ah, poor James! (*Stops as if communing with the past and then says shrewdly*) Mind you, I noticed there was something queer coming over him latterly. Whenever I'd bring in his soup to him there I'd find him with his breviary fallen to the floor, lying back in the chair and his mouth open. (*Lays her finger against her nose and frowns.*) But still and all he kept on saying that before the summer was over he'd go out for a drive on a fine day just to see the old house again where we were all born down in Irishtown and take me and Nannie with him. If we could only get one of them newfangled carriages that makes no noise that Father O'Rourke told him about – them with the rheumatic wheels – for the day cheap, he said, at Johnny Rush's over the way there and drive out the three of us together of a Sunday evening. He had his mind set on that . . . Poor James!

AUNT The Lord have mercy on his soul.

Eliza takes out handkerchief and wipes her eyes. Puts it back into her pocket and gazes for some time into the empty fireplace.

ELIZA He was too scrupulous always. The duties of the priesthood was too much for him. And then his life was, you might say, crossed.

AUNT Yes. He was a disappointed man. You could see that.

Under cover of another silence Stephen goes to the table and sips his sherry and then returns to his chair in the corner. Eliza falls into a deep reverie. They wait respectfully.

ELIZA (*begins slowly*) It was that chalice he broke . . . That was the beginning of it. But still . . . They say it was the boy's fault. But poor James was so nervous, God be merciful to him!

AUNT And was that it? I heard something.

ELIZA (*nodding ponderously*) That affected his mind. After that he began to mope by himself, talking to no one and wandering about by himself. So one night he was wanted for to go on a call and they couldn't find him anywhere. So then the clerk suggested to try the Chapel. So then they got the keys and opened the Chapel and the clerk and Father O'Rourke and another priest that was there brought in a light for to look for him . . . And what do you think but there he was, sitting up by himself in the dark in his confession box, wide-awake and laughing-like softly to himself? (*Sighing but very vigorously in an incantation*) Wide-awake and laughing-like to himself . . . So then, of course, when they saw that, that made them think there was something gone wrong with him . . .

SWALLOWS

Swallows was broadcast on BBC2 on 27 March 1975.
The cast was as follows:

SERGEANT Michael Brennan
SURVEYOR Frank Kelly
MICHAEL Richard Oliver
BIDDY Julie Hamilton
PRIEST Harry Webster

Directed by Robert Kidd
Produced by Barry Hanson

I INTERIOR. PUB

The Sergeant and the Surveyor come into the pub. They are flustered from the rain, both with their raincoat collars buttoned up, and they are hatted. A small peat fire glows in the grate, beside which the publican, Michael, is seated on a chair, painting the lower half of the wall.

SERGEANT (*rubs his hands as they go up to the counter*) A terrible day, Michael. Not fit for a dog to be out in. What can I offer you, Mr Hogg?

SURVEYOR No, let me get this one, Sergeant.

SERGEANT No, this one's on me. Seeing it's your first time in these parts. Two large Powers there, Michael, when you have the time.

SURVEYOR Thank you, Sergeant, but a small one for me.

Michael lays his paintbrush carefully on the paint can, lazily rises from the chair and goes behind the counter. His face is very lively behind the laziness and drowsiness. He pours the drinks, using on old small pewter measure.

MICHAEL I hear yous were measuring the road up at the quarry.

SERGEANT (*cautiously and testily*) How might you have heard that now?

MICHAEL (*testily too*) Ways and means. Oh, ways and means. Not even the Guards can do anything unknownst in this place.

He pours the drinks very slowly in order to control the conversation, though the caution is also in character, as is the slow painting while sitting on the chair. He is avid for information, giving information to get more, but pretending not to be.

A terrible accident it was. Poor Michael, God rest him, no more than eighteen and wheeling his bicycle up the hill at the quarry, on his way to Carrick for a haircut, when bang, into the next world via the bonnet, without as much as by-your-leave.

Michael has poured two measures into one glass. Though a small whiskey has been ordered he says as he pours the first measure into the second glass, hoping for the larger sale:

The same as this I suppose?

SERGEANT Go on. You might as well.

SURVEYOR (*covers the glass with his hand*) No, no. A small one for me.

They take water from a half-pint glass Michael has filled from a tap under the counter. The Sergeant very little water, the Surveyor a considerable quantity.

SERGEANT Here's to your health, Mr Hogg. (*Checks himself as he raises his glass, and puts it back on the counter.*) By the way, Michael, this is Mr Hogg. Mr Hogg: Mr Kelly. Mr Hogg is the State Surveyor.

Michael immediately wipes his right hand in his apron. From the Sergeant's impressed tone it is clear that the Surveyor's visit is an unusual high spot in his daily duties. They shake hands.

MICHAEL You're welcome to these parts, Mr Hogg.

SURVEYOR Thank you. (*They raise their glasses a second time.*) Your good health, Sergeant.

While the Surveyor sips at the whiskey the Sergeant empties the glass in one gulp. The Surveyor looks at the empty glass the Sergeant puts back on the counter with some astonishment.

SERGEANT (*coughing*) That hit the spot all right.

SURVEYOR (*tentatively*) Will you have another, Sergeant?

SERGEANT I suppose the same again. (*Seeing the Surveyor's almost untouched whiskey*) Are you having nothing at all yourself?

SURVEYOR Just a soda for me. You remember I have to play tonight.

Motions to Michael to fill the Sergeant's glass. He begins to take the wallet from his inside pocket. To do this he has to unbutton his raincoat. As he does, it becomes obvious he is in full evening dress. He is somewhat embarrassed by this as he is a stickler for the niceties.

I'm afraid it's not very suitable attire for either the time or the weather, but it was positively shining when I left Dublin this morning, and I thought to change to save time when I got to the hotel in case the measuring took long. But thanks to those drawings you made the time it took was negligible. Your good health, Sergeant. (*He pours a little of the water into the glass and raises it.*)

SERGEANT For nothing. I had a taste for figures at school.

MICHAEL Oh, the Sergeant's a very clever man. (*Then ironically*) We were very lucky they left him so long in these parts.

SERGEANT (*bridling*) Some don't count it so lucky when they're caught with the house full a few hours after closing time.

MICHAEL We won't go into that now. (*Wiping the counter with a cloth. Smiling ironically still*) But everybody's agog as to how the case will go. (*More seriously*) The poor woman's nerves they say are in an awful condition, having to pass that wooden cross his people put up, on her way to school and back. What use was it putting it up if it disturbs the poor woman so? I say the living have remindedness enough of their last ends and testaments without putting up wooden crosses on the highways and byways and it won't bring poor Michael back to life and going to Carrick for his haircut, but after *measuring* the road, Sergeant, (*he concentrates his whole attention on the slow wiping as he speaks*) do you have any better idea as to how the case will go? They say her defence will be that the sun blinded her as she came round the quarry.

SERGEANT (*looking long and disapprovingly at the wiping*) Now Michael, if myself and yourself knew how the case would go the judge and lawyers'd be out of a job, now wouldn't they?

MICHAEL (*feeling called to heel, grumbles*) Every man's entitled to his opinion. Opinions never did harm.

SERGEANT (*finishing his second whiskey*) One for the road, Mr Hogg?

SURVEYOR No, thanks, Sergeant, but have one yourself.

SERGEANT A pint of stout for the road then, Michael.

Michael slowly pulls the pint of stout, wiping the excess cream off the top with a wooden ruler or a

*knife. After each round he takes the change from
a cardboard shoe box on the shelf.*

They say the trouble with England is that you can't get a
decent pint there. They pull it too fast. They won't take
the time.

SURVEYOR I've heard that said though I'm not a pint
man myself.

MICHAEL Well, there's lashings of time in these parts,
and that's sure-fire, more time than there's sense. There
then, Sergeant, I hope that meets to your satisfaction.

SERGEANT Out of the top drawer, Michael. You could
take a knife and fork to it.

MICHAEL (*ironically*) We aim to please, Sergeant.

*After wiping the froth clear with the knife, Michael
puts the pint on the counter and goes back to the
chair and sits and starts to paint.*

SERGEANT Good health. (*Raises his pint.*)

SURVEYOR (*lifting his whiskey*) Good luck, Sergeant.

*The Surveyor leans on the counter, watching Michael's
painting with amused condescension.*

SERGEANT (*to Michael*) No use a man working himself
into a sweat, Michael.

*Michael stops painting to face the Sergeant. Paint
drips from the brush on to the floor.*

MICHAEL No man'd know that better than yourself,
Sergeant.

SERGEANT (*getting himself into deeper trouble*) They say
a proper painter only uses half the paint the likes of us use.

MICHAEL (*feeling he has got his own back on the Sergeant*) Now Sergeant, would you be by any chance insinuating that I'm not a proper painter?

SERGEANT (*only too anxious to concede*) I meant a man who does nothing else but paint, though you caught me there, all right, Michael.

They all laugh, the Surveyor indulgently at both of them, and the mood relaxes.

MICHAEL (*feeling the balance restored in his favour after the rebuke over the case*) I got you there sure enough, Sergeant. (*Scrapes what paint has fallen from his brush on to the floor with his boot, moves his chair, and resumes the slow painting.*)

SERGEANT Whatever about me and you being professional, Michael, Mr Hogg here is a real musician. He has his fiddle with him in the car. After I get Biddy to give us something to eat he's consented (*very conscious of the formality of the word*) to play a few things down at the barracks. (*Very proud of the fact that the Surveyor is going to play down at the barracks but at the same time it is information given to attempt to conciliate any of the needle left between himself and Michael.*)

SURVEYOR (*self-satisfied*) No, no. I am looking forward to playing but you exaggerate, Sergeant. I had the choice of becoming a professional but you see I chose security (*taking a tapewheel out of his raincoat pocket and holding it up before returning it to the pocket. Michael does not look up but goes on painting slowly*) to the vagaries of an artistic career.

SERGEANT Never mind – all men have to eat – but once a priest a priest forever.

SURVEYOR (*full of self-complacency*) Sometimes indeed

I think if I had to make my living from music it might lose half its magic for me.

The Sergeant has most of his pint finished and he excuses himself:

SERGEANT Excuse me, I won't be a minute.

He goes to the lavatory through a small door in the far corner of the bar from where Michael is painting. The Surveyor is obviously ill at ease with Michael. He faces Michael's back, leaning one elbow on the counter. He coughs.

SURVEYOR When do you mostly get customers, Michael?

MICHAEL (*his back stiffens but he goes on painting*) Late. (*Long pause to see if the Surveyor will react.*) Sometimes what drink you sell wouldn't pay to keep the fire going but in the summer of course there's the tourists.

SURVEYOR (*attempt at heavy wit*) Well, you should certainly have the place spruced up for the opening of the season.

MICHAEL Ah yes. (*Pauses to think. Very sarcastically*) Ah yes. You see it's a matter of planning and foresight. Yes, planning and foresight. (*Continues to paint all the time. Very aggressively*) The Sergeant too was a dab hand on the fiddle when he came to this place first. Many's the good night he gave us.

SERGEANT (*coming through the door*) I heard you, you blackguard. What was it but jigs and reels? Not to be compared with Mr Hogg's music and playing.

MICHAEL You can blackguard away but you can't deny we had many's a good night.

SURVEYOR We must both play then after we sign the formalities.

SERGEANT No, no. (*Hurt and embarrassed*) I haven't
played for years. Who wants to hear someone sawing
away when you can walk up to the wireless and turn it
on. I suppose we better be making a move. (*Very slap-
on-the-back voice to hide his hurt*) Will we be seeing you
at the function tonight, Michael?

MICHAEL I doubt it, Sergeant. The one night you lock
up and leave is the very night they'll develop a thirst and
come hammering at the door and herself can't cope with
them any more.

SERGEANT Good luck, Michael. I might call in on my way.

MICHAEL Fine, Sergeant.

SURVEYOR Goodbye, Michael.

*They go out of the door. The camera lingers on
Michael painting slowly away in the empty pub after
the door has closed.*

2 INTERIOR. KITCHEN

*The Sergeant and the Surveyor come into the kitchen. It
is a large soulless room. There is an old sewing machine
under the window close to the door where they come in.
A curtained black cabinet where the Sergeant keeps his
whiskey and medicines stands in the opposite corner.
A table is in the centre of the cement floor, a knitting
machine clamped to its end, at which Biddy sits as they
enter, busily adjusting her needles. A sideboard with a
large ornamental mirror is along the wall parallel with
the length of the table. Facing it the other side of the
table is an old iron range. Next to the mirror is the
scullery door. Past the door is a dresser with cups and
plates. Facing the sewing machine across the length of
the room is another window, under which stands a*

smaller table. It has a white bread box on it. There is one large decrepit armchair close to the fire, and wooden chairs at the tables. Close to the medicine press, on a little shelf on the wall, stands an old wireless. Above the iron range there is a very long mantel. In its centre a little red oil lamp is burning before a picture of the Sacred Heart, and beside it the Sergeant's old violin case. There is an assortment of boxes on the mantel but it is all covered in dust, and the whole mantel never touched except to change the oil in the lamp.

Biddy doesn't hear them enter as she is deaf and intent on her machine. The Surveyor has the violin case in his hand and enters first, obviously taken aback by the deaf woman. The Sergeant, who has a sheaf of official papers in his hand, moves past him, and then faces him. Biddy still doesn't notice.

SERGEANT It's only Biddy. She's deaf as a post, but pay no attention as she'll not hear a word we say. She knits socks for the parish, night and noon at the damned sock machine.

The Sergeant goes up to Biddy and touches her on the shoulder. She is very startled as she comes out of her world of silence and the machine. The chair falls back as she strives to get up in her confusion.

BIDDY (*shouting*) You're back.

She is now on her feet and the Sergeant gently picks up the chair and puts it back on its feet. Biddy notices the Surveyor for the first time. The Sergeant places his hand on her shoulder and she follows his lips to the exclusion of all else as he speaks. He moves his lips carefully as he speaks. He is used to her reading his lips for long.

SERGEANT Don't worry, Biddy. This is only Mr Hogg, the State Surveyor.

BIDDY (*turns to Surveyor in loud blurred voice*) You're very welcome, I'm sure, Sir.

SURVEYOR Thank you. Very nice to meet you.

She shakes the hand he offers very vigorously. He grimaces and flexes his fingers to see if they are not damaged in the handshake as she lets go.

BIDDY (*to Sergeant*) Yous will be wanting something to ate, won't yous?

SERGEANT (*to Biddy*) Yes.

The Sergeant turns to the Surveyor, while Biddy's eyes fasten back and forth on both of them:

Excuse me a minute. It's easier if I settle this in the scullery. You can leave the fiddle on the table and make yourself comfortable.

The Surveyor sits down but holds rigidly to his violin. The Sergeant guides Biddy towards the scullery. Its door is between the mirror and dresser with cups and plates.

3 INTERIOR. SCULLERY

The scullery is a small room. It has a large table and shelves and small window, before which is a basin in its iron stand. There is a small mirror and shaving gear in the window. The outside door is open. Hens have come in and stand perched in a circle on a sawn barrel close to the outside door. The outside door is open. The Sergeant, in a rage, closes the door behind him on the Surveyor.

SERGEANT I told you once and for all if you insist on keeping those damned hens of yours you must never forget to keep the doors shut.

*The hens, with the closing of the door, scatter with
fright, all out of the door, except one, which flies
straight at the window and knocks the mirror, which
falls on the side of the basin and smashes on the floor.*

Oh Jesus tonight! (*Putting his hand to his face.*)

BIDDY We'll have seven years now without a day's luck!

SERGEANT Never mind the mirror. We have a visitor.

*He has seized her shoulders and compels her to focus
on his lips.*

BIDDY (*reading his lips in terror*) We have a visitor.

SERGEANT Keep your voice down.

BIDDY Keep your voice down.

SERGEANT (*turning his face away*) Oh my God! (*And
back again*) We want something to eat.

*The hen is trying to fly out through the glass. The
Sergeant seizes it and flings it out the door. Goes back
to Biddy.*

BIDDY (*reading the lips but less hysterical*) We want
something to eat. (*Then thinking, returning to normal*)
There's bacon and eggs.

SERGEANT Get something decent. Hop round to the
shop and see if he has any ham and cheese.

BIDDY What if his ham is crawling and the price he
charges.

*The Sergeant takes a coat off a peg on the wall and
forcibly pushes her into it.*

Will I pay cash or get him to put it in the blue book?

SERGEANT (*takes a small notebook covered with blue*

uniform cloth from a nail on the wall and pushes it into her hand) The book! The book!

BIDDY (*moves to gather up the broken glass of the mirror*) We'll never have a day's luck.

SERGEANT (*seizing her*) Never mind the mirror. Here!

He takes a cap from another nail on the wall, puts it on her head, and pushes her towards the door.

BIDDY Cheddar and ham then.

SERGEANT Cheddar and ham. And don't forget to close the door after you, for God's sake, this time.

He practically pushes her outside by a slow violent closing of the scullery door.

Oh my God!

Pushes his hand through his receding hair as he turns to open the door that leads back to the Surveyor.

4 INTERIOR. KITCHEN

The Surveyor has removed the violin from the case. The frayed black silk in which it was wrapped in the case is on the table.

SERGEANT If you live like pigs you can't expect sweet airs and musics all the time.

He closes the door behind him. (Either the Surveyor doesn't hear, too intent on tuning the strings, or he chooses to ignore it.) He goes to the curtained press in the corner between the wireless and sewing machine and takes out a full bottle of whiskey and places it on the table. He jokes as he opens the door of the press and takes out the whiskey:

I call it the medicine press.

*Then he goes to the dresser and takes a jug of water.
He fills a large glass and the Surveyor comes out of
the tuning to restrain him.*

SURVEYOR Just a little for me. (*Places the bow near the
glass to restrain him.*)

SERGEANT (*taking the jug of water*) How much?

SURVEYOR Up to the top, Sergeant.

*The Sergeant pours a token drop in his own glass,
which is almost full of whiskey. After he takes a
stiff swallow he notices the lovely old violin in the
Surveyor's hands.*

SERGEANT Is it old, your fiddle?

SURVEYOR Very old, but I have it only four years.
I try to get to the continent every summer and I was
in Avignon four years ago, an evening an old Italian
musician was playing between the café tables, and the
moment I heard its tone I knew I'd have to have it. I
followed him from café to café until he'd finished for
the evening and then invited him to join me over a glass
of wine. Over the wine I asked him if he'd sell. First he
refused. Then I asked him to name some price he
couldn't afford not to take. I'm afraid I'm ashamed to
tell you the price. I tried to haggle but it was no use.
The last thing he wanted was to sell but because of his
family he couldn't afford to refuse that price if I was
prepared to pay it. With the money he could get proper
medical treatment – I couldn't completely follow his
French – for his daughter who was a consumptive
or something. He'd try to get by with an ordinary
instrument around the cafés. I'm afraid I paid up on the
spot, but the experts who have examined it since say it

was dead cheap at the price, that it might even be a genuine Stradivarius.

SERGEANT The experts know. You go to the priest for religion. You go to the doctor for medicine. Who can we trust if we can't trust the experts? On the broad of our backs we'd be without the experts.

SURVEYOR The Italian street musician was playing Paganini that first evening in Avignon. I adore Paganini's music.

He starts to play.

SERGEANT I never heard better. Not even on the wireless.

SURVEYOR Isn't the tone something?

SERGEANT It's priceless, that fiddle. You got a bargain.

SURVEYOR A man of extraordinary interest is Paganini. He was born in 1782 in the depths of Genoan poverty. But his genius brought him wealth and fame, so much so that when he came to London the rabble there tried to touch him in the way present-day rabbles nearly tear pop stars apart. To the very end he was true to his genius, improvising marvellously during his last hours on his Guarnerius. The Church though had serious doubts as to his orthodoxy and refused to have him buried in consecrated ground. He had to lie for five years in some field until the Church in her usual politic fashion relented and had him laid to rest in a village graveyard on his own land.

SERGEANT And the Church bumming herself up all the time as patron of the arts. Why don't you drink up? You have more than earned it.

SURVEYOR No thanks. No. It's the driving, the new laws.

SERGEANT Well I'm the law in these parts, for whatever

that's worth, and there's the function tonight. You could play there. It'd give the ignoramuses there a view past their noses to hear the playing the like of that Paganini. You could stay the night here in the barracks afterwards. Biddy could make up the bed. There's tons of room.

SURVEYOR No, no. I'm sorry. I have to drive to Galway tonight.

SERGEANT That's misfortunate but, ah well, what's one man's poison. (*Fills his glass to the brim.*) I was never one for forcing. But that's no reason for me to stint my own hand.

SURVEYOR Would you like me to play one of the old tunes? One of the tunes you used to play at the dances?

SERGEANT Very much.

SURVEYOR Is there anything in particular you'd like?

SERGEANT *The Kerry Dances. The Kerry Dances.*

SURVEYOR Can you just hum the opening part for me to make sure?

The Sergeant hums slowly. Confidently the Surveyor takes up the playing.

SERGEANT That's it, that's it, that's it for sweet sure. (*As the tune finishes*) It's a great pity ignoramuses around here couldn't be made to hear music the love and the like of that tonight.

SURVEYOR Is that the violin you used to play? (*Indicates with his bow the violin case one side of where the blood-red Sacred Heart lamp glows on the mantel.*)

SERGEANT Not since the dances have I played, not for years.

SURVEYOR Take it down anyhow. Once you see it the desire may return.

The Sergeant, reluctant but hypnotised by the playing and whiskey and the Surveyor's careless ease, takes it down. Dust covers the Sergeant as he takes it down. He tries to dust himself and the violin case with an old cloth.

SERGEANT (*complains*) At the rate Biddy goes banging at the range that mantelpiece will be fit to grow turnips soon.

When they open the case one string of the plain little violin has snapped and the bow is slack.

SURVEYOR It'd play again all right after proper repairing. Wouldn't it be a fine pastime for you in the long nights?

SERGEANT (*rattled and exasperated*) Arrah, play to deaf old Biddy, is it now, when you can walk over there and turn on the wireless?

He looks reflectively and fondly on the old violin the Surveyor has returned to its case.

It had a sweet note too in its day. I had no need of the whiskey to hurry the hours in those days, though we got some as we played, sitting up on the planks between the barrels, fiddling away as they swung past, shouting up to me, 'Rise it, Jimmy. More power to your good elbow, Jimmy Boy.'

Noise of opening and banging on the outside door. The Sergeant puts a hand to his head.

Oh my God, it's that woman again.

Biddy enters, dishevelled. She has left the cap and coat in the scullery but she still has the blue book in her

hands. As she speaks the Sergeant removes the book
from her hand and throws it on the sideboard, in
front of the mirror.

BIDDY Wet to the skin I got. And I told him his ham
was crawling and if it wasn't crawling it was next door
to crawling, and I told him if I was deaf itself God still
gave me the benefit of a good nose. You will have to do
now with what's in the house.

SURVEYOR A simple cup of tea will do me very well.

SERGEANT You'll have nothing for the inner man that
way. You can have bacon and eggs I'm sure.

SURVEYOR I'll have to have a full dinner this evening.
To eat much now would spoil it.

SERGEANT (*offers the whiskey bottle which is more*
than half depleted) You can't even be tempted to have a
drop of this stuff itself?

SURVEYOR No thanks. I'll just finish what I have in
the glass. Is there anything else you'd like me to play
for you?

SERGEANT Play something you'd like to play yourself.
That Paganini was as good as I ever heard.

BIDDY Will bacon and eggs do yous then?

SERGEANT (*groans*) Tea and brown bread instead.

SURVEYOR I'll play Kreisler then. I've been studying
Kreisler.

He plays.

SERGEANT As good as I ever heard. You're as good as
any professional. Maybe we might be able to persuade
you to change your mind and stay the night yet after all.

SURVEYOR There's nothing I'd like better than to stay the night and play.

SERGEANT That's great. You can stay then?

SURVEYOR No, no. It's unfortunately impossible. I have to be at the Wavecrest Hotel in Galway at six.

SERGEANT You could use the station phone to cancel it if you want.

SURVEYOR No. Every time I get a case in the West I stay at the Wavecrest Hotel. Eileen O'Neill is manageress there. She is the best accompanist I know; she could have been a concert pianist but like me she preferred ordinary security to the vagaries of an artistic career. She has already taken the evening off. It's why I changed into this suit: in case I was delayed, and we could start to play as soon as I got to the hotel. We've been both studying Kreisler, the piece I played just now and others, and I can hardly wait to see how they'll play. (*Already imagining her and looking inward*) This evening she'll probably wear the long dress of burgundy velvet with the satin bow in her hair as she plays.

The Sergeant imagines the room with the girl in the long dress at the piano playing by candlelight. The shot is seen in the whiskey bottle.

She is beautiful too.

Takes the wallet from his inside pocket and hands it to the Sergeant. He lingers over it out of politeness; she is not as beautiful as what he saw reflected in the glass.

SERGEANT (*as he hands it back*) Is that Eileen O'Neill?

SURVEYOR Yes. We hope to get engaged soon.

SERGEANT If I'd known that I'd not have pressed you so hard to come to the old function. You are lucky.

Through all this Biddy has been preparing tea and has laid the table.

BIDDY Your tea is drawn now if yous want.

She sits on the armchair and starts to examine reams of wool. The Sergeant pours the tea but neither of them have much desire to eat. As they nibble at a slice of bread and sip tea the Surveyor asks with a hint of sympathy, leaving behind his usual vanity:

SURVEYOR Did you ever think to get married yourself, Sergeant?

SERGEANT Yes, I suppose. I've come close enough once or twice to taking the plunge. And I suppose if I had it might have softened the cough. I've often heard marriage softens a man's cough. I suppose the old cough will finish you off eventually anyhow.

SURVEYOR That's too pessimistic a way of looking. You should take up the violin again. Music, how does it go, soothes the savage breast. You should take it up again.

SERGEANT Maybe you're right but I don't think I'll take it up now.

The Sergeant pushes aside his chair and the Surveyor rises too. As soon as they both rise Biddy gets up and clears the cups, etc., from the table. They stand over the table and sign the papers the Sergeant had initially come in with.

SURVEYOR *(as they finish, putting the cap back on his pen)* Leaving Michael's curiosity aside, how do you think the case will go? From the evidence she would appear not to have a leg to stand on. Do you think will the State be able to get manslaughter?

SERGEANT *(with a certain dignity born of hopelessness)*

Not a chance. Her family is too well connected. She'll lose her driving licence for twelve months and there'll be an order from the bench for the bend to be properly signposted.

SURVEYOR (*taking the violin case in his hand after putting on his coat*) Fortunately, Sergeant, you and I don't have to concern ourselves with justice or injustice, only with the accurate presentation of the evidence. And I can't thank you enough for those drawings you made of the accident. It would have taken me all day otherwise.

SERGEANT They're for nothing, for nothing.

SURVEYOR Till we meet on the court day. (*Holds out his right hand. The violin case hangs in the left.*)

SERGEANT I'll see you to the car.

The Surveyor looks towards Biddy but she is intent on washing dishes at the far table. They go out together as they came in.

5 INTERIOR. KITCHEN WITH OIL LAMP LIT

The scene is the same as before, except an oil lamp is lit in the centre of the big table and the blinds are drawn. Clothes – the Sergeant's suit for the function – are draped over the back of a wooden chair, turned to the fire. The Sergeant stares into the fire, the almost empty whiskey bottle and a glass by his hand.

BIDDY Will you want anything to ate before the function? (*She has obviously finished getting ready the Sergeant's things for the function, and is anxious to get back to her knitting.*)

SERGEANT (*waking out of his reverie*) No, Biddy, no.

BIDDY Your civvies are aired now if you want to change.
(*The Sergeant nods as he looks at the clothes over the
chair.*) And your shoes are polished. Is there anything
else?

SERGEANT No. Nothing else.

BIDDY I'll put a hot water jar in your bed. I'll not wait
up as no doubt it'll be the small hours before the
function's ended.

SERGEANT Thanks, Biddy, thanks.

*His eyes wander to the old fiddle lying open in its
case, almost like in a coffin, the curves of the violin
like a woman's body. He lifts it out, and his body
assumes an intensity as if he could smash it on the
floor; but he controls it and replaces it in the case,
closes the case, and slowly returns it to its place beside
the Sacred Heart lamp, dusting his hands of the dust.
He then takes his shirt and trousers from the chair
and goes with them out of the door. Biddy is firmly
seated in front of her sock machine at the end of the
table and pays him no attention. When he comes back
through the doorway he has on his brown trousers
and white shirt and shoes and socks. He returns to
the fire and slips on his vest and jacket. He takes his
necktie and the glass and bottle of whiskey back to
the table. He fills the glass to the brim with the last of
the whiskey, turns and holds the bottle to the lamp to
see if any dregs are left, but it is empty and he leaves
it back on the table. He lifts the very full glass and
raises it to Biddy, the necktie in the other hand, but
she does not look up from the machine.*

A man has a need of a little support to face into that
crew. (*Toasts to the unheeding Biddy and then starts to
mimic, still facing Biddy*) 'Something will have to be

done about Jackson's thieving ass, Sergeant, it'll take the law to bring him to his senses, nothing less, and those thistles of his will be blowing again over the townland this year with him dead drunk in the pub, and is Biddy's hens laying at all this weather, mine have gone on unholy strike, and I hear you were measuring the road today, you and a young whippersnapper from Dublin, and the poor woman's nerves I hear are in an awful condition, having to pass that wooden cross twice a day, it won't bring him back to life, poor Michael, God rest him, going to Carrick for his haircut, and did you ever see such a winter, torrents of rain and expectedness of snow.'

As he finishes knotting his tie he sees a shadowy function in the mirror. Fully dressed now, he turns towards Biddy again.

But tonight, Biddy, we'll give them a taste of higher things. Glasses of wine and Avignon and the sun and Mister Paganini.

6 SCHOOL ROOM. COUNTRYWOMEN'S ASSOCIATION MEETING

Scene in mirror. Like a schoolroom, the desks cleared back, and in the centre of the room a long table made by putting several tables together, covered with a white tablecloth, and laden with drink and plates of ham and chicken and fruitcake. A large fire blazes in the middle of the room and a few women flushed with the social excitement of the occasion hover about the table, waiting to clear empty plates and bring new dishes from an outer room. The priest sits at the head of the table. The Sergeant sits three places down to his right.

A hushed murmur.

SERGEANT He came out of a back-of-beyond very much like here (*heads turn*) except it was in Italy. And he became so famous that when he came to London crowds tried to touch him as nowadays they do with the pop stars, but he stuck to his artistic guns to the very end, improvising marvellously during his last hours on his Guarnerius. (*The speech becomes as much a vicious parody of the Surveyor's as the first was of local speech.*) I wonder what Guarnerius all of us here will be improvising on during our last hours before they hearse us cross Cootehall bridge to old Ardcarne. Well at least we'll be buried in consecrated ground – for I doubt if good Father Glynn there at the head of the table will have much doubt as to our orthodoxy – which is more than poor old Paganini got, for the Church wasn't sure that he had the right way of thinking and had him buried like an old dead cow in some field for five years, but they then relented and let him be buried in a village graveyard on his own land.

Clapping determined to stop it and the priest rises.

PRIEST I am sure we all very much regret Mr Hogg wasn't able to join us tonight and want to thank the Sergeant for his very interesting story of the Italian composer, not forgetting how much pleasure the Sergeant himself has given at former functions by his own playing.

Loud applause.

7 INTERIOR. KITCHEN WITH OIL LAMP LIT

Shot of Biddy turning and turning the handle of the sock machine but now only the empty bottle and glass are in front of the mirror.

Slow fade to black.

THE ROCKINGHAM SHOOT

The Rockingham Shoot was first broadcast on BBC2 Northern Ireland on 10 September 1987. The cast was as follows:

AIDAN REILLY Bosco Hogan
MRS REILLY Marie Kean
JOHN REILLY Ian McElhinney
MARY ARMSTRONG Hilary Reynolds
CANON GLYNN Niall Tóibín
MAGICIAN Tony Rohr
SERGEANT Oliver Maguire
GUARD MULLINS John Olohan
GUARD CASEY Gerard McSorley
FIRST TEACHER Libby Smyth
SECOND TEACHER Carmel McDonnell
MULLOY Ronan Wilmot
WHITE Dick Holland
COLLINS William Walker
GAMEKEEPER John Keyes
DUBLIN DETECTIVES Tony Coleman
                   Michael Gormley
THE CANON'S HOUSEKEEPER Lucie Jamieson

The Children
Ian Browne   Kevin McBrien
Selena Carty   Pauline McCartney
Darren Chapman   Deirdre McCrea
Majella Corrigan   Shay McMahon
Niall Donnelly   Sinead Murray
Julian Fegan   Brian O'Connor
Joanne Ferguson   Sonya Parkinson
Damian Keown   Neville Stronge
Elizabeth Kidney   Nigel Stronge

Directed by Kieran Hickey
Produced by Danny Boyle

1 EXTERIOR. COUNTRY CHAPEL. DAY

Election posters are seen on a tree in front of a church.

CLANN NA POBLACHTA
VOTE NO. 1
REILLY, A.

A political meeting in the early 1950s. From a small car draped in the tricolour, Reilly is addressing the people who are coming from the chapel. Reilly is standing on the front seat of the car, his body emerging from the open roof so that the car becomes his platform. He is speaking passionately to his apathetic audience.

REILLY A chairde Gael,[1] polling day has come and gone. I want to thank those of you who voted for me in the election. We did not win this time . . .

HECKLER And you won't win the next time either.

Laughs.

REILLY We did not win this time but there will be another day. A vote for me was a vote for freedom. And look at us today – speaking an alien tongue, aping alien ways, bowing and scraping as if we did not believe in our freedom – only slaves could allow such waste and shame. Seo ár lá. Seo ár dtír. Tá an lá sin againn anois. Sin ár lá. Go raibh míle maith agaibh go léir.[2]

1 My Irish friends.
2. This is our day. This is our country. The day is now. It is our day. Thank you all very much.

*He raises his arm in salute to his audience, who begin
to drift away when he switches to Gaelic.*

2 EXTERIOR. ROCKINGHAM HOUSE. DAY

Establishing shots of house and lake.

3 EXTERIOR. GATES AND SCHOOL. DAY

*Pan from gates of Rockingham House to a small
National School opposite. Reilly's car is parked outside.*

4 INTERIOR. CLASSROOM. DAY

REILLY Agus anois, tógaigí amach[3] *The Deserted
Village* by Oliver Goldsmith. Who can remember the old
soldier from last week? Tusa.[4]

He points to a boy who cannot answer.

Seas amach.[5]

*The boy stands out to the side. To another boy,
Collins.*

Peadar.

COLLINS
'The broken soldier, kindly bade to stay,
Sat by his fire, and talked the night away;
Wept o'er his wounds, or tales of sorrow done,
Shouldered his crutch, and showed how fields were won.'

3. And now, take out.
4. You.
5. Stand out.

REILLY Maith an buachaill.[6] Imagine this cane now is a crutch. Who'll show how the old soldier won all those battles? Ó Briain – tusa.

Reilly points to another boy who takes the cane he gives him. The boy walks up and down in front of the class carrying the cane as a crutch, then as a rifle and finally firing with it.

BOY Bang, bang, bang.

REILLY Sin a bhfuil anois. Ciúnas.[7] I want you to pay this poem particular attention. I've been looking through past examination papers and I think the portrait of either the parson or the schoolmaster has to come up on this year's paper. Goldsmith is very close to us. He was born – where?

CHILD Pallas.

REILLY In?

CHILD 1728.

REILLY Close to?

CHILD Ballymahon in the County Longford.

REILLY When he was eight he attended what is now the Bishop Hudson Grammar School in Elphin. He wrote *The Vicar of Wakefield* and a play, *She Stoops to Conquer*. Most of the great playwrights in English were Irish; I'd have you remember that.

He looks through the classroom window at the gates of Rockingham House.

Goldsmith called his poem *The Deserted Village* because people were leaving the land and small villages. A

6. Good boy.
7. That's all for now. Quiet.

thriving happy way of life was being ruined. (*Almost to himself*) It is not unlike today.

He opens a textbook and motions to the boy at the side to sit.

Suigh síos, amadán.[8] Now we come to the village schoolmaster – a person very like my poor self. (*The children smile.*) Róisín, take it up on page one hundred and fifty-four.

GIRL (*reading*)
'There, in his noisy mansion, skilled to rule,
The village master taught his little school;
A man severe he was, and stern to view . . .'

REILLY (*takes over from the girl*)
'I knew him well, and every truant knew;
Well had the boding tremblers learned to trace
The day's disasters in his morning face;
Full well they laughed with counterfeited glee,
At all his jokes, for many a joke had he;
Full well the busy whisper circling round,
Conveyed the dismal tidings when he frowned;
Yet he was kind, or if severe in aught,
The love he bore to learning was in fault.'

How would you explain that?

GIRL The only reason he was hard on the children was because he wanted them to learn.

REILLY He loved learning and he wanted them to have that learning. Which would you prefer, to have him or me for schoolmaster?

CHORUS You. You.

REILLY Counterfeited. Counterfeited.

8. Sit down, you idiot.

*A little later. Written on the blackboard is: 'A simile
is a poetic figure of speech whereby one thing is
compared directly to another.'*

Have you all copied that down? Tonight I want you to
go through the poem and pick out all the similes for me.
And for Wednesday I'll want an account of the character
of the parson and the schoolmaster. That's what I'm
really expecting to come up on the paper this year. And
I want you to mark these spellings. I want all those
spellings off by heart for tomorrow. Otherwise I may
have to administer a taste of this.

Reilly takes up the cane from his desk and flexes it.

5 EXTERIOR. PLAYGROUND. DAY

*The children from all three classes are playing during the
school dinner break. The youngest are supervised in a
singing game by a woman teacher. Some boys are
playing 'tig' and others are washing and polishing
Reilly's car. The older girls are skipping, watched by the
second woman teacher. Other children sit eating lunches
of sandwiches and bottles of milk.*

6 EXTERIOR. PLAYGROUND AND WALL. DAY

*A group of older girls leave the playground and run
towards the estate wall. As they climb over it we see a large
coloured tent standing in the bracken just beyond the wall.*

7 EXTERIOR. TENT. DAY

*Outside the tent, boys from Reilly's class are miming
beating while others watch.*

ROCKINGHAM BOY In the shoot, we're strung out in a line, every fifty yards. We have sticks. Every line is under a gamekeeper. He has a whistle. When he blows it again we stop dead still.

COLLINS Deer, foxes, badgers, hares, rabbits, squirrels, woodcock, everything comes out of the bushes. But they only shoot the pheasants.

SERGEANT'S SON How do you know that?

COLLINS We were there last year and we're going again tomorrow. That's how.

8 INTERIOR. TENT. DAY

Six girls run into the tent. There are bare trestle tables and stacked chairs inside.

FIRST ROCKINGHAM GIRL This is where we work.

GIRL What do you do?

FIRST ROCKINGHAM GIRL We lay out the sandwiches and the drinks and clean up afterwards.

GIRL (*enviously*) Can you eat any of it?

SECOND ROCKINGHAM GIRL Not while you're working. You're not allowed to eat anything while you're working.

THIRD ROCKINGHAM GIRL But in the evening we have everything they eat in the big house.

SECOND ROCKINGHAM GIRL Soup with cream, duck, ice cream, chocolate, pineapple.

FIRST ROCKINGHAM GIRL We have some in the big kitchen before it goes upstairs.

SECOND GIRL (*enviously*) Master Reilly won't let you go this year. He'll make you go to school.

SECOND ROCKINGHAM GIRL It's all arranged. He can't stop us.

9 INTERIOR. CLASSROOM. DAY

A list of words in Gaelic lettering is seen on the blackboard: 'An Rialtas, An Parliméad, An tOireachtas, An tUachtarán, An Dáil, An Seanad, Oll-Tógachán, Teachtaí Dála, An Taoiseach, An Tánaiste, Na hAirí Stáit, Rialtas daonfhlathach, Ríocht.'

REILLY Agus cén saigheas tír í?[9] What kind of country is Ireland? Rialtas daonfhlathach.

CHILDREN Rialtas daonfhlathach.

REILLY A democracy. And what kind of country is England? Ríocht.

CHILDREN Ríocht.

REILLY A monarchy. King and country. That will do for today. You can put your books away. That is the kind of country and how we rule ourselves. Now I have something I want you to listen to carefully. (*Pauses.*) I am informed that the British Ambassador, Sir John Maffey, is coming for the shoot. As in other years, the peasants will beat the pheasants out of the bushes for the milords to go bang-bang. I know some of you here can earn a half-crown for the day as a beater. *This* year I want you to show that we live in a free country and are proud of it. Tomorrow I want you to turn that half-crown down. Tomorrow I want to see every single one of you in school. Do you understand that?

CHILDREN Yes, sir.

9. What kind of country is it?

REILLY I'll see every single person here in school tomorrow, then. Let there be a small blow struck for freedom.

Reilly's raised hand is turned to begin the blessing in Gaelic before the prayers. The children stand.

10 INTERIOR. BARRACKS. DAY

The dayroom of a small Garda station. A large wooden table in front of an open fire, a number of wooden chairs about the table. There are heavy ledgers and an inkstand on the table. Baton cases and handcuffs hang from hooks along the wall. Above the fire there's a wooden mantelpiece and to the left of it a telephone on the wall. Beneath the telephone is a stripped iron bed. The bed rests along the wall that has been cut off from the dayroom. It is the prisoner's cell, but as they hardly ever have a prisoner it is used as a storeroom.

The Sergeant is sitting at the table, preoccupied with his paperwork. Guard Mullins enters with two mugs of tea. He hands one to the Sergeant and turns to look out of the window as he hears a car drive up.

MULLINS (*looking through window*) Huh, huh, speak of the devil. It's Sir Oracle and Casey with him. You'd think coming bottom of the poll would have taken some of the wind out of his sails. It's only made the man worse.

In the background Reilly helps Guard Casey take his bicycle from the boot of the car.

SERGEANT The war is still going on for Master Reilly. (*Mimics*) 'Not only Gaelic but free. Not only free but Gaelic as well.' All unfinished business.

MULLINS Still, he's a good teacher. You have to hand him that.

SERGEANT If you are clever he'll get you results. But if you are average or slow you can go whistle. My crowd are all slow.

The car drives off. Guard Casey enters.

MULLINS I thought you'd be out there spouting Gaelic for the next two hours at least.

CASEY No. No. Master Reilly has better Irish than I have, but he'll never have the *blas*.[10] That's what is killing him. You can only get the *blas* from the cradle. Nothing would do him but to put the bike in the boot. 'Caith suas ar an motor é. Ní thógfaidh sé second.'[11]

MULLINS You got a lift out of him anyway. It's more than he ever gave me or the Sergeant.

SERGEANT You can say that again.

CASEY (*feeling the censure*) Ah, Reilly's all right. He has his own ways, but I can't fault him. I'm fluent myself in two languages and I haven't a thing to say in either. (*Goes and signs the ledger on the table.*)

SERGEANT (*quietly, gently*) Did he say anything about the shoot, Ned?

CASEY He's wild against the shoot, Sergeant. He says it's a disgrace to keep the children away from school.

MULLINS He had the boys from the sixth and seventh classes out saving his brother's turf on Gloria Bog for several days last summer.

SERGEANT Oh, but *that*'s different.

10. Accent
11. Put it up on to the car. It'll take only a second.

CASEY He'll definitely kick up this year.

SERGEANT This place is going to be amok with the
Special Branch crowd from Dublin guarding the bloody
Ambassador. We'll have our hands full enough without
Master Reilly.

11 EXTERIOR. ROAD. DAY

*Reilly drives from school to the small traditional
farmhouse where he lives with his mother and brother.
On his way he drives past the demesne wall of
Rockingham, and also the lake with its view of the
great house.*

12 EXTERIOR. REILLY FARMHOUSE. DAY

*Reilly takes his schoolwork and newspaper from the car
and enters the house.*

13 INTERIOR. REILLY FARMHOUSE. DAY

*Reilly is surprised to find a handsome, well-dressed
young woman, Mary Armstrong, when he enters the
house, as well as his brother and mother. His brother is
a strong, uncomplicated, decent man with a gentle,
humorous face, but nobody's fool. He is naturally easy-
going and tolerant, in direct contrast with his brother,
but determined and unbending, even dangerous, once he
is provoked. He and Mary Armstrong are engaged, but
they have not announced it yet. It is her first visit to the
house, a kind of sounding before they decide to announce
their engagement. All are naturally nervous. Reilly reacts
away from the unexpected stranger as he enters the
room, but quickly reads the situation and behaves with*

natural courtesy and considerable charm. Mary Armstrong
rises as Reilly comes into the room, and he goes forward
to take her hand.

JOHN You know Mary Armstrong, Aidan.

REILLY You're very welcome to the house. Of course
I know Mary. She even promised me her vote in the
elections. (*Laughs.*) Her first preference, too . . . But that
I think I owe more to my brother than to politics.

The unease is released in hearty laughter. Mary
blushes.

MARY Well, you're right as far as Daddy goes. You vote
either Right or Wrong with Daddy. Fianna Fáil is right
and everything else is wrong. (*More laughter.*)

JOHN Joe Armstrong is nothing if not steadfast.

REILLY Everybody knows where your father stands.
He's a lovely man.

Mary remains standing.

Why aren't you sitting? Surely you're not going?

MARY I was on my way when we heard the car, and it
was Mrs Reilly made me stay till you came. Johnny has
been always at me to call when I'm passing and we've
no end of eggs lately.

MOTHER Look what Miss Armstrong (*Mary substitutes*
'Mary' but is ignored by the mother) brought. They're
wonderful, but it's far too much.

She shows a bowl of eggs, turning the newspaper they
are wrapped in back to show their colour.

REILLY They're wonderful and far too much.

MARY Goodbye, Mrs Reilly.

Mary and John leave. Mary and the Mother take formal leave of one another, but Reilly shakes her hand with great charm and friendliness.

MOTHER Goodbye.

REILLY Now that you have found your way to the house we'll think badly of you if you don't come here often.

MARY Goodbye, Aidan.

Exit John and Mary. John looks gratefully at his brother as he and Mary leave. Reilly moves to the scullery to wash his hands.

MOTHER I suppose it won't be long now till Johnny is taking Miss Armstrong into the house.

REILLY (*very cautiously, even respectfully*) Why? Was there something said?

MOTHER There was no need for anything to be said.

REILLY The Armstrongs are a very decent family. There is always a place for a young pair of hands about the house.

MOTHER There's never enough work for two women in any house.

Reilly returns to the table and opens out his newspaper. His Mother takes his food from the oven and puts it before him. Long, painful silence.

REILLY Well. It's about time I shook myself and got a house of my own. If the arrangements here don't suit you, you could come and live with me.

MOTHER I'd never get used to a new place at my age, and God knows it is time you should be leaving me as well. There is a time for everyone to take up their own life.

Reilly looks at her with total loyalty and deep love.

REILLY You need have no fear of me leaving you. For better or worse, you need have no fear of that.

14 EXTERIOR. GROUNDS OF ROCKINGHAM HOUSE. DAY

The house and lake at dawn. The shooting party is seen. At the gamekeeper's whistle, the beaters set off. Children from Reilly's class are prominent among them. Pheasants fly up from the undergrowth. The shooting party fire. Birds fall. The dogs collect the game.

15 EXTERIOR. SCHOOL. DAY

The sounds of shooting are heard.

16 INTERIOR. CLASSROOM. DAY

The room is nearly half empty. Vacant seats can be seen as Reilly completes the roll call.

REILLY Tomás Ó Coileáin.

No reply.

As láthair.[12] Peadar Ó Maoileoin.

BOY Anseo.[13]

REILLY Ruairí Ó Muirí. (*No reply.*) As láthair. Tadgh Ó Súilleabháin. (*No reply.*) As láthair. Róisín Saidléir.

GIRL Anseo.

REILLY Ten absent.

12. Absent.
13. Present.

All the Rockingham children are absent. The noise of shooting is clearly heard.

Tógaigí amach an leabhar Gaeilge, leathanach tríocha a haon.[14]

He closes the roll book angrily and goes to the window, which he slams shut to keep out the noise. Through the window we see Guards at the gate of Rockingham. The children take out their Irish books and turn to the correct page.

There are some difficult spellings on that page. When I'm finished I'll pick ten. We'll see how you do. Anois ná cloisim focal.[15] (*He sits at his desk.*)

The gunfire continues in the silence as they study, and Reilly goes through the homework. It has an unsettling effect. A whistle is heard. Shooting stops. A boy raises his hand to ask permission to go to the lavatory.

BOY Bhfuil cead agam dul go dtí an leithreas, a Mháistir?[16]

REILLY Tá. Brostaigh ort.[17]

17 EXTERIOR. SCHOOL YARD AND WALL. DAY

The boy runs from the school to climb the estate wall. From there he watches the shooting party and the beaters walking past the tent on their way to the next shooting area.

---

14. Take out your Irish book, page thirty-one.
15. Now I don't want to hear a word.
16. Please, Sir, may I go to the lavatory?
17. Yes. Hurry up.

18 INTERIOR. CLASSROOM. DAY

The boy comes back into the school, but Reilly hardly notices him.

BOY (*whispering to the boy sitting beside him in the desk*) I saw the whole shoot, the men with the guns.

SECOND BOY From where?

BOY The back wall.

SECOND BOY How many?

REILLY (*looking up sharply*) An cloisim éinne ag caint?[18]

The classroom freezes. Reilly returns to the homework exercises, but the two boys do not resume their conversation. The distant gunfire continues.

19 EXTERIOR. ROCKINGHAM HOUSE. DAY

The sound of the shoot is heard.

20 INTERIOR. TENT. DAY

Three girls are working in the tent. They are arranging sandwiches and bottles for the lavish cold buffet.

21 INTERIOR. CLASSROOM. DAY

There is now a list of ten words on the blackboard which Reilly has just written: 'Athraithe, Smaoinimh, Chosúlacht, Preabadh, Oscail, Corraithe, Ghualainn, Ascaill, Buidéal, Deichniúr.'

18. Do I hear anyone speaking?

REILLY Have you copied those down? Excellent. Repeat them now for me. (*He calls out a sentence containing the first word.*) Tá mo shaol athraithe go mór.

The children repeat the key word as Reilly calls it out at the end of each sentence:

CHILDREN Athraithe.

REILLY Tá mé ag smaoinimh.

CHILDREN Smaoinimh.

REILLY Bhí an chosúlacht orthu.

CHILDREN Chosúlacht.

REILLY Bhí a chrói ag preabadh.

CHILDREN Preabadh.

REILLY D'oscail sé an doras.

CHILDREN Oscail.

REILLY Ag éirí corraithe.

CHILDREN Corraithe.

REILLY Chuir sé a lámh ar ghualainn.

CHILDREN Ghualainn.

REILLY Faoin a ascaill.

CHILDREN Ascaill.

REILLY Bhí buidéal beag aige.

CHILDREN Buidéal.

REILLY Deichniúr acu a bhí ann.

CHILDREN Deichniúr.

Reilly and the class repeat the lesson.

22 EXTERIOR. SCHOOLYARD. DAY

The children are playing.

23 INTERIOR. CLASSROOM. DAY

Reilly is having lunch in the classroom with the two woman teachers.

REILLY You've heard the martial noises from our own little England all morning.

FIRST TEACHER They'd be hard to miss.

SECOND TEACHER The children were concentrated on nothing else. It was almost impossible to teach.

FIRST TEACHER I gave up. I gave them copying work. It was hopeless.

REILLY In my classes not a single pupil from the estate is present. They're all beating the bushes, skivvying in the kitchens. I warned them yesterday not to be absent.

FIRST TEACHER All the little ones are in.

SECOND TEACHER Just to get them off their hands.

REILLY My crowd will certainly have some accounting to do tomorrow. Yes. They will certainly have some accounting to do tomorrow.

24 EXTERIOR. ROCKINGHAM ESTATE. DAY

The boys are beating the bushes and trees. Birds fly up in the air. The shooting party fire.

25 INTERIOR. TENT. DAY

The three girls are clearing up after lunch. They giggle as they eat some left-over sandwiches.

26 EXTERIOR. ROCKINGHAM ESTATE GROUNDS. DAY

The boys from the school are finishing their day's work and arranging pheasants in braces on the side of an estate road. The gamekeeper supervises them.

27 EXTERIOR. ROCKINGHAM ESTATE. EVENING

Rockingham House and lake at dusk.

28 EXTERIOR. BARRACKS. EVENING

The usually quiet place is in turmoil. The detectives guarding the British Ambassador have come from Dublin and have turned the country station into temporary headquarters. They are all in plain clothes. Their cars are also unmarked. A number are hanging around outside and there is coming and going.

DUBLIN DETECTIVE (*in a sarcastic Dublin accent*) His Excellency is safe yet, anyhow.

FIRST MAN All we have to think about is our duty.

DUBLIN DETECTIVE It's freezing out there. Bring a double pair of socks.

SECOND MAN What time do you expect the ball to be over?

FIRST MAN Two or three o'clock.

DUBLIN DETECTIVE That's no use to us. The
Ambassador is sleeping the night in the house.

FIRST MAN And we'll have to be there until he leaves.

SECOND MAN When do you think that'll be?

GUARD MULLINS Ask me another.

*Guard Mullins and the Dublin detective move into the
dayroom.*

29 INTERIOR. BARRACKS. EVENING

*A group are playing cards on the dayroom table. The
Sergeant and Guard Mullins are the only ones in uniform.
The Sergeant has been busy since early morning and
looks harassed and tired. Mullins and the Dublin
detective enter.*

DUBLIN DETECTIVE (*to group at table*) May I join
you? What is it?

OTHERS Poker.

*An older detective is showing the Sergeant's son the
workings of his revolver.*

30 EXTERIOR. BARRACKS. EVENING

Reilly drives up and enters.

31 INTERIOR. BARRACKS. EVENING

*Reilly enters. As the boy sees Reilly he flees towards the
living quarters of the barracks. Reilly becomes uncertain
as he enters. The Sergeant has enough on his hands*

without Reilly. Reilly goes up to the Sergeant and hands him a note.

REILLY I come to report those absences. A whole section of the school went missing for this shoot.

SERGEANT Thanks. (*He takes the note and puts it on the mantelpiece. He wants to get rid of Reilly.*) I'll get Guard Casey to look into it.

REILLY (*aggressively*) *You* should look into it. It's gone on year after year. It's about time it was stopped.

SERGEANT (*coldly*) To be absent for a day is hardly a crime.

REILLY I call it an affront. You'd think we were still a subject people. People did not give their lives for children to go on beating peasants out of the bushes for our overlords!

SERGEANT *Pheasants*, I think.

REILLY Peasants or pheasants. There is little difference.

SERGEANT (*coldly and angrily*) In law there is an almighty difference. Remember these people work for the estate.

As Reilly prepares to leave, the head gamekeeper from the estate enters the dayroom. With him is a boy from Reilly's class carrying ten pheasants.

GAMEKEEPER With Sir Cecil's compliments. Where do you want them left, Sergeant?

SERGEANT Just hang them up over there anywhere, Dick.

GAMEKEEPER Right.

SERGEANT And thank Sir Cecil for me.

GAMEKEEPER Goodnight, Sergeant.

SERGEANT Goodnight, men.

Reilly stops and reads from a card attached to the pheasants as he is on his way out:

REILLY 'With the compliments of Sir Cecil and Lady Stafford King-Harmon.' It seems that more than the people of the estate are on the Rockingham payroll.

SERGEANT (*going up very close to Reilly*) You look after the school, Master. I'll manage the barracks.

The Sergeant violently closes the door on Reilly. It opens again immediately.

REILLY (*jeers at the door*) Pheasant for the peasants, how are you? (*Reilly again leaves.*)

DETECTIVE Who is that, Sergeant?

SERGEANT The local teacher, and a would-be politician as well.

DETECTIVE He seems sort of excited.

SERGEANT We have the same trouble with him every year. The shoot just seems to set off an alarm clock.

DUBLIN DETECTIVE PLAYING CARDS There was a moon last night as well.

They all laugh.

SERGEANT He's a very good teacher, but he can't do anything by half. The poor fellow believes he can change the world.

32 EXTERIOR. ROCKINGHAM HOUSE. NIGHT

The Rockingham Ball. Rockingham House and the immediate grounds are lit up like a marvellous white ship above the quiet water. Until very late the dance music drifts out over the whole silent countryside.

33 EXTERIOR. ROCKINGHAM HOUSE. NIGHT

Guards and detectives are on sentry duty outside the entrance porch.

34 EXTERIOR. LANEWAY NEAR ROCKINGHAM LAKE. NIGHT

Mary and John are walking arm in arm. In the background the house rises above the lake.

MARY It's a week and a year since we started going out. The G.A.A. dance was on the Sunday before the Rockingham shoot.

JOHN (*putting his arm round her shoulder*) By this time next year we'll be together in our own house.

MARY I don't know if your mother will ever take to me.

JOHN Then it's her lookout. I'll build a second house. I doubt if it will ever come to that, though. Aidan is talking of buying a house. Even before he got the scholarships and went away to college he was always a sort of God to her. She'll not live without him, but that's no worry of yours.

MARY (*kisses him*) Tá mé i ngrá leat.

JOHN What does that mean?

MARY (*laughing*) Did you not learn Irish at school?

JOHN I've forgotten every word of it except *tá* and *níl* and *anseo*.

MARY Then ask Aidan. What does 'Tá mé i ngrá leat' mean?

JOHN Come on. What does it mean? Come on. Don't be making a fool out of me.

MARY I'd like nothing better, if it were possible.

JOHN Come on. (*He draws her passionately to him.*) What does it mean?

MARY (*as they kiss*) 'I love you' . . . (*He laughs.*) Now you're laughing. Is that what I get for telling you?

JOHN Well, I'd surely have a nice head on me asking Aidan *that*.

All through the scene the lighted house across the water is seen and the music from the ball is clear.

35 INTERIOR. CLASSROOM. DAY

The blackboard reads: 'Éire Gaedhalach Éire saor. Ní tír gan teanga.'[19] *All the seats are full. Reilly is calling the roll.*

REILLY Domhnall Ó Baoill.

BOY Anseo.[20]

REILLY Tomás Ó Coileáin.

BOY Anseo.

REILLY Peadar Ó Maoileóin.

19. Ireland Gaelic, Ireland free. No country without its language.
20. Present.

BOY Anseo.

REILLY Ruairí Ó Muirí.

BOY Anseo.

REILLY Tadgh Ó Súilleabháin.

BOY Anseo.

REILLY Roisín Saidléir.

GIRL Anseo.

Reilly enters the total in the book. He closes the book and speaks with heavy sarcasm.

REILLY So the little Rockinghams are back from the big shoot. (*He mimics*) 'Yes, milord. No, milord. Good shot, Sir John. Good shot, Sir Cecil.'

Ó Coileáin (*An intelligent looking boy from Rockingham stands*) . . . or perhaps should I say Collins. You usually have enough to say for yourself. Can you explain why you weren't at school yesterday?

COLLINS We were kept because of the shoot, Sir.

REILLY Did I not tell you to be in school?

COLLINS Yes, Sir.

REILLY That counted for nothing?

The boy does not answer. He is frightened. Reilly turns to the general classroom.

Of course, that counted for nothing. The British Ambassador was coming. (*He rises and stands to address the class.*) When did this country win its freedom?

It is a well-rehearsed question. The children chant their answer in unison.

ALL In 1921, Sir.

REILLY After how long?

ALL After centuries of oppression, Sir.

REILLY Did anyone from this parish give his life for Ireland?

ALL Yes, Sir.

REILLY Who?

ALL Paddy Moran, Sir.

REILLY Paddy Moran. Anyone here related to Paddy Moran? (*A few tentative hands show.*) Put up those hands proudly! No one here is ashamed of Paddy Moran!

The hands rise higher. Reilly is pleased with his performance. As if it is a surprise, he calls:

Now, I have a surprise for you. Take out your copy books. You've no objections to a spelling test I trust. Some people not here yesterday may find it a little difficult, but . . . Are you ready?

Reilly begins to call out the ten words from the lesson of the day before. The children begin to write them down. Those who had been present the day before find the task relatively easy and they conceal their writing with their hands so that any Rockingham children sitting beside them cannot copy the words. The Rockingham children are dismayed and obviously lost.

Athraithe . . . Smaoinimh . . . Chosúlacht . . . Preabadh . . . Oscail . . . Corraithe . . . Ghuallainn . . . Ascaill . . . Buidéal . . . Deichniúr.

Agus arís . . .[21] (*He repeats the ten words.*)

21. And again . . .

36 EXTERIOR. ROCKINGHAM ESTATE. DAY

As Reilly continues to repeat the words, we see estate workers dismantling the tent, others picking up cartridges from the site of the shoot, and, finally, the tent being collapsed.

37 INTERIOR. CLASSROOM. DAY

Reilly has been looking out of the window. He turns to face the class.

REILLY Finished correcting? Now, who got them all right? (*Most of the children who have been present the previous day raise their hands.*) That is excellent. It shows what a little attendance at school can do. One spelling wrong? Two spellings wrong? (*More of those children who had been at school the previous day raise their hands.*) You people are safe. Now, three spellings wrong? Four? Five? (*Nobody stands.*) Six? Seven? Eight? Nine? . . . All the spellings wrong? (*All the ten Rockingham children are standing.*) Seasaigí amach.[22] It seems that not much was learned from the Rockingham shoot.

> *The children come forward to be beaten and line themselves in front of Reilly.*

Cailíní.[23]

> *Three girls step forward.*

FIRST GIRL We had to stay away, Sir.

REILLY Oh, you're not getting this for staying away. This is for spellings.

> *The first girl, second girl and third girl are each given two strokes of the cane. The line of boys waits.*

22. Stand out.
23. Girls.

This will be a lesson to you.

The first boy comes up.

FIRST BOY Sir, we thought it was no harm, Sir.

REILLY The day of reckoning isn't the day of thinking.

Reilly gives him two strokes on each hand. The boy pulls back his hands and starts to rub them. Reilly pulls each one forward and beats them in succession.

Come on, come on. Take your medicine.

The second boy comes up.

You should think of this when you're doing your lessons.

The second boy is given six rapid strokes. The third boy, Collins, refuses to come on to the rostrum.

COLLINS It's not fair.

Reilly grabs him and hauls him up. The boy struggles. Reilly swings him against the desk. In the struggle the globe falls to the ground. Reilly starts to beat him very hard.

REILLY I'll give you fair. (*Continues beating.*)

After the beating he hurls Collins back towards his place. The remaining four boys wait. Reilly pauses.

(*Muttering*) Not seeing to your studies. Not doing your duty.

Reilly calls up the first of the four. He begins a violent beating. These boys are struck savagely and their beating is ritualistic. The first group of beaten children watch this punishment and listen to Reilly as his voice rises and falls during the beating:

Come on . . . Wilful waste is woeful want . . . Come

on, next . . . Why is wilful waste woeful want? . . . You pay the piper, I call the tune; remember that . . . Come on, next . . . Éire Gaedhalach, Éire saor [24] . . . What, what? . . . Ní saor gan Gaedhalach, ní Gaedhalach gan saor [25] . . . Remember me . . . Poor little fellow . . . That's the way, that's the way.

For the final blows, Reilly has to physically hold the children. The last child is pushed away after his beating. By now Reilly is dishevelled, out of breath and sexually aroused. Shocked to discover this, he furtively pulls his jacket closed and shamefacedly stumbles over to a chair in the corner where he sits, shaking and wiping the sweat from his face. Then a half-stifled, angry rhythmical sobbing rises as the beaten children writhe in their seats, press folded arms into their bodies, in and out, in numbness and anger and pain.

38 INTERIOR. CAR. SUNSET

The sound of the crying continues as Reilly sits immobile in his parked car beside the lake. He stares at nothing.

39 INTERIOR. REILLY FARMHOUSE. NIGHT

The Mother is sitting in darkness waiting for Reilly to come from the town. He enters, switching on the light.

REILLY You're up very late, Mother.

MOTHER I was waiting up for you.

REILLY You know you shouldn't do that.

24. Ireland Gaelic, Ireland free.
25. Not free unless Gaelic, not Gaelic unless free.

MOTHER Why didn't you come home for your dinner?

REILLY I ran into a few people down in Bennetts.

MOTHER There were men here looking for you. They said they'd be back.

Reilly is alert, as if he guesses their errand.

REILLY Did they say what they wanted?

MOTHER They just said they wanted to see you.

REILLY Did you know them?

MOTHER I didn't see their faces. They wouldn't come in. I had a feeling they were up to no good. I got a strong smell of drink. (*Sound of footsteps approaching the door.*) There, they're back. Why don't I say you are not back? For them to call to the school tomorrow?

Loud knocking.

REILLY No, Mother. I'll see to them. They'd have seen the car, anyway. (*He goes to the door.*)

40 EXTERIOR. REILLY FARMHOUSE. NIGHT

Three men are outside: Mulloy, Collins and White.

MULLOY We want to know why you beat our children for staying away for the shoot.

REILLY No children were punished because of the shoot.

COLLINS You should have seen their hands.

WHITE What you did to them wouldn't be done to a dog.

REILLY They hadn't done their homework.

COLLINS Only the children from Rockingham were beaten.

WHITE Their hands were bleeding.

MULLOY The women couldn't get them to stop crying all evening.

REILLY I'm sorry about that. I'm very sorry.

MULLOY (*seizing Reilly by the collar*) You're sorry? You've every reason to feel sorry.

REILLY The cane was shredded but I didn't notice it.

MULLOY It's the cane you should get yourself straight across the face, and then you'd see how it feels.

Reilly is unafraid. He is cold and angry, feeling keenly the indignity of his position. Mulloy forces him back violently against the door.

REILLY You can beat me up if you want but that will resolve nothing. I said I was sorry.

MULLOY It's more than sorry you'll be before it's finished.

JOHN (*coming out of the darkness*) What the hell is going on here? What's going on here at this hour of night?

Mulloy releases Reilly, his aggression losing its impulse.

REILLY (*sarcastically*) These gentlemen have come to see me on school matters.

JOHN (*interposing himself between his brother and the men*) That can all be sorted out in daylight. This is no hour at any house.

MULLOY You haven't seen the end of this. You haven't seen the end of this by half.

WHITE We'll fix you for this if it's the last thing we ever do.

MULLOY And if you so much as leave a finger, leave one frigging finger on any of our children from this day out, you'd better be able to get out of this country quick.

JOHN That'll do now, men. Goodnight, men.

The men leave and the brothers re-enter the house.

41 INTERIOR. REILLY FARMHOUSE. NIGHT

The two brothers enter the kitchen. The Mother breaks the extreme tension.

MOTHER Are you all right, Aidan?

REILLY (*angrily*) Of course I'm all right. It's just the indignity of having anything to do with those louts.

JOHN (*with definite criticism*) You seem to have got them fairly roused.

MOTHER Aidan does far too much for them. He tries to raise them up when he should leave them in the gutter where they belong.

REILLY (*irritably*) I'm going to bed. I wish there was some place where you could be completely away from people.

He goes into the bedroom, slamming the door behind him. The Mother glares at John.

42 INTERIOR. CLASSROOM. FOLLOWING MORNING

Reilly has completed the roll call. There are three absent when he tots the names in the attendance book.

REILLY Anyone know why those three are absent?

A big boy answers aggressively and challengingly:

BIG BOY They had to go to the doctor. Their hands were cut, Sir.

Hands go up.

REILLY What now?

GIRL There's someone in the porch, Sir.

Reilly gets up.

REILLY (*to class*) Look at that page on the Treaty of Limerick.

He goes out to the porch and closes the door firmly.

43 INTERIOR. SCHOOL PORCH. DAY

The Sergeant is waiting for Reilly. He begins abruptly.

REILLY Sergeant?

SERGEANT The estate manager from Rockingham has made a complaint. He alleges the children from the estate were beaten in school for being absent during the shoot.

REILLY They were punished, but for reasons of school work and discipline.

SERGEANT Some of them were so badly beaten that they had to be taken to the doctor.

REILLY Oh, I'm sorry to hear that. The cane was shredded at the time, but I didn't notice it until afterwards. Not that I expect that to be taken into account. You'll all dance to Sir Cecil's tune anyhow.

SERGEANT It hasn't even got to Sir Cecil's ears yet. If it does, you could be in big trouble. The manager was worried about some of the men wanting to take the law into their own hands.

REILLY I did have visitors to the house late last night.

The Sergeant waits to see if Reilly will add anything but he does not.

SERGEANT Listen. I'll tell you something for nothing.

REILLY (*sarcastically*) I always appreciate that, Sergeant.

SERGEANT (*coldly*) The manager wanted me to prosecute you. I said I wouldn't do that, but you're not out of the woods yet. He can still take it to the courts as a civil suit, so I'd go easy if I were you.

REILLY Are you threatening me?

SERGEANT Remember that the people who set up this State were big people. *They* allowed room for everybody.

REILLY (*sarcastically again*) When I want a lesson on the foundation of the State, I'll certainly not forget to consult you. Have you any more profundities to contribute?

SERGEANT (*pulling on his gloves*) No, that's the lot, I'm afraid. Except for one small thing. (*Reilly looks at him.*) I'm warning you here and now to watch it.

The Sergeant leaves Reilly in pent-up anger, frustration and with much to think about, perhaps to fear. He is too disturbed to return to teaching. Noise has been rising throughout his talk with the Sergeant. He rushes back to the classroom.

44 INTERIOR. CLASSROOM. DAY

Reilly enters and shouts:

REILLY Cúinas![26] (*The noise stops abruptly.*) I don't want to hear a sound while I'm out.

26. Quiet!

45 EXTERIOR. SCHOOL DRIVEWAY. DAY

*The Sergeant is in conversation with a tall bedraggled
man (the Magician), in hat and overcoat, holding a
bicycle at the school gate. There is a suitcase strapped
to the carrier. Two large oilcloth bags hang from the
handlebars. Where the lamp would normally hang, there
is a large cane basket. The man is a stranger and the
Sergeant is clearly checking on his business in the area.*

SERGEANT Master Reilly. Just go right in. He'll see you,
I'm sure.

> *The Sergeant mounts his bicycle and rides off. The
> man approaches the school.*

46 EXTERIOR. SCHOOLYARD. DAY

*Reilly is walking in front of the school and smoking
a cigarette. When he reaches the corner he stops. The
Magician appears round the corner of the school. He
leans his bicycle carefully against the school wall and
approaches Reilly. He has a large birthmark on his face.*

REILLY Yes?

MAGICIAN I was at the priest's and he gave me this.
(*He hands him a note.*)

REILLY This place is getting a bit like O'Connell Street.
(*Reading the note*) A travelling showman? (*Showing
obvious distaste.*)

MAGICIAN I was a teacher once, too.

REILLY Was teaching too much of a constraint on your
talents?

MAGICIAN No, just misfortune. (*Drinking gesture.*)

REILLY What is it you do?

MAGICIAN I do magic, jokes, stories, in Irish as well as English. Quizzes.

REILLY Why should I allow you to waste the school day?

The Magician hesitates in the face of this hostility. Reilly glances at the priest's note.

MAGICIAN Everything is educational.

REILLY I'm sure nothing is educational. When would you propose to come?

MAGICIAN Tomorrow if it'd be all right, just after dinner.

REILLY And how much would you expect them to pay?

MAGICIAN Would a shilling be too much to ask? (*Almost pleading*) It's almost as low as I could do it for. You see, I give prizes as well.

REILLY (*curtly*) We'll see you tomorrow then.

MAGICIAN God bless you, Sir.

He offers his hand to Reilly, who ignores it. The Magician returns to his bicycle and wheels it away. Reilly, in a fury, tears up the note from the priest.

47 INTERIOR. REILLY FARMHOUSE. EVENING

The Mother is polishing Reilly's shoes. He comes out of the bedroom to finish dressing in a dark blue suit.

MOTHER Was there any more trouble in the school today?

REILLY No.

MOTHER Do you think will there be trouble?

REILLY No. (*Then relenting*) Anyhow the Canon will soon put a stop to it.

MOTHER Please God.

She hands him his shoes and starts to move to the scullery. Reilly sits down to lace up his shoes.

I was right about Johnny and Miss Armstrong. They are going to be married next May.

REILLY (*looks at her*) That's still a good way off.

MOTHER Don't let on I told you. He'll want to tell you himself.

REILLY Of course not. Where is he?

MOTHER He's fencing that gap in the far meadow. (*Reilly starts to laugh to himself.*) What's so funny?

REILLY Nothing much. Something they used tell us in college: 'All tragedies end in death, all comedies in marriage.'

MOTHER I don't see very much funny in that. (*She goes into the scullery.*)

REILLY I suppose it's not so funny. (*He continues almost to himself*) They stuff you full of all sorts of useless things in college. 'All comedies end in marriage' . . . (*Bitterly*) And they might have added for good measure that all vocations end in farce. (*Pause.*) We thought we'd make this country a better place by becoming teachers. Certainly not the most lucrative of the professions. It was our country. In our own hands for the first time. We'd make it the New Jerusalem. Now look at what it's

come down to. (*Still to himself*) I should have been a
lawyer. A lawyer. Not a doubt. Someone who lives off
the natural stupidity and greed of the people.

Mother returns from the scullery.

MOTHER Not a lawyer, Aidan. I'd not like to see you
a lawyer. I've not seen the inside of a courthouse yet
though I'm old.

REILLY You're not that old, Mother. Now, I don't want
you to worry about John getting married, or anything.
I'm starting seriously to look for that house. It's going to
be well away from here. Then you can live with John or
come to live with me. You'll have your pick of two
houses.

MOTHER Maybe it is a third house I'll have, one I have
no wish for.

REILLY (*anxiously*) Now, Mother. (*Firmly but with love*)
You always disliked it – quite rightly disliked it – when
other people took that line of talk. You'll live for years
yet, Mother.

MOTHER Please God. Please God.

REILLY And I'll find us some place where we'll be well
away from people.

48 EXTERIOR. PRESBYTERY. NIGHT

*Reilly's car is seen approaching the presbytery. The house
is two storeys and very large, with heavy knockers
on the front door. Reilly gets out of the car, carrying
a bottle of whiskey in brown paper, and knocks.*

49 INTERIOR. PRESBYTERY. NIGHT

The Canon's housekeeper opens the door to Reilly.

REILLY I come to see the Canon.

HOUSEKEEPER Oh, it's yourself, Master. (*She leads him towards the Canon's room and shows him in.*) Master Reilly to see you, Canon.

50 INTERIOR. ROOM IN PRESBYTERY. NIGHT

A large Victorian room, carpeted, heavy mahogany furniture, Victorian reproductions, religious pictures, books behind glass, a big coal fire in the open grate.

CANON Show him in, Bridget. Show him in. You're welcome, Aidan. I thought I'm in trouble now, a sick call or something, and it turns out to be your good self.

REILLY You asked me to drop in one of these nights, Canon.

CANON Did I now? (*He is obviously used to forgetting.*) It'll come back to me later. The old mind is not what it used to be, jumbled, slipping.

REILLY I wanted to see you myself, Canon.

Puts down the whiskey on the table. The Canon takes it up, and removes the brown paper.

CANON You shouldn't have done that. You know that. You do too much already. There was no need to bring anything. (*Looks at the bottle*) Redbreast. The best.

REILLY The last several times I came I've been drinking your whiskey. There's a time for everything.

The Canon takes the gift whiskey to a cupboard where he puts it carefully away. He brings a glass to

*the table where Reilly waits and pours whiskey from
a bottle already there.*

CANON I drink mine neat but . . .

*The Canon moves the jug towards the teacher, who
fills his glass almost to the brim with water.*

I don't know how you can taste it at that, but every man
to his own strength. Good health.

REILLY Good health.

They move to sit on opposite sides of the fire.

CANON You said you needed to see me, Aidan.

REILLY (*bluntly*) I'm in trouble, Canon.

CANON What sort of trouble? (*He grows watchful, but
is easy, being used to dealing with such situations.*)

REILLY There was the shoot in Rockingham.

CANON I know. The British Ambassador was there. I
wasn't invited to the do, but that is their business. I have
nothing against Sir Cecil. He pays me dues handsomely
and regularly, though he doesn't have to. He has his own
church.

REILLY The children go absent every year to beat out
the pheasants for their guns and to skivvy in the kitchens.
I warned them this year not to stay away from school,
but they still went.

CANON (*shrewdly*) You beat them for this? That's the
trouble, then?

REILLY I didn't punish them for being absent. They
knew no lessons when they came back.

CANON You really beat them for being away, though?

REILLY I wouldn't admit it to anybody but yourself, Canon.

CANON You'd be wise not to.

REILLY I went too far. I was upset.

CANON They are threatening law, then?

REILLY More or less, but I doubt if it'll come to that.

CANON (*irritably*) What do you expect me to do? Don't you see that this puts me out on a limb? Try to see it from my point of view, especially with the estate involved.

REILLY I worked myself to the bone for this parish for years. (*Rises.*) I think I deserve some consideration.

CANON I know you do. Do you think I'd be listening to you otherwise? Sit down. (*Reilly returns to his chair.*) You're going to have to learn to relax. Some of those speeches you made during the election did you no good at all. You're going to have to learn to . . . You're going to have to learn that you can't bend human nature to an ideal, no matter how good that ideal is. When I was young, I was very fond of poetry. I knew a great deal of verse by heart. I used to recite it sometimes when I was with the other young priests. (*Smiles.*) 'Wherewith being crowned, crooked eclipses against its glory fight, and time that gave . . . and time that gave . . .' I thought its beauty and truth were obvious. Then, I got one of the greatest shocks of my life. I was walking along a country road during the holidays with the best friend I had then, a Father Kelly. I was reciting something – John Donne it was – and I turned and saw his face purple with rage. 'There you go again, Jimmy Glynn,' he said, 'showing off. Showing yourself off as usual.' I'll never forget it.

REILLY (*quietly but not contritely*) I admit I went too far. It won't happen again.

CANON It *can't* happen again.

The Canon stands and puts his drink on the mantelpiece.

REILLY What will you do, Canon?

CANON You're lucky that all who work on the estate are Catholics. You can forget about it. (*Pause.*) You might as well have another drink. You probably need it more than I do.

REILLY Thank you, Canon.

He pours Reilly a drink. They drink together.

CANON By the way, did that travelling showman call to the school, the fellow on the bicycle?

REILLY Oh, yes!

CANON He told me he had a brother, a monsignor, in Donegal.

REILLY He told me he was a teacher once himself.

They laugh. The tenseness is now gone.

CANON Are you going to give him a chance?

REILLY Yes. He's to – what's the phrase? – 'tread the boards' tomorrow.

CANON I'm glad. I like to give those fellows a hand when I can. I sometimes feel that we might all be in their shoes except for the grace of God. I suppose in that sense we are all the same under the great sun of heaven. What's that it is? 'And time that gave . . . time that gave . . .'

REILLY (*insensitively completing the quotation*) '. . . doth now his gift confound.'

51 EXTERIOR. SCHOOL DRIVEWAY. DAY

The Magician is seen approaching on his bicycle and the excited children crowd around him when he reaches the gate, the bigger children vying with one another to wheel his bicycle.

52 INTERIOR. CLASSROOM. DAY

The partitions have been rolled back and the desks arranged for the concert. The two woman teachers are hanging black cloth over the windows and looking out at the Magician's arrival.

REILLY Our comedian has landed.

WOMAN TEACHER The children are treating him like a celebrity.

REILLY Some celebrity! He reminds me a bit of the country itself.

53 EXTERIOR. SCHOOL DRIVEWAY. DAY

The Magician's approach continues, more children rushing to join the procession behind him.

54 INTERIOR. CLASSROOM. DAY

There is an explosive flash. The children gasp. The Magician emerges through the curtains of a flimsy portable proscenium arch erected on the dais from which

Reilly teaches. A record starts to play from a portable gramophone. From his sleeve he produces a bunch of feathered flowers and throws them to the smallest children who form the front row of the audience. Reilly and the two woman teachers watch from the back of the room. The Magician next takes a walking cane, pretends to strike his hand with it and then shakes it out into a piece of black cloth. He then begins a quiz, using miming and hand gestures.

MAGICIAN What is the capital of Japan?

Hands are raised in the audience.

CHILDREN Tokyo.

MAGICIAN The longest river in the world?

More hands.

CHILDREN The Amazon.

MAGICIAN The highest mountain?

More hands.

CHILDREN Everest.

MAGICIAN As I was going to the fair of Athy, I met nine men and their nine wives and the nine wives each had nine children. How many were going to the fair of Athy?

CHILDREN Ninety-nine?

Eleven?

Eighty-one?

MAGICIAN One. The others were *coming* from the fair!

The children laugh and the teachers show their amusement also.

*The Magician next does a trick in which he produces
four pigeons from an apparently empty box. He takes
the birds behind the curtain and switches off the
gramophone. He emerges again.*

Who knows the seven deadly sins? (*Several hands are
raised.*)

GIRL (*fluently*) Pride, covetousness, lust, anger, gluttony,
envy and sloth.

MAGICIAN When God was handing out the deadly sins,
he gave one in particular to various nations. He gave
pride to the Spaniards, gluttony to the Germans, and
covetousness to the English. Which of the seven deadly
sins did he give to the Irish?

SERGEANT'S SON Envy.

Reilly is annoyed.

MAGICIAN Right. First time. I have a small story about
that. (*He begins to speak in Irish*) Tá scéal beag agam
faoi sin. Bhí dhá feirmeoirí Éireannach. Bhíodar i gcónaí
ag troid. Lá amháin tagann an Fairi maith chuig ceann
dos na feirmeoirí.[27]

*Reilly has not liked the apportioning of the deadly
sins, but his irritation turns to incredulity when he
hears the magician's faltering, ungrammatical Irish.*

REILLY (*from the back of the room, furious*) Stop! I
can't have you mangling our language like that, Sir. Tell
them the story in English. They know far more Irish than
you do.

MAGICIAN It's true I don't know it very well.

27. I have a little story about that. There were two Irish farmers.
They were always fighting. One day the Good Fairy comes to one
of the farmers.

REILLY (*roars*) You don't know it at all! (*He rushes up the room to the stage.*)

MAGICIAN (*weakly*) A lot of teachers ask for it. It's very popular with some.

REILLY Then they are worse than you are.

When Reilly, rushing from the darkened area of the room, finds himself on the stage, he is confused by the unfamiliar theatrical surroundings and dazzled by the light from the window. He stands there, bewildered by the Magician's takeover of his own territory. The Magician himself is frightened and confused by Reilly's violence. Then he realises that Reilly is even more unsure than he is.

MAGICIAN (*confused*) Was it all right up to that?

REILLY What?

MAGICIAN Was it all right up to that?

REILLY It was fine. I'm sorry. It's not your fault. (*He impulsively takes a handful of coins from his pocket and hands them to the Magician.*)

MAGICIAN Ah, no, no.

REILLY Take it, just tell the story in English. Go on, go on.

Reilly stumbles from the stage. On his way towards the back of the room, he accidentally catches against a black window curtain and pulls it from its fastening.

(*To the curtain.*) Gabh mo leithscéal.[28]

His shocked walk continues. He is now muttering to himself and he reaches a corner where he stands with

28. I beg your pardon.

*his back to the stage sobbing quietly. The Magician
waits. When he guesses that there will be no more
interruptions he begins his story again.*

MAGICIAN Your teacher was right. My Irish is poor. I'll
tell the story in English.

There were these two farmers, Paddy Mulloy and Paddy
Murphy. They were always fighting – they couldn't stand
one another – and they were poor. Then one day the
Good Fairy appeared to Paddy Mulloy and told him he
could have anything he wanted.

'Anything I want?'

'Anything at all, but with one condition: whatever I give
you, I have to give double to Paddy Murphy.'

'Would you be able to give me a hundred acres of good
rock land?'

'No trouble. You can have it in the morning, but I'll
have to give Paddy Murphy *two* hundred acres.'

'Hold on a minute there. That would never do. There's
no standing him and his few acres of sprat and rushes.
If he was given two hundred acres we'd have to leave the
country.'

'All right. We'll not give him two hundred acres. You'll
have to think of something else.'

'Could I have one hundred thousand pounds?'

'Sure. But remember Paddy Murphy has to get two
hundred thousand.'

'Stop! That's even worse. No one could stand the style
and conceit of him. He'd walk over everybody.'

'All right, you'll have to think of something else.'

Paddy Mulloy thought for a long time, and then he said to the Good Fairy: 'I know what I'll do, I'll have one of my hands cut off, and then he'll have to have *two* of his cut off. Won't he?'

(*To the children.*) Now, what do you make of that?

COLLINS Fierce envy.

MAGICIAN Right, there's envy for you. Now what do you want me to do next? I'll count to three to give you time to decide. Then you can tell me what you want. You'll have to hurry. I'm counting to three, not to ten. (*In a rush*) One, two . . . (*The children become anxious. Then, very slowly, holding up his hand*) . . . two and a half . . . two and three-quarters . . . three! Hands up!

The children raise their hands. Then, at first singly, they begin to call out.

CHILDREN Magic, magic. More magic.

Suddenly, the whole audience rises to its feet and shouts with one voice.

Magic, magic. More magic!

They wave their hands and applaud the Magician who smiles down at them. Reilly, fists clenched and arms folded across his chest, is still huddled in his corner. He turns as the tumult increases but is powerless to stop it. The gramophone record starts again.

Fade out.

THE POWER OF DARKNESS

After the melodrama of the same name
by Leo Tolstoy

Introduction

In the 1970s I was commissioned by the BBC to adapt Tolstoy's melodrama *The Power of Darkness* into Irish country speech. It was thought that the play would translate naturally into Irish speech because of a religious presence in the language and the relative lack of a class system.

I would have been glad of any work in those years, and was delighted with the Tolstoy commission. I admired the great novels, his autobiographies and stories like 'Family Happiness' and 'The Death of Ivan Ilych', but didn't know then that Tolstoy had written a play. The play was produced with a very strong cast and it was well received.

Generally when a play is produced or a novel published it frees the writer from the material. This did not happen with *The Power of Darkness*. Over the years I kept returning to Tolstoy's melodrama. This was without any thought of production or publication. I had come to feel that the language I used was too idiomatic and colourful, and had skimmed over what was at the heart of the play. The title is a perfect description of that heart, and it was a moral climate I knew well from my own upbringing. Religious doctrine was used to enforce an abject conformity, and once self-interest came into play evil was easily dressed up as good.[1]

1. In the Introduction to the 1991 edition of the play, McGahern elaborated further on this: 'The old fear of famine was confused with terror of damnation. The confusion and guilt and plain ignorance that surrounded sex turned men and women into exploiters and adversaries. Amid all this, the sad lusting after respectability, sugar-coated with sanctimoniousness and held

When *Amongst Women* was published, I adapted sections of the novel for the BBC. They were read by the late Tony Doyle and produced by Pam Brighton. Brighton, who had worked as a theatre producer, asked if I had ever written a play. I showed her *The Power of Darkness*. By that time the play had gone through many reworkings and she felt that it had moved so far from the original that it was practically a new play. She sent it to the Abbey Theatre. Garry Hynes was the Artistic Director, and she decided to direct the play herself as the Abbey's contribution to the Dublin Theatre Festival.

During the previews the play went well, but it was met with such hostility by the first-night audience that the actors found it difficult to act. The Dublin reviews reflected the same hostility.

I didn't come into the Abbey until late the next evening, and was met by Mick Lally at the door.

'God, John, we thought you weren't turning up. Have you seen the reviews?'

'No,' I said. 'I suppose they were bad.'

'Oh, they were much worse than that,' Mick said.

'What are you worried about, so?'

'No matter what they say, that play is alive,' Mick said. 'Andy O'Mahony liked it at one of the previews and has a show going out at 7.30. A car is coming for you in half an hour. *That*'s why I was worried. Get in that car and go out to RTÉ and talk about sex and sin and death – and

---

together by a thin binding of religious doctrine and ceremony, combined to form a very dark and explosive force that, generally, went inwards and hid. For anybody who might imagine this to be a description of a remote and dark age, I refer them to the findings of the Kerry Babies Tribunal in 1985. It is in the nature of things that such a climate also creates the dramatic hope, or even necessity, of redemption.' See *The Power of Darkness* (London: Faber and Faber, 1991), p. vii.

especially Resurrection – to see if we can keep these swing doors open.' The car came and I went out to RTÉ.

I was leaving for America the next day and had visions of the actors playing to empty houses. It is not a pleasant feeling and one I was unused to. When a book is published there is not anything like the same sense of responsibility and public vulnerability. Luckily, this did not happen. The play and the production received good notices from outside critics covering the Theatre Festival. A controversy started and by the time the run ended the actors were playing to full houses.

I have rewritten the play for this production, and though it has moved far from its roots, I hope the truth first glimpsed through Tolstoy's genius is still dramatically present.

John McGahern, August 2005

Plot

When the play begins, Peter King, a landowner, is dying. His considerable wealth was earned by his hardness and shrewdness in breeding and trading horses, but he lives in much the same way as the poor farmers he comes from. He has a twenty-year-old daughter, Maggie, from his first marriage, and his second wife, Eileen, is half his age. He expects them to work like servants, and he does not allow his money to spread ease or comfort.

His illness forces him to take on a young workman, Paul, the son of poor farmers who owe him money. Paul has a history of living at home, doing casual labour and womanising. He is a potent mixture of good looks, sexual egotism, weakness and vanity. His mother Baby says that women seem to go for him like bees to honey. She is perfectly in tune with her circumstances. Her decent husband Oliver, Paul's father, is deeply religious, but he appears as slow-witted and ineffective as she is oily and worldly-wise. An old soldier, Paddy, who is fighting a losing battle with the drink, is lured into the drama, and gradually becomes its moral voice.

The Power of Darkness was first performed on stage at the Abbey Theatre, Dublin, on 16 October 1991. The cast was as follows:

PETER KING Mick Lally
EILEEN Bernadette Shortt
MAGGIE Aishling O'Sullivan
PAUL Sean McGinley
OLIVER Tony Rohr
BABY Marie Mullen
PADDY Alan Devlin

Directed by Garry Hynes

This revised version of the text was produced for RTÉ Radio 1, and first broadcast on 4 September 2005. The cast was as follows:

PETER KING Mick Lally
EILEEN Cathy Belton
MAGGIE Lisa Lambe
PAUL Tom Murphy
OLIVER Seán Kearns
BABY Marie Mullen
PADDY Stephen Rea

Produced by Kevin Reynolds

Characters

PETER KING
a rich farmer and horsedealer

EILEEN
his second wife

MAGGIE
his twenty-year-old daughter by his first wife

PAUL
their young workman

OLIVER
BABY
Paul's parents, poor smallholders

PADDY
an old soldier, casual labourer

Act One

A very large kitchen/living-room at the back of the house. The window and door to the right of the stage look on to a large yard and a row of stables and old granaries and outhouses. The front door and the front of the house are never used except on rare formal occasions. At the back of the stage is a long stairs. Maggie is reading a book beside the Aga.

Sounds of a stick pounding the floor of an upstairs room. Sounds of exasperation as the man pounding the floor gets out of bed and drags himself across the landing to the top of the stairs. Sounds of disturbed horses from the outside stalls.

PETER Can nobody hear the horses before they'll break the place down? (*Louder*) Is there anybody there? Is there anybody there at all?

MAGGIE (*standing up*) I'm here, Daddy. It's me, Maggie.

She closes her book and hides it beneath the chair cushion as soon as Peter appears on the stairs.

PETER Could you not hear? How could you sit there and not hear? I could have been dying for all you'd care.

Noise of agitated horses.

The young stallion must be loose. Can nobody hear? And if he breaks into the mares . . . Where's Paul? Where's that stepmother of yours? Is there nobody to do anything? If I wasn't so sick I'd soon bring this whole house back to its senses.

MAGGIE I don't know where Eileen is but Paul's out on the road.

PETER God, O God! It's enough to drive a man insane. What's he doing out on the road?

MAGGIE He's talking to people.

PETER Talking to people! He'd need someone after him night, noon and morning. Who's he talking to?

MAGGIE They came in a Morris Minor.

PETER They came in a Morris Minor! O God, O God, O God! Will you run quick and get him to see to the horses before the stallion breaks the place down. Listen.

Crying of horses.

And they can't even hear.

MAGGIE I'm going now, Daddy. (*Exits.*)

Peter slowly descends the remainder of the stairs and drags himself over to the window.

PETER God, O God, O God, give me patience. This whole place will soon be in wrack and ruin.

Eileen enters through the porch.

Where have you been till now, Eileen? Didn't you hear the racket? There's the stallion or one of the horses gone wild. Do you pay no heed to anything any more?

EILEEN How could I hear?

PETER How could you not hear?

EILEEN You can lay off that now. I was out counting the sheep. You were crabbing about the sheep yesterday, the horses today, the cattle no doubt tomorrow. I haven't four hands, or eyes in the back of my head.

PETER Paul should have heard the horses. We'll have to show Paul the road. He does nothing, pays no heed to anything.

EILEEN How will you get back that loan you gave them to buy the tractor when he wanted to go to England if you show him the road?

PETER His father will pay it back. Oliver, his father, is honest and decent.

EILEEN (*fiercely*) Where, then, will you get another workman? Workmen don't grow on the hedges any more.

PETER We'd be better off on our own. God, O God, did you ever see the like? Out on the road, talking to people, and the horses wild.

EILEEN The horses are quiet. (*They listen.*) Paul has seen to the horses. There's work for two men here. If you let Paul go you'll get nobody. And I'm not going to do your draggin' for you round the winter with you up in bed dishing out the orders like Lord Muc.

PETER We'd get plenty to work.

EILEEN Why did you go to such lengths to keep him when he was going to England?

PETER God forgive me, but it was the last thing I wanted. Who wanted him kept but yourself?

EILEEN (*in a rage*) I wasn't going to drag for you then and I'm not going to drag for you now. I'm not going to be dog and saddlehorse like your first poor wife.

PETER (*shocked, blesses himself*) May God give her rest. May God forgive you.

Maggie enters.

MAGGIE Paul has the stallion tied up, Daddy. He said there was no danger.

PETER What's he up to now?

MAGGIE He's gone back to his mother and father. It was them he was talking to out on the road. They came in the Morris Minor. (*In a mocking voice directed at Eileen*) He says they want him to go home and get married.

PETER Can anything be believed in this place any more? I better go and see what's happening for myself, though I'm hardly able to walk. (*Exits.*)

EILEEN (*recovering from the shock but even more enraged, shouting after Peter*) Get rid of him, then, when he's away already. Well, I'm not going to drag for you. Get that into your skull, my lord. I'm not going to be your saddlehorse for this winter or any other winter.

MAGGIE What are you shouting at Daddy for?

EILEEN Shut your stupid gob.

MAGGIE I know why you're shouting at Daddy. You'd never shout at Paul.

EILEEN What are you saying? I'll soon teach your mouth manners.

MAGGIE (*running out*) It's Paul you want to be married to. That's why you're shouting at Daddy.

Eileen lunges towards her but she has slipped away. Eileen stands in a state of extreme agitation.

EILEEN (*to herself*) She was gone before I could get my hand on her. One of these days she's going to go too far.

Paul enters the room stealthily. Eileen doesn't notice him at first.

PAUL Eileen. (*Slopes towards her.*) My father has come
with my mother. The old fella says I have to go home
and get married.

EILEEN Why aren't you away, then?

PAUL So that's the way it is now? You want to be rid
of me?

EILEEN I'm not going anywhere. It's you that's clearing
out. That's all. I'm just here, to be lifted up or put down
as you see fit.

PAUL Easy now, Eileen. That's not fair. You know that
I love you. I gave you my word. That can never change.
Even if he forces me to marry we can still be together.
I'd only be marrying for the old performance.

EILEEN Do you realise who you are talking to? Do you
think for a minute that I'd want your wife's leavings?

PAUL How can I go against them? How can I go against
my father?

EILEEN That's right. Throw it all over on your poor
father. Who's behind it all but yourself and your old
girlfriend? What did you tell her when she came like a
tramp to the house looking for you last week?

PAUL (*weakly*) I promised her nothing. I warned her
never to show her face round the place again.

EILEEN What brought your father here, then? Who
brought him here but that girlfriend of yours and
yourself? One thing I can tell you for certain is that your
poor mother didn't bring him here.

PAUL I swear that's not true. How could it be true?
Why would I be bringing him here?

EILEEN You're a grown man now. You'll have to get that into your head. A horse can be brought to the water but he can't be made to drink.

PAUL How can I go against my father?

EILEEN Tell him you won't marry her and let that be the end of it.

PAUL What if she says she's in the family way and that I'll have to marry her?

EILEEN Was it you put her that way, then?

PAUL There were others but now they are trying to peg it all over on me.

EILEEN Did you tell her you'd marry her?

PAUL (*affronted*) Tell her I'd marry her? I did in my bollocks. I may be cabbage-looking but I'm not that green.

EILEEN Then you've nothing to worry about.

PAUL If she says to my father I promised to marry her?

EILEEN Then she's telling it on her own. She's lying.

PAUL What if he believes her?

EILEEN The more fool him. You're not in short pants. Tell him she's lying. She'll not be the first to try to nail her man that way and she'll not be the last.

PAUL (*watching Eileen carefully and apprehensively*) I'd hate to go against my father. There was a fellow from Cloone who went against his father like that a few years back and he came to a terrible pass. I'd have no taste for that.

EILEEN What happened?

PAUL A tree he was cutting with his brother kicked.

A branch broke his back.

EILEEN Then stay away from trees.

PAUL They say you never have a day's luck once you go against your father.

EILEEN That's all auld raiméis.[1] I've made myself low as the dirt, and all for you, and don't you forget all we spoke of together. I'm telling you, if you leave me now I'll not be answerable for what I'll do.

PAUL If I'd wanted to leave I'd have gone that time to England. You know too well that I only stayed because of you. You know nothing kept me but you.

EILEEN (*changing tone*) Don't forget what I told you then, either. You can hear everything here in this house. It'll not be long now till you're the master of everything here.

PAUL No one wants to step into another's poor shoes. I'd never want to even think about that.

EILEEN But you'll not forget everything we spoke of together, either?

PAUL How could I forget you? I've never cared for anybody the way I care for you.

EILEEN (*embracing Paul passionately*) Nor I, either. I care so much that sometimes I get afraid.

The door opens. Baby enters, blesses herself. Paul and Eileen draw apart.

BABY What my eyes saw they didn't take in. What my ears heard they've already forgot. Well, I suppose people are only young once, but it might be as well to know,

1. Nonsense.

Sonny Boy, that your master is out there. He's out of his mind with looking for you.

PAUL I came in for a halter.

BABY I've noticed that those sort of halters are usually found close to good-looking women . . . No. Baby notices nothing.

PAUL Is it true that I have to get married, Mother?

BABY What would you want to go and take on a wife for, when you can hardly look after yourself? The whole thing is a figment of your old fella's ranting and raving. Now, run off with your halter and leave this whole business to cooler councils.

PAUL I can't understand what's going on.

BABY Then don't try to understand.

PAUL What am I to do, then?

BABY Don't you hear Peter calling you? Go out to Peter.

Paul exits, closing the door behind him.

EILEEN Can you tell me what's going on? Is he leaving or isn't he leaving?

BABY Arrah, what would he be leaving for? Isn't he all right and more than all right where he is? Am I right or wrong?

EILEEN I won't lie to you. I don't know how I'd be able to go on living here if Paul was to leave.

BABY Poor Peter, it's plain to the world, is on his last legs. You're a young woman, the best part of your life still ahead of you. What's happening is only healthy, and wouldn't I be a strange sort of mother to stand in her son's light?

EILEEN I don't care about anything as long as he doesn't have to leave.

BABY Then you don't have to worry your head, love. That's just the raving of yon old amadhaun[2] of mine. Once an idea gets set in his head, nothing short of a crowbar is fit to dislodge it.

EILEEN Who started it all, then?

BABY Well, our lad is sort of harmless like his father, and he's good-looking. The women seem to go for him like the bees to the honey. Who am I telling? You know a bit about it yourself, love. Before he came here he was working in town as one of the week-on, week-off fellas. They used to go into the American Bar. There was this girl working in the bar they were said to have got out of some orphanage run by the nuns. You know the sort.

EILEEN Was that Rosie?

BABY Rosie. Whether anything happened or not I wouldn't know. But anyhow that old amadhaun of mine got wind of something about the town. It wouldn't surprise me if it was all put around by herself. They all know how gullible my old boy is.

EILEEN She can't be let get away with it.

BABY Well, anyhow, my old boy got all in a tatter. 'He must marry the girl. He'll have to do right before God.' I tried to get him to see there might be more than one side to the story, but you might as well be trying to humour a jackass. Well, if the front door doesn't open, always try the back door, because you have no use going against the men once they get an idea. You must know it well yourself. You have to pretend to see it their way. 'Well,' I said, 'if that's the way it is he'll have to marry her; but first we'll

2. Fool

have to try to find out his side of the business.' So, love, here we are.

EILEEN What if he still orders Paul to marry her? Paul is still sort of in awe of his father, afeard to go against him in anything.

BABY Order, is it? Why the man wouldn't know how to order his breakfast. Baby only brought him here to get him turning in circles. There'll be no marrying. You can take it from me. Baby knows which side of her bread is buttered.

EILEEN Last week the same Rosie came here looking for him. You know, in some ways Paul is very soft.

BABY Softness is one thing. Marrying is another. The girl hasn't a thing to her name but the clothes she stands up in. Paul may be a bit soft but no son of Baby's is all that far astray.

EILEEN If Paul left I'd be finished. I couldn't live here now without him.

BABY Who are you talking to? Isn't it only natural? There was never much jizz in poor Peter the best day ever he was, and there must be a lot less now.

EILEEN The very sight of him makes me sick, and he's never done complaining.

BABY I know, love. They get that way. What I'm afraid of – and there's talk – that he might hand everything here over to that sister of his. We'd be all high and dry if that was to happen. I brought you these in case they might be needed. (*Looks around and whispers. She hands Eileen some pills.*) This will put him so sound asleep that the devil wouldn't wake him. And this – I don't like to say what it does – can put an end to poor people's troubles before they realise they have any. There is many a funeral that's followed by a fine wedding. I brought them just in case they are needed. The whole world can see the poor man is on his way out, anyhow.

EILEEN I'm not sure . . . I don't know . . . I'm beginning to be frightened.

BABY I brought them just in case. You can never think too far ahead in this world.

EILEEN It frightens me . . .

BABY Maybe if the man was blooming it'd be different. As it is, he's betwixt and between, neither in this world or the next. Sure, it's an everyday occurrence nowadays. Doctors give it as a kindness every day of the week, though they can't say that they do. They do it in these new hospices every day . . .

EILEEN I couldn't do it. I'd never bring myself . . .

BABY Just as you like, love. I'll take them back.

EILEEN Is that all there is to it? It's just like giving medicine?

BABY With a nice cup of tea, love.

EILEEN I'm not sure what I'm doing. I'm not sure if I should be even taking them in my hands.

BABY I promised the man some money.

EILEEN Here. Take the money.

She hands over money and goes to hide the drugs in a box.

BABY Now, love, don't let them out of your sight.

EILEEN Nobody will look in here, but later I'll put them in a safer place.

275

BABY That's the kind of talk I like to hear. But if by any misfortune they saw the light, all you have to say is that they're for dogs that go around killing sheep. Actually, they work very well on dogs.

The door opens.

PETER (*offstage*) Come in, Oliver, and take the weight off your feet.

Peter and Oliver enter.

Now, Oliver, there's no use beating round the bush. We'll have to get this straight once and for all.

OLIVER Well, you know, whatever is right – you know. All I want done is whatever is right. Eileen!

He takes his cap off to Eileen. She shakes his hand.

EILEEN Oliver, you're welcome.

PETER Sit down. We'll have to think this thing through. Do you want Paul to finish up here and go home and get married?

BABY I don't see what all this rush into marrying is about. If he leaves here and gets married what'll he live on at our place? As it is we haven't enough for ourselves.

PETER You have to decide that. You have to make up your own minds. I can't help you in any of that.

BABY What hurry is on him to marry? To listen to that man of mine here you'd think the world was coming to an end if he didn't marry.

PETER He could do worse than to marry. Marriage often gives a man a more serious outlook on life.

OLIVER It could be managed, you know. I've got a job in town.

BABY A plush job at that. In the bonemeal factory. You should get the whiff off him when he comes home. It'd make you throw up.

OLIVER It is a bit of a noseful, I admit. But it pays off, you know. Paul could do the shuffling round the house and I'd be bringing something in from the factory.

PETER You've decided that your son should leave here, then, and stay at home. That seems all right with me. There's just the matter of the loan. I'd expect that to be paid back if he was to leave.

OLIVER Of course, Peter King. It wouldn't be – you know – honest otherwise. All we'd ask is to be given some time.

PETER That's easily arranged. You'll not be rushed.

BABY We're jumping too far ahead. The marrying part hasn't been settled at all yet. If she was a girl of a family we knew, it'd be different. But how can we take her word for everything?

OLIVER You're blackening her now. She did no wrong. It was our son who did the wrong.

PETER What wrong did he do?

OLIVER Well, you know, you know, did with her what shouldn't be done.

BABY Will you whist for a minute, you auld amadhaun? It's little you know about women. She set her cap at him from the very beginning. Now she's saying that it was him led her up the garden path.

PETER If that's true it does him no credit either.

BABY But everything rests on her word up to now, a word nobody would take but that auld simpleton there. Doesn't the whole of the country except himself know that she was the next best thing to the town bicycle.

OLIVER There you are – you know – twisting, twisting
. . . wronging the girl, you know, blackening her.

BABY (*mimicking*) 'You know, you know, you know'
. . . You don't even know what part of Ireland you're
in. Don't take our word for it, Peter King. Go and ask
anybody from the town about the girls that work in the
American Bar and you'll soon get an earful. It's that kind
of bar. They pick them specially.

PETER Well, if that's the kind she is, maybe you should
be slower to rush into anything. Marriage is a serious
matter. It's easier to get into than to get out of.

OLIVER She's being blackened, I tell you. I know that
she's decent, and I feel sorry for her.

BABY Will you look at him? Isn't he an ornament?
Sorry for a one that'd chase after anything that moved
in britches and no care at all for his own son.

OLIVER I know what I say is right.

BABY That must be a great comfort to you, when the
whole world can see that you're talking through your
drainpipe.

OLIVER You can twist things in people's eyes but you
can't twist them in God's eyes.

BABY You might as well be talking to a jennet.

OLIVER She is a hardworking girl. She's young and –
you know – she has her health. We're not as young as
we were once. You know, you know – we're getting on.
We could do with a young pair of hands round the place.
But the main thing is that the wrong done to the girl
must be put right before God, all the more so because
she has neither father nor mother nor brother to fall
back on.

BABY It's plain that she had no trouble in pulling the wool over your eyes, you auld gulpin.

OLIVER Isn't she a human being the same as ourselves? Isn't she equal in God's eyes? There's no other way to look at it.

BABY Away on his rocking horse again.

PETER Take it easy. Now, Oliver, some of these girls aren't everything they make out to be either. What we should do is send for your son and ask him – straight out – what happened. He won't lie to his father.

BABY That's the first sensible words I heard today. We have no need of Paul at home. Any time there's a rush we can get Paddy, the old British soldier, for a day or two. Paddy will work for the price of a few drinks.

OLIVER Often, Peter King, we twist things to favour ourselves and refuse to take God into account. And what we think to be best for ourselves turns out to be the worst because we left God out.

PETER Of course we must include God. It wouldn't be right if religion was left out.

OLIVER If we leave God out of it everything sooner or later takes a turn for the worse no matter how well it seemed to favour ourselves in the beginning. If we do it God's way it may appear hard at the time but we're right in our minds – you see – you see – that's the main thing. We're happy. We're doing God's will. The lad should come home and marry the girl. I'll keep the job in the factory. We'll manage with the help of God. Other people do.

PETER That's enough. Go and get Paul. We'll put it to him straight.

Paul enters.

PAUL (*aggressively*) I was sent for?

PETER Where have you left your manners? Is that a way to address your father?

OLIVER It seems there's – you know – you know – a rumour going round about you, Paul.

PAUL What sort of rumour? The country is full of rumours.

OLIVER About – you know – yourself and Rosie, the orphan girl.

PAUL That's nothing new. There's always old gossip and rumours.

OLIVER Is it true or not true? You must tell the truth before God. Have you been – you know – you know – yes, fooling with the girl?

PAUL I haven't an idea of what you're getting at.

OLIVER Yes. Fooling with her, committing sin . . .

PAUL We all had a bit of fun with the girls. There was never anything serious.

PETER Don't try to slither. Give your father a straight answer.

OLIVER You can twist things before men but not before God. She's an orphan. She has no one to stand up for her. She has neither father nor brothers. There's all the more need to be straight and decent.

PAUL There's no slithering. I've told you nothing because there's nothing to tell. (*Getting excited*) Why didn't she say anything about Billy Molloy? Why has everything to be pegged over on me?

OLIVER Think before it's too late. A lie can't be hid from God.

PAUL There was nothing between us but a bit of fun. And may God strike me dead if I lie. (*Silence. Then still more excitedly*) Why are you trying to peg over everything on me when all the fellows had a bit of a fling?

BABY Do you see now? He'd believe everybody before his own son.

PETER It's all settled, then?

OLIVER Remember, if a man does wrong he may escape for a year or ten years. But sooner or later it catches up with him. God catches up with him. That poor girl – you know. What will she do with her child, and her all alone in the world.

PAUL That can't be thrown over on me.

BABY Once your auld fella gets an idea into his head it can't be got out. It's a waste of breath trying to say anything.

PETER (*to Oliver*) What do you say?

OLIVER He must do as he thinks right, but I only wish, I only wish . . .

BABY You only wish. You only wish. Paul will stay where he is. We haven't enough for ourselves at home.

PETER There's just one last thing. He's no use to me over the winter if he's not going to stay at least a year.

BABY Of course he can stay for the year – and more than the year. As we said, we can get Paddy who is beside us for a few days to do the little that has to be done round our place when the rush comes.

PETER He's stopping for the year, then?

OLIVER For the year, Peter King, but I don't know. I'm not easy.

BABY It's all settled. Signed, sealed and delivered from this very day. I know he'll be treated decently.

PETER If that is all settled I'll see you out as far as the road. Paul, I want you to check those horses. If they were seen to properly in the first place they'd not be going wild like they were a few hours ago. As it is they'll be unsettled now for days.

Everyone exits but Paul. Maggie enters.

PAUL (*to himself*) He'd have you working till you drop. The rest would have you turning in circles till you wouldn't know whether you were coming or going.

MAGGIE (*startled at finding Paul alone*) You might at least have lit the lamp, Paul. It's got very dark in here.

PAUL I don't need any lamp to admire you, Maggie.

MAGGIE Go off with yourself. I won't fall for that old guff. And there's another poor woman looking for you. This place is getting as bad as O'Connell Street with the amount of people looking for you.

PAUL Who is it?

MAGGIE The same girl that was here looking for you last week.

PAUL You're coddin' me, Maggie.

MAGGIE Go out and see for yourself, then.

PAUL What does she want?

MAGGIE She wouldn't tell. She asked me if it was true that you were leaving to be married. I told her I didn't know. You better go out to her. She said she'll not leave till she finds out.

PAUL Did they see her on the way out to the car?

MAGGIE No. They didn't see. She's waiting for you down by the stable.

PAUL Why should I go out to her?

MAGGIE She said she'll come in if you don't. (*Laughing, embarrassed*) She was asking me if they were trying to make a match between Paul and Maggie. The poor thing didn't know I was Maggie. She is all upset.

PAUL What would you say to that, Maggie?

MAGGIE Say to what?

PAUL Say to marrying me.

MAGGIE I'd do no such thing.

PAUL Why not?

MAGGIE Because you'd not be let. (*Laughs.*)

PAUL Who's to stop me?

MAGGIE You'd not be let. Eileen wouldn't let you. Your eyes would be tore out of your head if you tried. You'd get what poor Daddy's getting now.

PAUL I better go out to her. I'll soon give her the road. You'd think she'd have got the message by now.

MAGGIE Be nice to her, Paul. She's in trouble.

PAUL I'm going to tell her to clear out with her bag and baggage and never to darken this place again. A stop has to be put to this fooling.

MAGGIE You're nothing but an animal, Paul.

PAUL She has to be shown the door. I'll soon give her the message. Why has she to come and pick on me?

MAGGIE Isn't she a girl the same as I'm a girl? That's what you'd do to me if you got the chance. I shouldn't have compared you to an animal. People like you are far worse than animals. (*Exits.*)

PAUL Once a man gets mixed up with women he never knows whether he's coming or going. He'd be far better to go out into the fields and eat grass with the horses. I better go out and see her. God, when these women come a-bulling you'd think there wasn't a fence up anywhere in the country.

Act Two

The same scene, some months later. Eileen is cooking and washing. A hard knocking comes from upstairs. She looks towards the ceiling in exasperation.

EILEEN He never lets up. You'd need a whole army to dance attendance on the man. (*Demanding knocking continues.*) He'd want you to be ten places at once.

Maggie comes quickly down the stairs with her coat on.

Were you upstairs all this time? Beautifying yourself again? Where are you away to now?

MAGGIE (*resentfully*) I was with Daddy.

EILEEN What does the man want? He's knocking again. Did he not tell you what he wants?

MAGGIE It must be you he wants. He told me to go to Aunt Martha's and not to waste a minute.

EILEEN (*frightened*) What does he want with Aunt Martha?

MAGGIE He wants her to come here. (*Starts to sob.*) He says he's on the way out.

EILEEN I'll see what he wants but you stay here. Make sure those pots don't boil over.

MAGGIE (*aggressively*) He told me to go and not waste a minute.

EILEEN I'll see what he wants, but you better be here when I come down.

Eileen goes upstairs. She is not long. Returns very slowly.

He's not well. I'm going myself to Aunt Martha's.

MAGGIE He told me to go.

EILEEN I'm telling you different. I'm going to Aunt Martha's and I want you to go and get Paul. Tell him he's needed in the house. Tell him to hurry.

MAGGIE I don't know where Paul is. Daddy told me not to waste a second getting to Aunt Martha's.

EILEEN (*very slowly and fiercely*) Paul is out in the fields. He's working the tractor. You'll be able to find him by the noise of the tractor. Tell him I want him this minute.

MAGGIE I was told to go for Martha.

EILEEN Go before I have to tell you twice. Go!

Maggie exits reluctantly. Long pause after she leaves. Eileen has bought time by this stratagem but she is desperate and at a loss for what to do next. Her relief is palpable when Baby enters.

EILEEN Baby! God must have sent you. You didn't come a minute too soon.

BABY What's wrong, love? You don't look well at all.

EILEEN I'm nearly demented.

BABY Poor Peter is still holding on, I suppose.

EILEEN Still holding out and I don't know which way to turn. I can feel them beating all around. I'd be better off in Portlaoise. He's just tried to send for Aunt Martha.

BABY What could he want Martha for?

EILEEN He feels he's going. I fear he wants to hand the money . . . and the whole place over to her.

BABY (*quickly*) The money is still in the house, then?

EILEEN Peter never trusted banks. He always said the taxman had a habit of peeping into banks. He keeps it in the safe upstairs. You'd need six men to move that safe.

BABY Where is the key kept?

EILEEN Round his neck, but you'd want the combination. The key is no good without the combination.

BABY What, love, is the combination? Forgive ignorance, love.

EILEEN Numbers you need to open the lock with. They're kept on a slip in his wallet.

BABY I'm afraid combinations came after poor Baby's day, but where is the wallet?

EILEEN It's either on him or it's hid. I don't know what way to turn.

BABY Has Peter as much as they say? They say he's a millionaire.

EILEEN He made a lot of money with the horses. They say he was the best judge of a horse for several counties around, and he never spent.

BABY Listen, girl. I've come to the conclusion that if you don't shift yourself quick you'll wind up with nothing in the heel of the hunt, after wasting the best years of your young life on the man.

EILEEN I don't know what way to turn. Paul is no use. He's frightened. You can't talk to him.

BABY Never mind about Paul. If you let this chance slip

you're done for. You'll have to brighten yourself if you don't want to be out on the road. Has he had the priest and all that?

EILEEN The poor priest has a pass beaten to the place. He anointed him yesterday for the fourth time. You know how funny poor Father Young is. He said when he came down the stairs yesterday that Peter has enough oil on him now to float a battleship.

BABY It's good the priest was here that many times. Everything should be seen to be done by the book.

EILEEN We thought he was going yesterday. We even started the Rosary.

BABY Where has Paul been during all this?

EILEEN Paul is like a child. He's no use. He's out on the tractor. I sent Maggie for him just before you came. She'll have her work cut out to get him to the house but it's better than her going for Martha. I'll get you a quick cup of tea first. You must be parched. It's a sight for sore eyes to have you at hand. I didn't know what way to turn when you came in the door.

BABY I'd love a hot cup of tea. (*Sitting down.*) Did you hear about the wedding we had back our way?

EILEEN No. What wedding?

BABY This will be music to your ears, anyhow. Old Ritchie Coyne married the Rosie that had Paul tormented. At least that's one bit of baggage out of our way. She was damaged goods of course, but it appears Ritchie doesn't mind that. Years back there was an old fellow like Ritchie living beside us, who married a girl with a limp. He said he didn't mind the limp, since he didn't marry her for jumping ditches.

EILEEN Ritchie's old, isn't he? I suppose he has money.

BABY It's a comfortable enough place, but there's four children there already and with his appearance who else would have him, place or no place?

EILEEN It seems it turned out lucky for everybody, then?

BABY And it shut up my old gander as well. He had my head light about the poor girl that had neither father nor mother. You could never get it into his skull that it's the breed of them. Anyhow, that bit is all settled now. (*In a whisper*) Have you tried him with any of the medicines I gave you?

EILEEN I wasn't able. I gave him the white pills once and he was like a sheet afterwards.

BABY They have no strength at all. How many did you give?

EILEEN Two. In tea.

BABY You might as well be giving him cod-liver oil. Did he remark on the taste?

EILEEN He said it had a bitter taste. I had to tell him how when you're sick everything tastes bitter. (*Hysterically*) I don't know why you gave me those things at all. I've hardly slept since I got them.

BABY Now don't go blaming anything over on Baby. You took them of your own free will. If anything were to go wrong Baby would never have heard tell of them. But, not to change the subject, I heard people talking about you the other day. They were remarking how Peter could go and leave you out on the road after sucking your young life dry. I heard people say it would be hard to blame you no matter what you tried. They all know how hard Peter is.

EILEEN Sometimes I feel so surrounded that I could do away with myself. I feel them beating around the place.

BABY I know, love. But we haven't much time. We have to find the money. Then we'll give him a nice drink of tea. The poor thing will be off like a bird.

EILEEN I'm afraid. Isn't it better that he be let go natural?

BABY (*viciously*) What's natural? Is it natural that he's trying to bring his sister in over his lawful wife before turning you out on the road?

EILEEN I don't know. I don't know how we got into this.

BABY If you don't shift soon you'll find yourself out on the road and his sister will be cracking the whip.

EILEEN I'd still have my rights as his wife.

BABY If he gives her charge of the money you'll find your rights won't be much use.

EILEEN (*panicking*) I better go for Martha before he starts knocking again. She'd be here already if Maggie had gone.

BABY Are you out of your mind? Here. Do what I tell you. Put on the kettle. We'll give him a nice cup of tea and tell him that Martha is on her way.

EILEEN Suppose anything would happen?

BABY There's no time for supposing. Just do what I tell you. Put on that kettle.

EILEEN (*in awe and fear*) I'll put on the kettle.

BABY That's more like it. (*In a whisper*) Don't say a word about this to Paul. He's useless like that. He'd get all in a tizzy. He's more like his auld father in some ways than you'd ever think.

*Eileen stops in terror as Peter starts descending the
stairs. His steps are slow and stumbling, as if he could
fall. Baby retreats into the shadows of the room so
that she can observe. Peter is too ill to notice her.*

EILEEN What on earth brought you down? You could
kill yourself on the stairs.

PETER Did you not hear me knocking? Is there no way
to make you hear? I might as well be dead up there for
all anybody cares.

EILEEN Don't you know you're not fit to come down?
Now we'll have to get you back up.

PETER What could I do but come down when nobody
would answer. Did Maggie get back from Martha's yet?

EILEEN She didn't go yet. I told her I'd go myself.

PETER I warned her to go at once. Where is she now?

EILEEN I sent her out to get Paul. You're not fit to be
here on your own and when she gets Paul I'm going for
Aunt Martha myself. Maggie isn't fit to go all that way
on her own.

PETER She's more fit than what's left round here.
There's no heed passed on me no more than a dog, no
heed passed on my daughter either. I want my daughter
to go. I want her to go this minute.

EILEEN Of course I'm not trusted to go. I'm just the
skivvy round here.

*During the argument Baby stands in the shadows,
a silent and sinister figure, unnoticed by Peter. Peter
slumps into a chair.*

BABY (*whispering*) Take care would you let Maggie go!
We haven't a minute. See if that wallet is above in the
room. If it's on him we don't have to worry.

PETER Who's that I hear?

EILEEN Paul's mother has just got here.

As Baby shifts to engage Peter, Eileen climbs the stairs.

BABY I just came over to see Paul and to see how things are getting along. I'm sorry to hear you're not well.

PETER Paul's mother. You're welcome. I'm afraid Paul has got out of hand.

BABY I'll give Paul a bit of my mind, then, to see he does everything you want. My husband asked to be remembered to you. You've been always good to us.

PETER I'm afraid I'm finished.

BABY There's no use talking like that. Worse than you have got better.

PETER No. I can feel myself going.

BABY Well, even if it's true, everything is well taken care of. You've had the priest. You're leaving a fine family behind. They'll be comfortable. Paul will help them to manage for a while.

PETER There's no one to manage. They're all wild with foolishness. I know all about it. Everything I've worked for will soon be scattered.

BABY You're still the master. Can't you leave clear orders behind?

PETER (*distracted*) Has Maggie gone for Martha yet?

BABY She'll go the minute she gets back.

PETER Martha should have been here by now. Where's Eileen gone to?

BABY She went upstairs for something. You can hear her. She's on her way back down.

Eileen comes down the stairs.

EILEEN (*whispers to Baby*) I have the wallet.

BABY Keep it out of sight. (*To Peter*) Peter, you'll have a drink of something. It'll give you strength.

PETER I'm not sure I'm able to take anything.

BABY If you don't take something your poor strength will soon go. Anybody can take tea.

PETER I'll try the tea, then. Has Martha come yet?

BABY She'll be sent for in a minute.

PETER I'm finished. Everything I worked for will be scattered.

BABY There was a man up our way who thought he was done for and he mended in a matter of days. There's no use in that kind of talk.

PETER No. I'm going. I know it.

BABY I'll get you a nice drink of hot tea with lemons and sugar. Are there any lemons?

EILEEN They are on the dresser.

Paul enters. He doesn't see Peter.

PAUL So you are here, Mother? Is everything all right at home?

BABY Well enough, thank God. We've our health.

PAUL How did you find the man here?

BABY Can you not see your poor master? (*She points to*

Peter.) Have you no word for him?

PAUL Are you feeling any better, Peter?

Either Peter doesn't hear or doesn't answer.

EILEEN Where's Maggie?

PAUL She's gone for her Aunt Martha. She said her father told her to go.

PETER (*finding the energy to be peremptory*) Is that you, Paul? I want you a minute.

Eileen and Baby whisper together.

How is it you're in the house at this time of day?

PAUL Eileen sent Maggie out for me.

EILEEN I told him that already.

PETER Isn't Maggie gone for Martha?

PAUL She's gone now. She went after telling me I was wanted.

PETER Who wanted you in the house?

EILEEN I wanted him. I couldn't be here on my own with the state you're in.

PETER It took her all that length to get away. You can trust nobody. What's going to happen to everything? What's going to happen?

BABY Seeing you're here, Paul, why don't you help Peter over to the big chair by the table where he'll be more comfortable.

Paul helps Peter to his feet.

PAUL I'll carry him over. The poor thing is as light as a feather.

PETER Paul!

PAUL What is it now? (*As if expecting another rebuke; but he is taken aback by the uncharacteristic tone.*)

PETER I may never have a chance to speak to you again. I feel I'm going. I want to ask your forgiveness for any wrong I've ever done you. I've said many a hard word to you in my time. Forgive me before I go.

PAUL What's there to forgive? I'm in need of forgiveness myself.

BABY Have you no heart, son? Your poor master is asking your forgiveness.

PAUL Of course I forgive, but there's nothing to forgive.

PETER For the love of God, forgive me.

PAUL (*emotionally, sentimentally*) God will forgive you. You've never done me any wrong. It's me that should be asking your forgiveness.

Peter is set down by the table. Eileen makes his drink.

BABY (*to Peter*) We have your drink almost ready. You'll start to feel better as soon as you have the drink. (*To Eileen*) Here's the tablets. (*She pushes them into Eileen's hand. Eileen cowers away.*) Put them in the drink. Stir them well.

EILEEN I can't. I'm not able. I don't know what I'm doing.

BABY Steady yourself, woman. (*Hisses*) Put them in the drink. Stir them with the spoon. We've no time. If Martha gets here we're done for.

Trembling and shaking, Eileen drops in the tablets. They stir the cup and give him the drink. Eileen takes the drink to Peter, who is too ill to notice her extreme agitation. She stands in a horror of fascination, watching Peter drink.

EILEEN Does it taste all right?

PETER It tastes sort of bitter.

EILEEN That must be the lemon.

BABY It needs more sugar. We must have forgot the sugar. (*She gets the sugar, puts it in the drink and stirs it vigorously.*) It'll taste better now. That'll make a new man of you.

PETER (*tries to speak*) For the love of God . . .

He collapses in the chair.

BABY The poor thing is gone. Isn't he far better off than the way he was? In the end the poor thing went away like a bird. (*She feels round his neck for the key.*) The key is not in the wallet. It's here around his neck. Get a scissors. Quick!

Eileen hands Baby the scissors and she cuts the string round Peter's neck.

There's the key.

PAUL (*begins to cry*) The poor man asked for my forgiveness when it is me that should be asking for his. He trusted me in his house. (*Staring in recrimination at Eileen.*) He trusted me in his house and look how we paid him back.

BABY Enough of that old stuff. We'll need your help.

EILEEN I can't move, I'm that afraid.

BABY If you don't move soon you'll have the whole of your life to think about moving.

EILEEN What can we do?

BABY Take the key. You have his wallet. Open the safe.

Get the money. Give the money to Paul. Paul will hide the money.

EILEEN I'm frightened.

BABY You've no time to be afraid.

PAUL I don't want any poor man's money.

BABY Hurry. Both of you. He was going to put both of you out on the road and you'll be still out on the road if you don't hurry. That was a quare kind of forgiveness. I'll stay here in case Martha or Maggie comes back. Hurry. We haven't a minute to lose.

Eileen and Paul climb the stairs. Baby remains with Peter, watching the door like a hawk. Upstairs, there is the noise of them trying to open the safe.

(*Calling up the stairs.*) What's keeping you? We haven't all day.

EILEEN I'm coming.

They come down the stairs. Eileen is carrying a cloth bag.

BABY You got it open?

EILEEN I thought it would never open, and then it opened all of a sudden.

BABY You have all the money?

EILEEN All that was there.

BABY Did you lock the safe again?

EILEEN No. We didn't think.

BABY For the love of God, woman, will you go back and lock it quick. Give Paul the money. Paul will stay here with the money. (*Eileen hands the money fearfully*

297

to Paul and goes back up the stairs.) Well, Paul, we'll have to watch out for your end of it now.

PAUL How – my end of it?

BABY The way you're to live.

PAUL I got by up to now, didn't I?

BABY Well, if you did, it was poorly. Now you've a chance to be somebody in the world.

PAUL I don't know what you're getting at.

BABY Oh, I'm only looking to your future and hoping that when the good times come you won't forget your old mother.

PAUL What's that got to do with anything?

BABY Don't think to pull the wool over your poor mother's eyes. I see what's going on. First, you have to go and hide that money so that nobody but yourself knows where it is hid. You are up to your neck in this, Sonny, whether you like it or not. I saw all that was going on.

PAUL The money isn't mine. It's no business of mine.

BABY Sometimes you can be as dim as your auld father, but if you breathe a word of this to anyone you're a goner. Even you know enough to know that.

PAUL I don't know what's going on. You women have me that I don't know whether I'm coming or going. What has the money to do with me?

BABY Women, you know, are very changeable. Once you have the money, the whip is in your hands. Do you get me now? You've had your fun here. Now you have to shake yourself.

PAUL You women would drive a man out of his mind. The poor man is dead. I can't even ask his forgiveness now.

Pale and distraught, Eileen comes down the stairs.

EILEEN (*wearily*) It's locked. (*She moves to give Baby the key.*) It's your key now.

BABY Baby wouldn't want anything like that to be found on her. Keep it or lose it. What use is it now?

EILEEN I'm going like a leaf. I better go with Paul and put the money safe.

BABY (*seizing her by the arm*) Are you out of your mind? Don't you know you'll be missed? Maggie will be here any minute. (*To Paul*) Are you paralysed or what? Are you a man or a mouse?

PAUL I'll hide it. I know places where an army wouldn't find it. I'm not as slow as you think.

EILEEN Where'll you hide it?

PAUL (*suddenly smiling*) What are you worried about, Eileen? I know how to make it safe.

EILEEN I'm shaking like a leaf.

PAUL (*his old jaunty, seductive self*) There's no need to be afraid. I'll hide it where an army wouldn't find it. (*Exits.*)

EILEEN (*Left alone with Baby, turns towards Peter*) He's gone. There's not a breath. What'll I do now? There's not a stir.

BABY Take it easy, love. Wasn't it a release for the poor creature? When you come to think about it, wasn't it a release for yourself, a release for everybody?

EILEEN (*shaking*) We'll have to get someone in to lay him out. What will they notice? I think we are all going to be lost.

BABY No need to send for anybody. Many's the poor body Baby has laid out. There should even be some warm water left in the kettle. No need to send outside for anybody. We'll keep it all well and safe within the house.

Maggie enters. She doesn't notice anything at first.

MAGGIE Aunt Martha was in town but I left word and she'll be over the minute she gets back.

BABY It's too late now, love. Your poor father, God rest him, is gone.

For a moment Maggie is stone-silent, and then she rushes towards Peter in a frenzy of grief.

MAGGIE What have they done to you, Father? Father, what have you done to yourself? What have they done to you?

Act Three

The same room. Winter. Heavy rain and wind outside. Nine months have passed since Act Two. Pots are cooking on the stove. Eileen is sewing. The door opens. Paddy enters.

EILEEN It's you, Paddy. I thought it might be Paul.

PADDY Only me and famished. Paul hasn't come home yet?

EILEEN I don't know what's keeping him. His father is expected this evening. It'd be a nice pass if he wasn't here when his father arrives, but even that would appear to be no bother to him nowadays.

PADDY (*laughing*) No bother in the world. Paul is letting the washers fly. He's living royal. He doesn't have to care. Paddy is here to do the work.

EILEEN (*sharply*) Have you all done outside?

PADDY Everything is done and not done by half either. The horses are all watered and fed. So is the cattle. The houses are all cleaned out and bedded.

EILEEN Paul should be doing that work. Peter had no need of a man till he got old.

PADDY Why did you marry Paul? That's when you made your big mistake. If you hadn't to marry him he'd have had to work. Never throw a dog a bone. (*Laughs.*) Hold bone in mouth and dog will follow.

EILEEN (*looks directly up*) I'm afraid I'm beginning to think it was a mistake, Paddy. Yet I loved him. I'm afraid I love him still.

PADDY Love! Love, is it? Love flies out the window. Marriage should be the eye-opener. I came home after I married and found my old dosey in bed with two men and she was that drunk she didn't know which bed she was in or who were the men.

EILEEN It'd be easy if love went away. All I know is that things can't go on much longer the way they are going.

PADDY I'd soon call a halt if I were in your shoes. Paul knows nothing about horses, and the horsey crowd have him in the palm of their hands. There's no worse crowd to get in with. Paul thinks it's great to be the master of a place that has the name of horses. Peter, God rest him, knew his horses and he was hard. He needed to be hard. Those horsey crowd would take the eyes out of your head and tell you you could see better without them. (*Laughs.*) Was it a fortnight ago that Paul came home in that hound's-tooth jacket with the silk hankie stuck in his pocket? (*Laughs.*) You should definitely call a halt before it is all too late.

EILEEN There's many a thing I feel like doing. But then I find I can do nothing. You don't know what I've been through, Paddy. It's only nine months since Peter went but it feels like years already.

PADDY It's you that has the dry hay – the money. You can always call a halt if you have the washers. People can't go far without the washers. That's what I'd do if I were in your shoes.

Silence. Paddy is waiting for Eileen to speak, but when she remains silent he says:

What brought Paul to town this time?

EILEEN He said he had to get money out of the bank for his father. If it wasn't that excuse it'd be some other. Nowadays he seems to live in the town.

PADDY Did Maggie go with him?

EILEEN Does he go anywhere without her? Doesn't he always take her to the town? (*Partly to herself*) You'd think I didn't exist. That's the love he shows now.

PADDY I heard some talk about buying a white dress. Is Maggie going to be married? If she was married and safe that'd be one thing less on your mind.

EILEEN (*with feeling*) I wish she was. If she's not married soon it will be too late.

PADDY Wasn't there a marriage arranged?

EILEEN There was but it fell through. They smelled a rat. People are no fools.

PADDY Oh, there could be a rat in that stack, all right. That's the kind of a rat that (*mimics a baby's cry*) when it comes out of the stack, could be awkward.

EILEEN She's saying now that her father wanted her to have the place and be married to Paul. She acts as if she owns the place. And if I as much as open my mouth they're both down my throat.

PADDY If I was you I'd call a halt. I'd call in the washers.

EILEEN I can't even do that. All that's keeping me going is that there is a marriage nearly arranged now with young Mikey Coyne. His old uncle married Rosie, the girl that worked in the bar that used to come here after Paul.

PADDY I knew Rosie well. I was often in the American Bar, but I'm afraid there's not much I remember. (*Laughs.*)

I used often have to inquire in the mornings if I was in myself the day before. Most times they used tell me I was.

EILEEN If we could get Maggie married, then life might get back to normal here. But neither of them seems to be in any rush. They haven't got enough of their cake yet.

PADDY I'm surprised you put up with it in the first place.

EILEEN I had no idea. I loved Paul. I thought he cared for me as well. They fairly pulled the wool over my eyes. They only started to come right out in the open in the last few weeks. I can't sleep at night. There are times I can't stop my hands shaking. (*Listening.*) Shish, I hear somebody outside. That must be them back. Don't mention a word of what was said.

PADDY I'll hop into the scullery here till I see what way the wind is blowing. (*Exits.*)

EILEEN On your life, don't go too far. If he turns out to be wild with drink, come back in at once.

A knock on the door. Oliver enters.

OLIVER God bless everybody here. Are you all well?

EILEEN We were expecting you, Oliver, but we thought you mightn't come because of the terrible night.

OLIVER There's the car, you know; it's like an old tent. When you have a thing on your mind, you might as well – how is it put? – get it over with. That's it, get it over with. Do it there and then. So it's me that's here. Here I am. Is Paul at home?

EILEEN He went to get money from the bank in town. He should be home any minute. We've been expecting him for the past hour. We thought it was Paul when we heard your knock.

OLIVER Our old tedder would have done another year or, you know, two, but nothing would do Paul but we get a new second-hand tedder. It'll be paid back, you know. We wouldn't want anything, you know, for nothing.

EILEEN You needn't worry. Paul will have it for you when he comes in. I'll leave it between the two of you. Now. You must be starving. You'll eat something. We were waiting for Paul. But you can eat something with Paddy. He's just slipped outside for something.

Paddy enters. Oliver is very startled to see him.

PADDY You're welcome here, Oliver.

OLIVER Good Lord, Paddy. You're the last person, you know, I was expecting to find here. We were going to look to see if you'd give us a few days next week.

PADDY I'm sort of surprised myself to be here, Oliver.

OLIVER What, you know, are you doing here now?

PADDY I'm working for your son. I'm more or less permanent here now.

OLIVER You're working for Paul, here?

PADDY I was working, as you know, in that last place but I fell by the wayside and they gave me the road. I ran into Paul in the town and he took me on. I'm permanent here ever since.

OLIVER Has Paul gone in for a new line of, you know, you know, business, that he has the need of a man?

EILEEN (*unable to contain herself*) He has plenty of business all right, spending money like water. He's never out of the town. He pays Paddy to do the work for him here.

PADDY Seeing that he has it, he might as well give it air. (*Laughing*) Money doesn't exist if it doesn't go round.

OLIVER That's not right. Too much money destroys everything in sight. It harms a man. You know – they think they're enjoying themselves when it's bringing them – you know – nothing but harm.

EILEEN You have no idea to what lengths it has gone. Everything is being let fly round here, from morning to night now. It's all one big spree.

OLIVER Money is – you know – the ruination of the world.

PADDY I know all about it. When I had money myself I was that polluted for weeks that I didn't know me own name. But now that the money is gone I've turned over a new leaf. The lack of funds is a great man for putting an end to the spree.

OLIVER And where, might I ask, is your good woman?

PADDY Good woman for sure, disappeared into nature. I have to admit I didn't search under too many bushes.

OLIVER How can you both let that happen? You both, you know, are married.

PADDY What else would you expect? An old soldier's wife for it! What do you expect from a mule but a kick?

OLIVER It all sounds – how can I say – a bit through other. It's not, you know, right.

Silence. Eileen sets the table.

EILEEN You should draw up to the table. Everything is near ready.

OLIVER Had Paul something to sell in town?

EILEEN No. He just has to get money out of the bank. Pull up to the table or your food will be cold.

They all sit down to supper.

OLIVER I hope Paul wasn't going to the town to get money for me.

EILEEN He's always in the town. The money was just an excuse to get to the town. (*Tidying up as the men continue their meal.*) If only his father would talk to him. He might get some sense. His father though is too good for this world. And the world thinks him a fool.

OLIVER Did you say something?

EILEEN No, nothing. Nothing at all.

OLIVER I thought – you know – I heard you say something.

EILEEN No. Nothing. (*She starts to wash up as the men finish their meal.*) By the way, did you hear any news of Rosie – the girl who used to work in the American Bar – since she got married?

OLIVER Yes, now that you mention it. I heard the women say something.

EILEEN Did they say how she's doing?

OLIVER She's doing all right. You know – she's a good girl. She works hard and the husband is a good steady old fellow.

EILEEN Do you know anything about a nephew of her husband's – a Mikey Coyne? There's talk of him and our Maggie. The match is more or less made.

OLIVER I might have heard talk but I didn't heed it, you know.

EILEEN We'd like to see Maggie settled. There's never enough room for two women in any one house. There might be more peace here if we were on our own.

OLIVER It's good, you know, to be settled, but she's plenty of time. She'll be married long enough. She's young. She has plenty of time.

EILEEN (*barely able to contain herself*) She has a few days. That's the length I'd put on it. A week at the very most.

PADDY (*who has been absorbed in eating*) Pay them no heed. Let that whack away. That meal was just beautiful, Eileen.

EILEEN You'd think he'd be here to meet his father. He didn't need the whole day in town. You'd think he'd be at least back by now.

Paul enters. He is overdressed, in a pantomime of a horsey gentleman. In spite of his good looks the general effect is garish and ridiculous.

PAUL Do you know who has come home? (*Eileen looks up from clearing the table in silence.*) Have you forgotten me that quick, Eileen? Do you know who has come home?

EILEEN Will you quit your cod-acting. In that get-up anybody would think you had escaped from a circus.

PAUL (*very severely*) Who has come home?

EILEEN Who else but yourself has come home? Will you come in and shut the door and don't be giving us our death. You're late as it is.

PAUL You must say: 'The master has come home.'

EILEEN Are you imagining you're Master Wrynn now?

A fine schoolteacher you'd make! An example to all and sundry. Don't you see who's here?

PAUL (*observing Oliver for the first time*) I'm not ashamed of my father. I'm proud of my father. (*Bows.*) How do you do, Father.

OLIVER Drunk. It's a disgrace before God.

PAUL Yes. I have to admit I had a glass or two. I met a friend, a most learned man.

EILEEN Can't you go and lie down?

PAUL Say: 'The master has come home.'

EILEEN Can't you go and lie down?

PAUL First, I'm going to have a civilised cup of tea with my father. So put on the kettle. Where's Maggie?

Maggie enters, fashionably dressed, carrying an armful of parcels.

Oh, she's here as well. Maggie! Come on over here to the light, Maggie, so that they can see you. Isn't she a knockout?

MAGGIE Everything was scattered about the back of the car. I couldn't find the red thread.

PAUL Oh, the thread is all right. Paddy will find it. I'd be most obliged to you, Paddy. As you can see, I'm a trifle un-cappassitated. I got a few bags of nuts for the horses from the creamery. We are a bit short till the lorry comes round. When you take out the bags, Paddy, will you throw your eye around for the thread?

OLIVER It's a disgrace. To put an old man out in the rain to lift hundredweights of nuts from the back of a car when you know you're far fitter to do it yourself. You're young, you know; poor Paddy is old.

PADDY (*rising*) That's form for the course round here. You sit back when you're young. You have to work till you drop when you're old. (*Exits.*)

PAUL Don't worry your head about Paddy. He'd do anything for those horses. He even sleeps with them. He's fonder of those horses than of any Christian. Nonetheless he's a gentleman.

EILEEN Do you want tea?

PAUL Yes. I intend to partake of a civilised cup of tea with my father. (*He turns to Maggie*) Have you all the parcels?

MAGGIE Except the thread – and this – this isn't mine. (*Puts it down angrily.*) There it is on the table, whoever it's for.

EILEEN He's gone and bought her more finery. Is there going to be any end to this?

PAUL (*trying to appear sober*) I've had a glass or two but I can hold it. That's the test of a man. You see, I remembered too about our old tedder at home. I got the money out of the bank to buy that new second-hand tedder.

OLIVER You're drunk. You don't know what you're saying or what you're doing.

PAUL I may appear somewhat intoxicated but I'm sober enough in my mind. I can settle the matter of the tedder right off.

OLIVER This is a disgrace – you know – a pure disgrace.

PAUL Here's the money. I'm not a son that'd see his father short. Take it. There's lots more where that came from.

OLIVER No. No. I can't take it.

PAUL (*seizes Oliver's hand*) Take it. You'll have to take it.

OLIVER I can't take it. You don't know what you're doing.

PAUL Take it. I'll not let you go till you take it.

EILEEN You better take the money. He'll give you no peace till you do take it.

OLIVER (*takes it shaking his head*) This isn't right. No good can come of it. It can bring no luck. It couldn't be – you know – lucky.

PAUL If you feel easier paying it back, then pay it back but I'll never ask you for the money. I'd never ask my father for money. Why don't you show us the presents, Maggie?

MAGGIE What's the use? I've already put them away.

PAUL Eileen here would love to see the new dress.

OLIVER This is a foolishness beyond words, you know, and trumpery.

Maggie unpacks and displays the dress.

MAGGIE I don't see the use of showing them here. It's silk and you can see the Chinese print. A fat lot they'd know around here about China.

EILEEN (*in a terrible rage*) Take your rubbish off my table or I'll soon clear the table.

PAUL Don't be jealous, Eileen. (*Laughing. Hiccups.*) Play cool.

EILEEN What are you ravelling about?

Sweeps the dress off the table.

MAGGIE (*picking up the dress*) You can throw your own things around if you want but keep your paws off mine.

EILEEN The table is for eating, not for showing off the belongings of a streepach.[3]

PAUL Take it easy, Eileen. I bought you a present as well. Play cool, ladies.

EILEEN Whose money do you think is buying these presents?

MAGGIE (*in a rage as well*) None of your money. That's for sure. You tried to get your hands on it but it didn't come off. I know all about it. (*Tries to push Eileen out of her way.*)

EILEEN Who do you think you're shoving? Keep your hands off me.

PAUL (*steps between them*) Take it easy. Easy on there. Play cool, lovely ladies, now, play cool.

MAGGIE (*to Eileen*) I'd keep my quiet about the money if I was you.

EILEEN Quiet about what? Out with it.

MAGGIE I know a thing or two, I'm telling you.

EILEEN How would you know anything? Never gets up before the Angelus. Only able to chase after married men.

MAGGIE It's better than poisoning them.

Eileen stops in shock and then throws herself at Maggie.

EILEEN What did you say? What is that you said?

PAUL (*holding her back*) Easy. Take it easy. Play cool!

3. Strumpet.

EILEEN You'll not make me afraid.

PAUL (*sobering*) You'll find yourself cooling outside the door if you're not careful.

EILEEN I'd like to see you throw me out of my own house. I'd soon get the Guards.

PAUL Out you go, then. You were warned. (*Opens the door.*)

EILEEN I'll send for the Guards. (*Exits. From without*) I'll do some harm before I'm finished. This has gone on long enough.

Door bangs.

OLIVER This is terrible. Do you know that you've put your own wife out of the house? This is terrible before God.

PAUL There's no need to look on it like that. You have to know how to handle these women. If you didn't take a stiff line they'd get up on a man. All she'll do is sit in the car or go down to Paddy in the stables. You don't have to put up an electric fence but you do have to know where to draw the line with these women. If you didn't know where to draw the line they'd get up on a man.

OLIVER I've never seen such conduct. God, you know, couldn't be in a house like this. God couldn't be in this house.

MAGGIE (*folding her dress carefully*) Look what she's done to my dress. Wait till I get my hands on her dresses. I'll flitter them to ribbons.

PAUL Didn't I put her out? Isn't that enough? What more do you want?

MAGGIE If you'd left her in I could be tried for what I'd do. Look at my dress! It's ruined.

PAUL Put it away.

MAGGIE If you hadn't gone and married her that time everything would be all right. The place would be ours now. She'll do the same to you as she did to my father.

PAUL There's no holding back these women once they start to turn wicked.

MAGGIE It's strung up she should be. It's in jail she should be.

OLIVER I can't stay on in a house like this. It's a disgrace. The devil is in this house.

PAUL There's no use in this fighting. Why don't we have an old song instead? It's a pity there's no music. (*Starts to sing 'Phil the Fluther's Ball'*.) What we need is a shot of whiskey. Or a drop of that good *poteen* we got off the Guards.

Door opens and Paddy enters.

PADDY This house isn't half tame. They'll do for one another yet.

OLIVER (*rising*) Here's my place, Paddy. You'll need to warm yourself. I'm off.

PADDY You'll do for one another yet.

PAUL We might as well have a thimbleful of something better than the tea. Where's Eileen gone to?

PADDY She's crying down in the stables. I'll go back in case anything happens. She's that out of her mind she could let loose the horses. (*Exits.*)

PAUL Why doesn't she come in? There's no need to take

these things too much to heart. (*Pours whiskey.*) What have you put on your coat for, Father? Pull over and have a cup of tea. What's got into everybody all of a sudden?

OLIVER I can't. I'm going. Here's your money back.

PAUL Where would you be off to? Pull over and have a cup of tea. Sleep the night here. The man that made time made plenty of time.

OLIVER I can't. If I did it'd be like saying that the house was all right, when it's plain that it's well on the way to ruin.

PAUL You're talking through your drainpipe, Father. How could it be on the road to ruin?

OLIVER It all began when you swore you did Rosie no wrong.

PAUL Are you still on about that ancient history?

OLIVER A sin is always a sin until you go on your knees and beg forgiveness. You can hide sin from people but you can't hide it from God.

PAUL Sit down and drink your tea, Father. (*Slurs*) Mother would soon bring you to your senses if she was here. Only for her you'd be in a friggin' monastery long ago.

OLIVER I can't. I'm going. I'd be living with sin if I stayed.

PAUL Are you scolding me now in my own house? I'm not a child any more. I didn't ask you here. You came here on your own bat. You wanted money for the tedder.

OLIVER I'd beg on the roads before I'd take such money. Here's your money. (*Places it on the table.*)

PAUL What are you getting all worked up for, upsetting

yourself and everybody else? The money is yours. You need the money and there is lashings where that comes from.

OLIVER Let me go. It'd be a sin to take such money. I have to go.

PAUL This is a nice state of affairs.

OLIVER Come to your senses, Paul. Repent your sin. It's never too late before God. (*Exits.*)

Maggie goes up to Paul, embraces him, and playfully tries to take the glass out of his hand.

MAGGIE I think I could do with a drop myself after all that.

PAUL (*drawing violently away from her in self-absorption*) I'm beginning to wish I was never born.

MAGGIE I love you, Paul. You know I love you.

PAUL Leave me alone. I wish I was bloody well never born. I better get Eileen in out of the stables. (*To himself, as he staggers to the door*) Being in with these women when they get riz is like being in with the devils in hell. They leave you with no taste for anything. A man would be better to go out into the fields and eat grass with the horses.

Act Four

A storeroom off the stables and close to the house and backyard which are all lit up. From the house, sounds of music and dancing and drunken shouting. Paddy enters from the stables to the left of the stage, holding a rope and bridle. He stands listening to the drunkenness, torn between temptation to drink and disgust.

PADDY They're all crooked in there at Maggie's wedding, the women worse than the men. They said I could go in any time I wanted. They don't know me. Once I get the taste of drink I'm a goner. There's no turning back. Then who'd see to the poor horses? (*Noises of people shouting and boasting.*) They must be starting to leave. Will you listen to the blowing? They are all big shots today. Big blows!

Paul enters from the house.

What's bringing you here, Paul? Your place is in at the wedding.

PAUL I can't stand it in there. I came out for air. Why don't you go in and have a good drink for yourself, Paddy? You've attended to the outside for long enough.

PADDY I'm not drinking, Paul. I've learned me lesson. Once I ever get the taste there's no turning back. I'm a goner.

PAUL Give me that rope and bridle. (*Goes to take the rope but Paddy resists.*) I'll see to the horses, Paddy. You go in and enjoy yourself while it lasts. Never mind about the turning back.

PADDY You'll not see to the horses, Paul. Your place is in the house. You're the man there. You don't need me to remind you. I'll see to the horses!

PAUL (*bitterly*) My place is more with the horses than anywhere in that house.

PADDY (*wrestling the rope free*) You're not getting that rope, Paul. You'll be missed in the house. You see. The woman is out looking for you already. Here's your wife.

Eileen enters from the house.

I'm going to see to the horses. (*He breaks suddenly free and disappears towards the horses*).

EILEEN I was looking for you everywhere. Then I thought you must have gone to the yard. (*Goes towards him excitedly.*) I feel it's you and me that are married. Our lives are just beginning. We can be ourselves at last. (*Tries to embrace him.*) Give me a small kiss, Paul.

PAUL (*pushing her away, more in despair than horror*) I don't know what's going on. I can't stand what's going on in there.

EILEEN Everything is going wonderful. Several are saying it's been the best wedding for years. Once it is over we'll have a whole life to ourselves again. (*Tries to embrace him again.*) There were times this morning I thought we'd never get Maggie to the church but it is all tied and sewed up by now, and our lives together are just beginning.

Baby enters from the house, obviously in search of them, energetic and anxious.

BABY Is this where you both are! Won't you have the rest of your lives for that carry-on? You'll be missed. Maggie is having these pains. I just managed to bundle her up to her room. She's having a miscarriage, or what I hope is a miscarriage. We're finished if they start to get whiff of anything. I said she was having a small turn. But we haven't a minute to waste.

PAUL (*speaking slowly, uncomprehendingly*) Before she went to the church she had these pains. (*Breaking down.*) She said she was only getting married to please me. How did I ever get into such a business?

EILEEN I knew it was near at hand. I was afraid it'd happen this morning.

Paul makes as if to go towards the stables.

BABY Where are you making off to now?

PAUL I was going to see if Paddy wanted a hand with the horses.

BABY Paddy wants no hand. You stay here. You'll be needed.

PAUL Needed for what?

BABY You'll find out soon enough. You'll be needed all right.

PAUL My head is going round in circles. You women are terrible.

BABY Straighten yourself now. Stay here with your wife. Don't let him move a foot. The room is locked and it's away at the back. I don't want her shouting.

Baby exits with amazing quickness. Paul and Eileen are left facing one another as open adversaries, Eileen coldly enraged.

EILEEN Don't stir a foot from here. You'll have work to do in a minute.

PAUL (*dismayed*) What work? You were all love a minute ago, and listen to you now.

EILEEN You and Maggie had your fun. Now you'll have to get rid of the fun.

PAUL I don't know what you are going on about. You have me that I don't know whether I'm coming or going.

EILEEN I'll soon put you straight. Maggie had a miscarriage. (*Paul starts to sob.*) You weren't so tender-hearted when you were battering me round the place, putting me out of my own home. We'll see now what kind of man you are. We'll soon see what you're made of.

PAUL (*in infantile fear and rage*) You want to get me into trouble. That's what you want.

EILEEN No one wants to get you into trouble. You got yourself into trouble. Now you'll have to get yourself out. Do you hear them in the house? You'll be in a nice how-do-you-do if they get to hear of your trouble. What will her new husband do then?

PAUL I'm going like a leaf. I don't know what on earth you women are up to. You have me going round in circles.

EILEEN (*quietly, fiercely*) Your mother will be here in a minute with your baggage. You'll do with it what you do with what the cat has. Or a dead lamb. You'll take it out into the fields with a spade or you'll throw it into one of the deep gripes. Here's your mother. We'll see now what you're made of. Now do what you have to do.

Paul recoils in horror. Eileen turns to Baby, who enters with a bundle of sheets.

PAUL What have you in the sheets, Mother?

BABY Something for you to do in a couple of minutes.

EILEEN Is she all right? Is she fit to be left alone?

BABY She's a bit weak now but in a few hours she'll be as good as new. She's young and she's healthy.

EILEEN How did you get to talk to her at all? She'd have tore the eyes out of my head if I as much as said a word.

BABY She was a bit high and mighty at first, but Baby soon told her what is what. People have a habit of coming to their senses when they are told what is what. You go back into the house now. You'll be missed.

EILEEN What will I say to them in the house?

BABY Tell them women's business and the excitement of the day, and it's probably nothing. Tell them that the doctor saw her already, and he said that she had to be quiet till he sees her again. They're that drunk they'll believe anything.

EILEEN I'll do that as long as this gentleman does his part.

BABY (*thrusting the bundle into Paul's arms*) Get rid of this bundle quick. Take it!

PAUL Is it alive?

BABY How could it be alive the way it came into the world? Take it! We have to be quick. Every minute it's here we're in danger. Leave it in some gripe. The sheets can be burned after.

PAUL What if we're found out?

BABY How could you be found out? In your own house. On your own land. We have no time to waste on this talk.

PAUL I'll not do it. Do it yourselves if you want. I'm

going to see to the horses. Paddy has been out there on his own long enough.

He makes a move to go to the stables but Eileen seizes him.

EILEEN You better take it. If you don't take it I'll tell everything that went on. I'll only keep quiet as long as you do your part.

PAUL (*taken aback by her fury*) What will you tell?

EILEEN Everything. Who took the money and spent it? You did. I gave the poison and you knew. You're up to your neck in this whether you like it or not. You can be very tender-hearted when it suits. But take it now and get rid of it if you want to save your own skin. I'm not in this on my own by any means.

BABY Easy there, love. He's not that foolish. Take it, son. You have this poor wife of yours wild.

EILEEN Take it or I'll bring everybody out this very minute. (*Makes as if to shout.*)

BABY Are you out of your mind, woman? Here. He's taken it. Can't you see? (*She shakes Eileen roughly.*)

PAUL (*taking the bundle, shrinking*) You can't make me do it if I don't want. Curse the day I had the misfortune to ever get into this house.

EILEEN You'll do it. Or I'll not be long calling the whole house out. I've slept with Peter on my mind long enough. Now you'll have something to sleep with from this day out. I have gone through so much already that I have nothing to lose. I slept with Peter on my mind through the night and got up to see you and Maggie make dirt of me through the day. I'm not going to be made dirt of any longer.

BABY Come on. We have no time to lose. We are on our own land. I'll go with you myself.

PAUL I'll do it myself. But did you ever see such people?

BABY (*to Eileen*) He was too tender-hearted as a boy, love. It'll be all right. It's just hard for him. Go in and see that they don't start looking for Maggie. I'll go with him. Go in, love, before they start talking. Once talking starts it's that much harder to stop.

Eileen exits.

PAUL (*holding the bundle out*) I don't know how I got into this. I wish I was never born.

BABY (*taking him firmly by the arm*) You had no say in it, Sonny. Neither had your old father. You've had your fun. Now you have to shape up. It's a good job old Baby is here. If Baby wasn't here things would soon be in a nice pass. (*Exits.*)

Into the empty stage Paddy enters, wildly drunk, carrying a bottle of whiskey and a rope ringed on his shoulder.

PADDY There's nobody here. They must have all gone back to the house. Listen. (*Noise of the wedding.*) Mad. All mad. All going to come down . . . a house of cards. (*Drinks.*) I'm going to do for this bottle. We were in the war, in the trenches. The bombs were dropping. (*Loses track of what he was about to say . . . Shouts*) Whatever it was it was all strenuous and continuous. (*He curls up in the corner and goes to sleep, snoring.*)

Act Five

The same scene. The noise of the wedding party can be clearly heard from the house, but it is winding down. Baby enters, leading a distraught Paul into the storeroom where Paddy lies snoring.

PAUL It might as well have been a child, and we threw it into the gripe.

BABY That was no child. It had months to go, son, and it is as well for us it had. These things happen. It's just like calves you find dead in the field. Often they're not half made or quarter made.

PAUL I wish I had been dead too before I was born.

BABY Take it easy, love. I know it was hard, but with Maggie married the good times will be here again. I hope you won't forget your poor old mother and all she's done for you when the time comes.

PAUL How could there ever be good times again after what has gone on?

BABY It may seem that way now but it'll change. What you need is a good stiff drink to steady your nerves. Then you'll be able to face into the crowd. They'll be away before long. Then you'll be sole master round here.

PAUL How can I face anybody ever again after what we've done? I can't face myself. The poor animals would never have done what we have done. The animals are decent.

BABY Your poor nerves are playing you up, that is all.

You were very excitable even as a boy. You don't have to face anybody. You can stay here in the hay until your poor nerves settle and I'll go and get you a good stiff something from the house. (*Exits*)

This scene is done haltingly, as if Paul is struggling with the words and barely comprehending what he is saying:

PAUL We threw it into a gripe. The sheets were soaked. (*Shivers and examines his hands.*) What did they do to Maggie? How can I face anything from this day out? What am I to do? What has been done to me? Once you get in with these women you can let go of your life. One evening I walked down the railway line with Rosie. I put my arm round her. She came closer. I'm not made of stone. I'm only flesh and blood. I only came here to work, to earn enough to buy a few things for the home place, but I couldn't turn in the place but Eileen was there. I don't know why I ever touched her. Peter did me no harm. Then when he died I married her and that wiped the wrong out. I didn't know then that she gave him the poison. I was never able to touch her after she told me she gave him the poison. There was the wet day here in the stable that Maggie tried to pull the bridle out of my hands. We were cod-acting. Then the bridle ring broke and we fell in the hay. I wouldn't have done anything if she'd said even a word. She went all soft in my hands. Ever since then it is only in the wildness of drink I've been able to live. If I'd gone with my father that time and married Rosie we wouldn't have much but we'd be happy. There'd be none of this on our minds. We'd have our own lives. Rosie, oh Rosie, why didn't you keep me? It was my one chance. Why didn't I know it was my one chance?

Baby enters with a bottle.

BABY Here, Paul. A good slug of this will soon steady your nerves, but don't take too much. They'll be wanting you to make a speech before they leave. You can drink as much as you want then once we have the house to ourselves again.

PAUL I want nothing to drink.

BABY A small slug will do you good, love.

PAUL It will do no good. Nothing will do any good.

BABY Here! (*Taking the bottle to him as to a child*) A small sup will warm you, love, start you back to yourself. I know it has been hard for you, love. You were never able for much that was hard, even as a child. We could never even get you to pull the neck of a chicken.

PAUL (*drinks*) Why have you done this to me, Mother? I can feel it burn as it goes down but it still does no good. Nothing will ever do any good from this day out. Mother, why can't you heal your poor son?

BABY Rest yourself, love. It'll take it a while before you start to feel it working. I have to go and get Maggie.

PAUL (*becoming alert*) Get Maggie for what?

BABY Soon she'll have to leave with her husband. That's when you'll have to make your speech.

PAUL How will she be able to leave?

BABY It's surprising what you can manage to do when you have to, when there's no other way out. She belongs to them now. She'll have to take up her bed and go with them.

PAUL What if she's not able?

BABY She'll be able. Women are able for a lot more than men. They have to be. Don't stay too long here.

They'll soon be looking for you to speak. (*Exits.*)

PAUL Putting Maggie out too, and she not able to walk. How did I get into the hands of such a pair of devils out of hell? There's Paddy's rope. (*Picks it up.*) He must have forgot it in the straw. I can throw it over the rafters. There's only one way out now. That way I won't have to face anybody.

Paul drops the rope at the sound of approaching steps. Baby enters.

BABY Get up, Paul. They're calling for you. Eileen had a terrible time getting Maggie down but now she's ready to leave. She says she won't leave until she sees you first. They're all calling for you as well. They want your speech.

PAUL What can I say to them?

BABY You know the old stuff backwards. How happy everybody is at the sight of a young couple starting out in life. Two fine families united. Wish them wealth and health and happiness and may all their troubles be little ones. The usual old malarkey. Once you get started the only trouble you'll have is to know when to stop. They're that cross-eyed they'll clap like lunatics no matter what you say.

PAUL I can't face them.

BABY What's wrong with you?

PAUL What did we throw into the gripe, Mother?

BABY An accident. Nothing. Something that happens every day in hospitals, and out of them.

PAUL I felt I was throwing a life into that gripe.

BABY That was your nerves. You'll have to pull yourself

together. You've cut your stick so you better shape up. You'll have to put a face on it whether you like it or not. Maggie had to do it and she had more to put up with than you. If you don't face into them at once they could start to think there's something wrong.

PAUL Who got me into this . . . hell?

BABY Nobody got you into anything. I'll give you a hand up. You don't even have to make a speech. All you have to say is that like many a better man before you you've had a glass too many but you want to drink a last glass to the happy couple. That's all the speech you'll have to make. They'll clap and thank you all the more for it being short. Come on, Paul. If you don't get up out of that straw we're done for. Here's your wife even coming for you.

Eileen enters, excited and tipsy.

EILEEN It couldn't have gone off better, but they're all now calling for Paul. Where has he got to? I thought I'd never get Maggie down that stairs.

BABY See for yourself, love, and if you can shift him you're a better woman than his poor old mother.

EILEEN Will you look at the cut of him? (*Laughs.*) But come on, I'll give you a hand. They're calling for you. Everybody says it's been the best wedding around in years.

PAUL What's so good about that?

EILEEN There was no expense spared. Everybody's happy. Come on, I'll help you up. (*She takes his hand, but he pulls it away.*) Maggie will soon be gone. We'll have a life together at last.

PAUL (*coldly*) Go back in. I'll come on my own.

EILEEN It's no time for acting the fool in the straw.

Everything is respectable again. You managed to act like a man in the end. I never thought you'd have the gumption. All you have to do now is go in. Then it'll be as if nothing ever happened. We'll have our own lives for the first time.

PAUL Go back to them. I want to put a few words of a speech together in my mind. It'll not take long.

EILEEN I better get back. Don't be too long, love. Everything is going wonderful now, but that could change.

PAUL I'll be there almost as soon as yourself. I'm on my feet now.

BABY See how he answers to the young bird's call while the old bird is powerless. Always the mother has to give way to the wife.

Eileen exits.

Will I wait for you?

PAUL No. Go ahead. I won't be a minute. I just want to think up a few words that'll send them away happy. It'll not take me a minute.

Baby exits.

I haven't long. They'll be back soon. I'll just have to get this rope over the rafter. (*Starts to gather in the rope but finds it tightens.*) The rope must have got tangled in something.

He gives it a few quick jerks and then a very strong pull. Suddenly a roar comes from within the heap of straw.

PADDY Hold on a minute there. You're not getting away with my rope!

A very drunken Paddy staggers out of the straw with the end of the rope knotted round his waist.

PAUL (*in amazement*) Why have you the rope tied round you like that?

PADDY To keep fuckers like you from running off with it. I might be cabbage-looking but I'm not all that green.

PAUL Paddy! Don't you know me? Paul.

PADDY Is it Paul? I have to inspect. You never know who's who nowadays. Begod, it's yourself all right, Paul.

Paddy staggers. When he recognises Paul he breaks out into hilarious laughter.

PAUL What's wrong with you, Paddy?

PADDY That's the best one yet. Trying to steal his own rope. (*Finding it all too comic*) Or did they send you out to feed the horses? Is that all they think of you now? They'll soon have you made into another Paddy. They can take Paddy out of the bog . . . (*finds this uproarious*) But they can't take the bog out of Paddy. You've had one royal time, Paul, but now they're sending you back to the bog.

PAUL (*anxiously*) Give me the rope. I'm in a hurry.

PADDY I'm giving nobody the rope. I might be fluthered but the one thing I'm not giving up is the rope. (*Falls down.*) The drink got the better of me that time but the next time I'll do for it. (*From the straw*) Maybe you're thinking of doing away with yourself? (*Finds this funny.*)

PAUL (*petulantly, but anxiously*) What's so funny about that?

PADDY Maybe you are thinking of doing away with yourself, Paul? (*Finds this even funnier.*) This is all getting out of hand . . . beyond the beyond . . . (*Roaring with laughter*) You might be stupid and from the bog, Paul, but you can't be that bog-stupid. You think I'm

fluthered, that I need a hand up out of the straw, but
I need no hand. And you're not getting the rope. Paddy
is no daw. Where the rope goes, Paddy goes. Do you
want to hear my history, Paul? I was a private – bad luck
to it – in the British army, fought from India down into
Burma. I was wounded three times, won the George
Medal and drank it in the same year, and you ask who
am I? You'd think I'm a big shot because I came through
all that war. But I'm nobody. I'm everybody and I'm
nobody. I swore never to touch a drop again and will
you look at me now? Do you think I'm afraid of you?
There's not a man on earth that I'm afraid of. I'm sure
only of one thing now: there's no turning back at this
stage. I'll not stop now till I've the shirt drunk off my
back. They gave me pack drill in the army because of
the drink. Left, right, left, round and round the square,
till the head started to reel, but that didn't stop me. I'm
afraid of no man because I speak my mind. 'Who are
you?' they ask. 'I'm me,' I tell them. They don't like that
because it's the truth. Once you have to pretend to be
anything other than yourself, it's a sign you're frightened.
And once you're frightened of any man, you're finished.
I'm frightened of no man. We all came up out of the
trench. The bombs were falling. The fucking Japs were
everywhere. I had a machine gun. (*Sprays the audience.*)
And then . . . and then . . . I don't know what it was
but whatever it was (*shouts*) it was strenuous and
continuous. Are you a man or a mouse, Paul? Are you
alive or dead? Did you hang yourself yet, Paul?

PAUL Did you say there was never a reason to fear any
man?

PADDY What reason could there be to fear? Aren't they
all made of the same dirt as ourselves? They all have to
die. Look at them. One is bow-legged, another has a
belly; someone else can run like the wind, and everybody

thinks that is wonderful. One man is as grey as a badger, another has a shining head of hair – and how long will that last? – and what difference will it make? They all have to shite. Doesn't it melt down to the same old story in the finish? All the young women think the sun shines out of their knickers, and fellas like you, Paul, run round as if you had the meaning of life in your trousers. What does it add up to? It adds up to fuck-all. What should you be afraid of them for? All they can make you do is die once, and if they don't you'll have to do it for yourself sooner or later anyhow. Tell the truth. Shame the devil. And tell them all to take running jumps. And whatever it was . . . (*pauses, forgetting what he was about to say*) it was always strenuous and continuous. (*Passes out.*)

PAUL He's passed out. He's not dead. He's snoring.

Paul seizes him by the rope and shakes him, but it is no use. Noise increases from the house as if doors are being opened. Footsteps approach. Paul turns to face them, like an animal at bay.

They are coming for me now. What will they do to me? What can I say?

Oliver enters.

It's you, Father. Help me, Father.

OLIVER I came – you know – to see where you are. The women say they can't get you to come in. They're calling for you to make a speech in there but, how can I put it, I think things are far from right in there. I fear God, you know, isn't in that house in there. And who is this, you know, with the rope? Is he dead?

PAUL It's Paddy, Father. He's not dead. He's drunk but he makes more sense than most people. He said no man should be afraid of another man.

OLIVER Paddy is misfortunate, you know. He shouldn't drink but I never found any harm in poor Paddy.

PAUL He said no man should be afraid of another man.

OLIVER He's right, you know, in that. You should only be afraid before God. If you are not afraid before God you can't be afraid before man. If you are right in the eyes of God, you need fear no man.

PAUL If only I heeded you in the beginning I'd never have gone wrong, Father. It all began when I wouldn't marry Rosie.

A clamour of 'Paul!' rises from the house.

OLIVER They're calling for you, Paul. You'll have to face them, you know.

PAUL I can't face them. I've done too much wrong.

OLIVER Then, you know, it's simple, what you have to do. You have to confess and God will forgive you. You don't have to fear anybody if you tell the truth before God.

PAUL I'll confess to them before God and then I don't have to be afraid to face them as men.

OLIVER Confess before God, son.

PAUL I'll tell the truth the same as if I was speaking to God. I've committed crimes – sins – and I want to confess.

OLIVER I'll go with you, Paul. I'll stand by your side.

Paul and Oliver exit into the house.

As noise of the wedding changes from calling for Paul to welcoming Paul with thunderous applause, Paddy wakes out of the straw.

PADDY What's going on here? You're not going off with my rope, Paul. The rope is still here anyhow. (*Silence.*) They have all gone. They must have gone into the house. Listen to the roars!

Shouts of 'Paul, Paul! Speech, speech!' to applause. All this is distant but clear, away from Paddy in the straw, who is close:

PAUL (*offstage*) The speech I have to give is not what is expected.

Murmurs of surprise, a drunken shout or two: 'You never lost it, Paul!' 'Good man, Paul.' Silence.

I've committed crimes – sins – and I want to confess. The first sin I committed was against Rosie. I promised to marry her, got her with child, and threw her over. Rosie, forgive me, for the love of God.

OLIVER (*offstage*) God will forgive.

Murmurs, shouts.

BABY (*offstage*) He's out of his mind. Get hold of him before he does harm. He doesn't know what he's saying.

OLIVER (*offstage*) He knows well what he's doing. He's confessing before God. Silence, good people.

PADDY He'll do for himself now. For all his show and blowing, Paul was never anything but a poor fool – a straw in the wind. Oliver must have got him to confess. Oliver was always religious, always steadfast. Listen. He's going on.

In the distance:

PAUL (*offstage*) The next person I have to ask for forgiveness is Maggie. Her father died no natural death. He was poisoned. I took his money. Before that I took his wife. Then I ruined his daughter's young girlhood after it was left in my care. And then I threw her child in a gripe.

OLIVER (*offstage*) These are terrible sins, but God will forgive you.

Cries of 'Arrest him!' 'Get the Guards!' 'The truth before God!' emerge from the general tumult that rises from the silence and shock.

PADDY They'll crucify him now. (*Repeats sarcastically*) 'God will forgive!' They are all for God when God is on their side. (*Reflectively*) Bound to come down . . . A house of cards. The poor fool will maybe get some peace after all that tattering around. He may have done for poor Eileen and Maggie as well, but old Baby will take some nailing. Baby will not hop up on anybody's cross. Still, if you get your soul cleared you have just the one small death, and then you're right . . . (*Laughs.*) What's this they say? . . . You're with kings and county councillors. If I could get my hands on a bottle I'd do for it now. In the war the machine gun went rat-a-tat-a-tat. We were coming out of the trenches. The bombs were falling. I can't remember another thing . . . Well . . . whatever it was . . . it was all strenuous and continuous . . . And then . . . and then . . . was only strenuous and continuous for a while . . . it went all silent, except for the crows.

Appendix

FRAGMENTS FROM A DRAMATIC WORK

MRS MCCANN Well what kept yous? Catechism is over, and the roll is held up. It better not be the same excuse today.

VOICES There was blasting at the quarry.

MRS MCCANN Are yous going to tell the truth or has the truth to be handled out of yous? Jimmy McDermot told me that that there was to be no blasting this week.

VOICES It was that we started late. The alarm didn't go off.

MRS MCCANN Why didn't you tell the truth in the first place. You know that lies is a breaking of the eighth commandment.

VOICES We were afraid, Mrs Watson.

MRS MCCANN Well you'll have reason to be afraid. Out with them now.

Sound of cane on hands.

And now, this third one for the lie.

*

RADIO ANNOUNCER Bail o Dhia oraibh go leir a chairde Gael O Phairc an Chrocaigh. Hello everyone . . .

Cheers.

And welcome to yet another All Ireland Final Day.

337

Stamp of feet.

VOICES Who's collecting the bets?

Mulligans fiver is shaking now.

Roscommon will never do it again.

Up Roscommon. No heretics in this house. Down with the begrudgers.

Cheering.

Shush now. Turn up the radio, Joe.

ANNOUNCERS VOICE

*

ANNOUNCER And No 3 is?

MORONEY Andrew Moroney.

ANNOUNCER And your occupation Mr Moroney is . . .

MORONEY Gentleman Farmer.

LISTENER'S VOICE And murder me slowly sideways, love. Did you ever such a spake? A Gentleman Farmer. It's worse than having a dog walking round on his hind legs.

*

OLD MR MORONEY The virgin queen usually emerges in a colony from which the old queen has flown. She starts her adult life by searching among the combs for any possible rivals, those still in the cells or having just come out like herself. Any she finds she stings to death through the walls of cell. It is, my dears, if I can suggest as much, just like life itself and almost equally inefficient.

Notes on the Texts

In the bibliographic notes below, the abbreviation BBC WAC refers to items held in the BBC Written Archives Centre, Caversham Park, Reading. NUIG refers to items held in the Archives Collections at the James Hardiman Library, National University of Ireland, Galway. UCDA refers to items held in the Deposited Collections at the UCD Archives, James Joyce Library, University College Dublin.

SINCLAIR

The text is that of the published script: 'Sinclair – a Play by John McGahern', *The Listener*, 18 November 1971, pp. 690–92.

The cast list is taken from a copy of the BBC recording script (TS), sent by McGahern to Niall Walsh, n.d.: The Niall Walsh–McGahern Correspondence, NUIG: P102/102.

THE BARRACKS

No script from the original 1972 BBC production of *The Barracks* is extant, either in the BBC WAC or in the John McGahern Papers at NUIG. However, a second production of the play in the following year used the same script originally prepared by McGahern for the BBC production. This was produced by John Lynch and broadcast on RTÉ Radio on 28 September 1973, starring

Thomas Studley as Sergeant Reagan and Neasa ní Anrachainn as Elizabeth. The text included in this volume is taken from a typescript used for this second production, held in the RTÉ Radio Drama and Variety Scripts collection, UCDA: P261/2038.

The cast list of the BBC production is taken from the listing in the *Radio Times*, 20 January 1972, p. 31. Accessible via the BBC Genome Project: <http://genome.ch.bbc.co.uk/>

THE SISTERS

The text is taken from a typescript screenplay: BBC WAC: T51/188/1 (17 pages). Two identical copies are held in the John McGahern Papers, NUIG: P71/747 and P71/748 (with handwritten notes).

The note on the 'Location' is taken from a different, probably earlier, version of the typescript held in the same file: BBC WAC: T51/188/1 (13 pages).

SWALLOWS

The text is taken from the BBC camera script held in the John McGahern Papers, NUIG: P71/756. McGahern's handwritten revisions in an otherwise almost identical copy of the script (NUIG: P71/755) have been incorporated in the text.

THE ROCKINGHAM SHOOT

The text is taken from a typescript with handwritten revisions: BBC WAC: TV Drama Scripts 1987, microfilm no. 545 (104 pages). The typescripts of *The Rockingham*

Shoot in the John McGahern Papers (NUIG: P71/764 and P71/765) probably represent an earlier stage in the play's development: much of the same material is present there but in a different sequence from that of the finished film.

THE POWER OF DARKNESS

McGahern worked on adapting Tolstoy's play for much of his working life, between *c.*1970 and 2005. During that period, he wrote a number of versions (for details of these, see the Introduction, pp. 39–51). Included in this volume is McGahern's latest revision of the play, completed less than one year before his death.

The text is taken from the recording script used for the 2005 RTÉ radio production (TS: private collection); the editor is indebted to the producer, Kevin Reynolds, for generously providing a photocopy. The text of a type-script in the John McGahern Papers, with handwritten corrections in McGahern's hand and marked with a Post-It note that reads 'Finished July 15 '05' (NUIG: P71/742), is largely identical; the RTÉ recording script appears to be a fair copy incorporating the handwritten corrections from NUIG: P71/742.

Some of the stage directions in the recording script are inconsistent or incomplete. Where this is the case, stage directions have been silently supplied, drawing where possible on the text of the earlier published version: *The Power of Darkness* (London: Faber and Faber, 1991).

McGahern's Introduction is that which accompanied the first broadcast of this latest version of the play on RTÉ Radio 1 on 4 September 2005. The text of the Introduction as it is printed here is based on two draft typescripts with handwritten revisions, probably McGahern's recording notes (TS: private collection), but it also incorporates some further amendments to the text of those drafts in accordance with the finished recording. The text of the Introduction was previously published in this form in *Love of the World: Essays*, ed. Stanley van der Ziel (London: Faber and Faber, 2009), pp. 283–4.

APPENDIX
FRAGMENTS FROM A DRAMATIC WORK

These fragments of a draft of an early dramatic work are a transcript of a three-page manuscript, on two different types of paper, with handwritten corrections by McGahern. The John McGahern Papers, NUIG: P71/1279.